what is this thing called philosophy of religion?

What is this thing called Philosophy of Religion? grapples with the core topics studied on philosophy of religion undergraduate courses, including:

- The meaning of religious language, including twentieth century developments.
- The nature of the Divine, including divine power, wisdom and action.
- Arguments for the existence of the Divine.
- Challenges to belief in the Divine, including the problems of evil, divine hiddenness and religious diversity.
- Believing without arguments.
- Arguments for life after death, including reincarnation.

In addition to the in-depth coverage of the key themes within the subject area Elizabeth Burns explores the topics from the perspectives of the five main world religions, introducing students to the work of scholars from a variety of religious traditions and interpretations of belief.

What is this thing called Philosophy of Religion? is the ideal introduction for those approaching the philosophy of religion for the first time, containing many helpful student-friendly features, such as a glossary of important terms, study questions and further reading.

Elizabeth Burns was a Reader at Heythrop College, University of London where she taught philosophy of religion from 2000–2017 and was, for five years, Dean of Undergraduate Studies. She is now a Reader and Programme Director of the University of London International Programmes in Theology at the central University of London and Director of Taught Programmes at the Cambridge Theological Federation.

What is this thing called?

The Routledge *What is this thing called?* series of concise textbooks has been designed for use by students coming to a core and important area of philosophy for the first time. Each volume explores the relevant central questions with clear explanation of complex ideas and engaging contemporary examples. Features to aid study include text boxes, chapter summaries, study questions, further reading and glossaries.

What Is This Thing Called Knowledge? third edition
Duncan Pritchard

What Is This Thing Called Philosophy of Language?
Gary Kemp

What Is This Thing Called Ethics? second edition
Christopher Bennett

What Is This Thing Called Metaethics?
Matthew Chrisman

What Is This Thing Called Global Justice?
Kok-Chor Tan

What Is This Thing Called Metaphysics? third edition
Brian Garrett

Forthcoming

What Is This Thing Called Emotion?
Dorothea Debus

What Is This Thing Called Philosophical Methodology?
James Andow

What Is This Thing Called Knowledge? fourth edition
Duncan Pritchard

Other titles in the series can be found at
www.routledge.com/What-is-this-thing-called/book-series/WITTC

ELIZABETH BURNS

what is this thing called philosophy of religion?

Routledge
Taylor & Francis Group

LONDON AND NEW YORK

First published 2018
by Routledge
2 Park Square, Milton Park, Abingdon, Oxon OX14 4RN

and by Routledge
711 Third Avenue, New York, NY 10017

Routledge is an imprint of the Taylor & Francis Group, an informa business

British Library Cataloguing-in-Publication Data
A catalogue record for this book is available from the British Library

Library of Congress Cataloging-in-Publication Data
A catalog record for this book has been requested

ISBN: 978-1-138-81777-7 (hbk)
ISBN: 978-1-138-81778-4 (pbk)
ISBN: 978-1-315-74549-7 (ebk)

Typeset in Berling
by Sunrise Setting Ltd, Brixham, UK
Printed and bound by CPI Group (UK) Ltd, Croydon, CR0 4YY

CONTENTS

ACKNOWLEDGEMENTS

This book began its life many years ago as a subject guide for students taking the philosophy of religion module by distance learning as part of a Bachelor of Divinity programme at what is now called the University of London International Programmes in Theology. The notes on which it draws have also been updated annually for the benefit of MA students at Heythrop College, University of London, to whom I am grateful for their many comments and questions.

I would also like to thank, in particular, my former colleague at Heythrop College Peter Vardy, who commissioned the subject guide from which this book has evolved, and my Head of Department, Peter Gallagher, without whose exceptional under-standing and encouragement this book would never have been written.

I owe a considerable debt of gratitude to three anonymous reviewers, and to the editorial team at Taylor and Francis for their forbearance as I struggled to produce the text in circumstances which turned out to be rather more difficult than I had anticipated.

My thanks are also due to Luke Hughes-Davies, Yasser Rasool, Mark Gatland and Charles Mather for their support during my treatment for and recovery from cancer, without whose interventions it is unlikely that I would have lived to write this book.

Finally, for their friendship and encouragement I would like to thank my colleagues at Heythrop College, in particular Anna Abram, Annabel Clarkson and Fiona Ellis, and at the Cambridge Theological Federation, especially Zoe Bennett, Charlotte Bentley, Liz Curry, Mat Ridley, Jenny Thorogood and Sharon Williamson, along with Marguerite Daw, Wendy Caton, Tina Hathaway, Jennifer Knight, Adrienne Sharman, Anne Peach and Anna Wheeler, and my family, Natasha Burns, Betty Burns and Paul Noble.

1

what is philosophy of religion?

• INTRODUCTION

Broadly speaking, philosophy of religion is a branch of philosophy which uses the tools of philosophy to ask questions about the nature and existence of the Divine, the supreme being or value. (This may be God or Allah, but the term is intended to be inclusive of traditions in which the ultimate being or value is something other than God.) Philosophy of religion is usually conducted from a neutral standpoint, whereas philosophical theology, from which it is sometimes distinguished, takes place within a religious tradition and examines how the doctrines of that tradition, both individually and together, can best be understood in order to provide philosophical support for the beliefs of that tradition.

When beginning to study the philosophy of religion, for at least two reasons it is important to have a clear idea of what philosophers of religion do, and why they do it. Firstly, if you are simply thinking about an inherited list of topics without much conception of what you are trying to achieve and why, it is easy to become bogged down in complex ideas and technical details and lose sight of your sense of purpose. Philosophy of religion can come to seem like an intellectual game which is of little or no practical importance. Secondly, what you think you are doing when studying the philosophy of religion can affect the kind of questions you ask, and the methods you use to try to answer them.

But before we can consider further what philosophy of religion is, and why we study it, we need to examine the meaning of its component parts – that is, 'religion' and 'philosophy'.

• WHAT IS RELIGION?

Although philosophy of religion is usually, in some circles at least, regarded as a branch of philosophy, it might be argued that you cannot be a good philosopher of religion unless you have a clear understanding of what it is that you are asking philosophical questions about. An inadequate understanding of the nature of religion can lead some to reject religion without considering that there may be many ways in which it is possible to be 'religious'. For example, the comedian Marcus Brigstocke gives a description of the God in whom he does not believe which includes the following: '[B]earded, bathed in light, lives up in Heaven, has a staff of angels . . . the fella with the booming voice' (2011: 87). Although all of these characteristics are derived from biblical and/or artistic attempts to portray the Divine, un-nuanced accounts of them such as that offered by Brigstocke may be at least partly responsible for the rejection of religious belief by the so-called 'new atheists'.

Since it is difficult to define religion in such a way that systems of beliefs and practices which are normally called 'religious' (for example, Theravada Buddhism) are included, while those which are not (for example, Marxism) are excluded, scholars often rec-ommend the 'family resemblance approach', according to which there is a range of features, no single one of which a religion must possess, but at least some of which any religion must possess. Various features have been suggested, but they might include at least some of the following:

1 Belief in an Ultimate Reality, the Divine (which may be personal and/or impersonal) and/or a system of doctrines which give ultimate meaning and purpose to human life.
2 Belief that the existence and nature of the Divine is revealed to human beings by means of sacred writings, religious experiences and/or human reason.
3 Belief that the Divine and/or the system of doctrines requires adherence to a specified code of behaviour.
4 A sense of dependence upon and reverence for something of ultimate importance and external to oneself.
5 The making of a commitment, often recognised by means of a ceremony, to a system of beliefs and a way of life.
6 The use of sacred writings, symbols, sounds and personal and community rituals which help believers to recognise and acknowledge the Divine and adhere to a specified code of behaviour.
7 The use of a building/place or the gathering of a community which provides 'sacred' space for communal worship and/or contemplation of the Divine, and the perform-ance of ceremonies and rituals.
8 The offer of 'salvation' – a better, and perhaps eternal, state of being. This might take the form of forgiveness following repentance of sins, freedom from fear, a new or renewed sense of purpose, continued existence after death or reincarnation leading eventually to *nirvana*, the end of suffering with the extinction of the individual.[1]

Reflection

To what extent does any religion of which you have knowledge possess these characteristics?

Can you think of a form of religious belief which could not be described in this way? Or a secular belief-system which could?

• DEFINING THE DIVINE

The type of religion which is most usually discussed by philosophers of religion is generally known as 'classical theism'. Broadly speaking, this is the view that God created time, the world and everything in it from nothing, and everything depends for its continued existence on God. On this view, God has a range of attributes, but most commonly is said to be a person or personal, omnipotent (all-powerful), omniscient (all-knowing) and good. There are, however, many other ways to understand the Divine, some of which, along with classical theism, are defined in the table which may be found in Appendix 1.

• WHAT IS PHILOSOPHY?

Like 'religion', 'philosophy' is difficult to define. Literally it means 'love of knowledge', from the Greek *philos*, 'love', and *sophia*, 'knowledge'. In recent years it has become common to distinguish between 'analytic philosophy' and 'continental philosophy'.

The analytic tradition of philosophy is said to have begun with the work of Gottlob Frege (1848–1925), G. E. Moore (1873–1958) and Bertrand Russell (1872–1970), to propose hypotheses and test them in the light of data in the manner of scientific enquiry, and to aim to achieve clarity and rigour. Arguments are often formalised to assess their deductive validity (whether they lead to a certain conclusion) or inductive strength (whether the steps of the argument make the conclusion more likely), and are assessed for explanatory power, simplicity and fit with background knowledge. Analytic philosophy is usually divided into sub-disciplines, of which philosophy of religion is one. Others include epistemology (the study of how and what we can know), methodology (the study of the methods commonly used in philosophical inquiry), logic (the study of good and bad reasoning), metaphysics (the study of abstract concepts such as the nature of being or time) and philosophy of mind (the study of the nature of mind and its relationship to the body and to the world more generally). All of these sub-disciplines overlap with and are used by philosophers of religion.

By contrast, philosophy in the continental tradition is based on the philosophy of Georg Hegel (1770–1831), Edmund Husserl (1859–1938) and Martin Heidegger (1889–1976), and adopts a style which is more literary than scientific. It aims not to say something precisely or to show that it is well established but to deconstruct common ways of thinking in order to show how they are socially and/or spiritually disadvantageous, and to provide a new vision which will inspire everyone to struggle for 'liberation'. Philosophers writing in this tradition may choose a view on the basis of its ethical and socio-political implications, the psychological motivations which caused it to be adopted or the extent to which it promotes particular values, or fits in with and informs our experience of human life. Continental philosophy therefore draws on various fields from the humanities, including literary and cultural theory, politics and psychoanalysis, and uses these as the model for philosophical discourse. Ultimately, it seeks not knowledge but wisdom, a way of thinking which focuses on the application of knowledge to practical issues, such as how to live a good and/or happy life. (This and the preceding paragraph are informed by Trakakis, 2007.)

These two philosophical traditions are now perhaps better characterised as philosophical styles because their identification with geographical locations is becoming less clear. The dividing line between them is also becoming less clear, since the work of some philosophers contains features of both styles of philosophical writing.

• WHAT IS THE PHILOSOPHY OF RELIGION?

Analytic philosophers of religion tend to focus on questions concerning whether the concept of the Divine is coherent by examining the meaning and implications of attributes which are commonly applied to the Divine, either individually or in conjunction with others. For example, the Divine is often said to be omnipotent, omniscient and good, and philosophers examine what it means to apply each of these to the Divine, and whether a Divinity who is omnipotent, omniscient and good can allow evil (the problem of evil). They also consider whether there is any evidence to justify belief in the existence of a Divinity who has these attributes, especially in the light of current scientific theories about the origin and continued existence of the universe.

Philosophers of religion working in the continental tradition tend to consider a wider range of possible ways of thinking about the nature of the Divine. They also tend to focus on practical ways in which religious belief can help us to address the problems of human life – in particular, the problem of how to deal with suffering, and the way in which we can focus on ethical behaviour as a means both to combat suffering and to live a meaningful life.

• STUDYING THE PHILOSOPHY OF RELIGION

Although studying the philosophy of religion can sometimes seem challenging, both because it may force you to question and perhaps threaten to undermine your existing beliefs about religion, whatever they may be, and because we can never be sure that we have reached the 'right' answer to our questions, I would suggest that the benefits of studying this subject far outweigh the difficulties, for the following reasons:

1 It is good to question our own beliefs about religion to ensure that we have the best possible reasons for what we believe and, therefore, how we choose to live our lives. Although studying the philosophy of religion may lead you to change some of your beliefs, beliefs which have withstood questioning are much more secure than those which have not been subjected to careful scrutiny.
2 Religion is a widespread and important cultural phenomenon. According to a recent study, the world currently contains about 5.8 billion religious believers, including 2.2 billion Christians, 1.6 billion Muslims, 1 billion Hindus and about 500 million Buddhists (The Pew Research Center, 2012). Religious beliefs are not just abstract concepts; they have a significant impact – both positive and negative – on societies throughout the world. It is therefore important that as many people as possible are able to contribute thoughtfully to discussion about them. Talk changes beliefs, which change behaviour. As the author of Ecclesiasticus said, many centuries ago: 'Discussion

is the beginning of every work, and counsel precedes every undertaking. The mind is the root of all conduct' (*The Holy Bible*, 1989, Sirach [second century BCE] 37:16–17).

3 As Charles Taliaferro (2013) suggests, philosophy of religion can enhance cross-cultural dialogue. It looks for both common and distinguishing features of religious belief and practice, and this may improve the relationship between religions, and between religions and secular institutions.

4 Although the philosophy of religion can never provide definitive answers to any of the questions which it addresses, it can help to rule out some possible answers, particularly those which might be regarded as superstitious or fanatical. Indeed, uncertainty about the answers to philosophical questions about religious belief might even be viewed as a positive feature of the discipline, on the grounds that certainty about such answers can lead to superstition and fanaticism. A developing international awareness of the shakiness of the philosophical ground upon which religious fanatics stand could therefore make a major contribution to the improvement of global security.

• HOW TO USE THIS BOOK

For the most part, the aim of this book is to provide you with the tools to formulate your own view, rather than to argue for a particular view. It focuses primarily on analytical philosophers' analysis of classical theism but endeavours to include arguments offered by scholars writing from the perspective of each of the world's major religions.

In Chapters 2 and 3, the difficulty of talking about the nature of the Divine in ordinary, everyday language is acknowledged in a discussion of several ways in which this problem has been addressed. Chapters 4 to 8 consider a range of common questions about the nature of the Divine, while Chapters 9 to 13 examine key arguments for belief in the existence of the Divine. Three significant objections to such belief are discussed in Chapters 14 to 16. The relationship between reason and faith is discussed in Chapters 17 and 18, and the book concludes with an examination of the philosophical questions which might be asked about belief in an afterlife, variously conceived, and a consideration of how we might best live with the knowledge of our own mortality.

Most of the texts discussed are available in one or more of the many anthologies of readings in the philosophy of religion and, where applicable, Appendix 3 lists original sources and anthologies in which they may be found. At the end of each chapter or section, a list of further reading is provided for those who wish to venture further into the debates. Since it is not always easy to differentiate between 'introductory' and 'advanced' further reading, I have divided these lists into online encyclopedia articles, extracts of books or articles available in anthologies, original articles in edited collections, articles which, for university students and alumni, may be freely available through JSTOR, and books. In at least some cases, this represents an ascending scale of difficulty.

In the lists of references and further reading, for works which have been published in more than one edition, the date of first publication is provided in square brackets. Where applicable, one reprinted version is given; others, where available, are listed in

Appendix 3. Where I have cited a reprinted text, the citation lists the publication dates of the most recent edition of the anthology (with page numbers) and recent (if applicable) and first editions of the source.

• NOTE

1 I am grateful to Charles Neave, Stephen Balogh and John Heyderman for suggested amendments to points 6 and 7.

• REFERENCES

Brigstocke, Marcus (2011) *God Collar* (London: Bantam Press).

Taliaferro, Charles (2013) 'Philosophy of Religion', *Stanford Encyclopedia of Philosophy*, http://plato.stanford.edu/entries/philosophy-religion/.

The Holy Bible, New Revised Standard Version (1989) 'The Apocryphal/Deuterocanonical Books of the Old Testament', *Sirach* 37:16–17 (Oxford: Oxford University Press), 115.

The Pew Research Center (2012) 'The Global Religious Landscape', www.pewforum.org/2012/12/18/global-religious-landscape-exec/.

Trakakis, Nick (2007) 'Metaphilosophy of Religion: The Analytic-Continental Divide in Philosophy of Religion', *Ars Disputandi* 7, 1: 179–220, www.tandfonline.com/doi/pdf/10.1080/15665399.2007.10819969.

• FURTHER READING

Original articles in edited collections

Caputo, John (2010) 'Continental Philosophy of Religion' in Charles Taliaferro, Paul Draper and Philip L. Quinn (eds) *A Companion to Philosophy of Religion* (Chichester: Wiley-Blackwell), 667–673.

Westphal, Merold (2010) 'The Emergence of Modern Philosophy of Religion' in Charles Taliaferro, Paul Draper and Philip L. Quinn (eds) *A Companion to Philosophy of Religion* (Chichester: Wiley-Blackwell), 133–140.

Article

Harrison, Victoria (2006) 'The Pragmatics of Defining Religion in a Multi-Cultural World', *International Journal for Philosophy of Religion* 59, 3: 133–152.

Books

Hartshorne, Charles and Reese, William L. (2000 [1953]) *Philosophers Speak of God* (New York, NY: Humanity Books).

Taliaferro, Charles and Marty, Elsa J. (eds) (2010) *A Dictionary of Philosophy of Religion* (London: Continuum).

Wildman, Wesley J. (2010) *Religious Philosophy as Multidisciplinary Comparative Inquiry: Envisioning a Future for the Philosophy of Religion* (New York, NY: State University of New York Press).

2

ways with words: the meaning of religious language

• INTRODUCTION

Since the nature of the Divine, if it exists, is so different from the nature of the physical objects and mental concepts about which we commonly talk, it is often talked about in non-literal language. In this and the following chapter we will examine some of the forms this language can take.

• SECTION A: THE NEGATIVE WAY

The negative way is a way of talking about the Divine by saying what it is not. We find this way of talking about the Divine in the Hindu tradition in which *Brahman*, the ultimate divine reality, is described only as 'not this, not this' (*Brhādaranyaka* Upaniṣad, III.9.26 (c. 700 BCE), quoted in Sen, 2008: 49). The negative way is more developed in the Abrahamic religions, however, probably as a consequence of the influence of the philosopher Plato (427–357 BCE).

Plato talked of 'the One' which can be neither thought nor spoken of, but his follower Plotinus (204–270 CE), the originator of the philosophy now known as Neo-Platonism, argued in the *Enneads* (253–270) that the One emanates (spreads out) down through a hierarchy of non-physical things (e.g. mind) until it reaches things which have a physical existence. He taught that human beings can make a spiritual ascent to the One by means of imageless or 'apophatic' meditation – that is, meditation which describes God in negative rather than positive terms. This way of understanding religious language can therefore lead to a form of religious experience which was particularly important in the tradition of medieval spirituality, especially in the teaching of Meister Eckhart (1260–1327), and in the anonymous work *The Cloud of Unknowing* (late fourteenth century).

The influence of Plotinus can be seen in the writings of Pseudo-Dionysius, an unknown author who may have lived in Syria towards the end of the fifth century (Ware, 1997: 63). In *On the Divine Names* (original date of publication unknown), Pseudo-Dionysius suggests that God's names cannot literally describe God because human language is unable to describe something which is perfect and unique. Rather, they point towards the Divine as the cause of all things. So, for example, when we say that the Divine is good, we mean that the Divine is the cause of goodness, and so on. But this affirmative way (a way of talking about the Divine using positive terms) seems to have been less important for Pseudo-Dionysius than the negative way. He claims that, the higher our understanding ascends in the direction of the Divine, the more restricted our language becomes, until we reach a point at which we can neither understand nor speak of what we experience. He argues that it is the negative way which can take us to this point. We move beyond words and concepts by denying them, and this eventually enables us to understand that God, who has no limitations, can never be adequately described by human words. This means that even words which seem to say something positive about the Divine – e.g. 'Sonship' or 'Fatherhood' – must ultimately be denied, because even apparently positive terms cannot adequately describe something which is beyond human language.

A similar approach can be found in the work of the Jewish philosopher Moses Maimonides (1135–1204). There is some disagreement among scholars regarding the interpretation and consistency of Maimonides' teaching on the negative way (Gellman, 2013: 121), but some of his key points may be found in Chapter 59 of the *Guide of the Perplexed* (1190). Here he claims that everyone agrees that the Divine cannot be properly understood by the human mind, and that, since whatever positive terms we might ascribe to the Divine are derived from those which we apply in our human world and we therefore can never fully grasp the magnitude of the divine nature, the most appropriate manner of approaching the Divine is that described in Psalm 65: 'Silence is praise to You' (Psalm 65:2). To attempt to describe the Divine by means of positive attributes would be like praising a human king who has millions of gold pieces because he possesses silver. The *Torah* (the law of God as revealed to Moses in the first five books of the Hebrew Bible) speaks in the language of humankind in order that humankind might understand something of the nature of the Divine, but we should use the divine attributes we find there only when reading the *Torah*, with the exception of those which have been established for use in prayer by 'the men of the Great Synagogue' (Maimonides, 1972: 272 [1963] [1190]). The attributes which we find in the *Torah* which are not permitted for use in prayer are of two kinds; either they describe divine action – God's effects upon creation – or they describe qualities which must exist in God, although we cannot understand the nature of those qualities.

Objections to the negative way

Although Thomas Aquinas (c. 1225–1274) was, to some extent, sympathetic to the negative way, on the grounds that negative terms enable us to express the difference between the Divine and humankind (1265–1274: Part I, Question 13, Article 2), he also raised objections to it. Alexander Broadie (1987) identifies the following from Article 2:

1 If even terms like 'good', 'wise', 'living' etc. must be understood negatively, how do we decide which names can be used to describe God? For example, could we not say that God is 'bodily', on the grounds that the term means something completely different from its usual sense?

Broadie suggests that, for Maimonides, in order to protect their faith, people need to be taught that names describing perfections can be applied to the Divine, but that names describing imperfections cannot. This still raises the question of how we are to distinguish between perfections and imperfections, and who makes this decision. For example, some might argue that disembodiment is an imperfection. Perhaps we could respond that, for human beings, disembodiment might be regarded as an imperfection, but for the Divine, which exists throughout the universe, embodiment might be a significant limitation – unless we adopt some kind of pantheism or panentheism, according to which the Divine is the universe, or the universe is part of the Divine.

2 When people say that God lives, they mean to convey more than the idea that the Divine is different from inanimate bodies.

Broadie notes that Maimonides distinguishes between the philosophically sophisticated and the multitude, and suggests that a philosopher will not accept a view simply because it is held by most people. So, although Aquinas might be correct to say that people do not understand God's attributes negatively, this does not necessarily mean that they are correct.

A third objection, however, is more difficult to counter:

3 If we can say only what something is not, this gives us little indication of what it is. For example, if we say that something is not green, not square, not metallic and not dead, this might indicate to us that we are talking about something which is alive, but not that we are referring to an elephant.

Reflection

What, in your view, is the most significant objection to speaking about the Divine in negative terms? Do you think that it can be overcome?

Conclusion

The negative way does, at least, remind us that the nature of the Divine, if it exists, is very difficult to describe in human language. Nevertheless, we can talk about it to a limited extent by listing things which it is not, even if there might be some disagreement about what these are. It is, nonetheless, the case that many religious believers do think that it is possible to speak of God in more positive terms. In the remainder of this chapter we will examine some common ways in which this might be done.

• REFERENCES

Anonymous (2001 [late fourteenth century]) *The Cloud of Unknowing*, trans. and ed. A. Spearing (Harmondsworth: Penguin).

Aquinas, Thomas (2016 [1920] [1265–1274]) *The Summa Theologica of St Thomas Aquinas*, trans. Fathers of the English Dominican Province, www.newadvent.org/summa/ Part I, Question 13, Articles 1–2.

Broadie, Alexander (1987) 'Maimonides and Aquinas on the Names of God', *Religious Studies* 23, 2: 157–170.

Gellman, Jerome (2013) 'Moses Maimonides/Rambam' in Chad Meister and Paul Copan (eds) *The Routledge Companion to Philosophy of Religion* (Abingdon: Routledge), 119–129.

Maimonides, Moses (1963 [1190]) *The Guide of the Perplexed*, trans. Schlomo Pines (Chicago, IL: University of Chicago Press), Chapter 59; reprinted in Isadore Twersky (ed.) *A Maimonides Reader* (West Orange, NJ: Behrman House, Inc., 1972), 270–274.

Plotinus (253–270) Enneads, extracts in *Plotinus, A Volume of Selections in a New English Translation*, trans. A. H. Armstrong (London: Allen and Unwin and New York: Humanities Press Inc., 1953), 60–62; extract reprinted in Ian T. Ramsey (ed.) *Words About God: The Philosophy of Religion* (London: SCM Press, 1971), 20–22.

Pseudo-Dionysius (1920 [original date of publication unknown]) *On the Divine Names* in *Dionysius the Areopagite: On the Divine Names and Mystical Theology*, trans. C. E. Rolt (London: Society for the Propagation of Christian Knowledge), www.documentacatholicaomnia.eu/03d/0450-0525,_Dionysius_Areopagita,_On_The_Divine_Names_And_The_Mystical_Theology,_EN.pdf.

Sen, Sushanta (1989) 'The Vedic-Upanisadic Concept of *Brahman* (The Highest God)' in Linda Tessier (ed.) *Concepts of the Ultimate* (New York, NY: St Martin's Press), 83–97; reprinted in Andrew Eshleman (ed.) *Readings in Philosophy of Religion: East Meets West* (Malden, MA: Blackwell Publishing, 2008), 43–51.

Ware, Timothy (1997) *The Orthodox Church* (Harmondsworth: Penguin Books).

• FURTHER READING

Encyclopedia articles

Corrigan, Kevin and Harrington, L. Michael (2015) 'Pseudo-Dionysius the Areopagite', *Stanford Encyclopedia of Philosophy*, http://plato.stanford.edu/archives/spr2015/entries/pseudo-dionysius-areopagite.

Gerson, Lloyd (2014) 'Plotinus', *Stanford Encyclopedia of Philosophy*, http://plato.stanford.edu/archives/sum2014/entries/plotinus.

Seeskin, Kenneth (2014) 'Maimonides', *Stanford Encyclopedia of Philosophy*, http://plato.stanford.edu/archives/spr2014/entries/maimonides. See especially section 4.

Articles

Bradley, Arthur (2001) 'Without Negative Theology: Deconstruction and the Politics of Negative Theology', *Heythrop Journal* XLII, 2: 133–147.

Buijs, Joseph A. (1988) 'The Negative Theology of Maimonides and Aquinas', *The Review of Metaphysics* 41, 4: 723–738.

Duclow, Donald F. (1977) 'Divine Nothingness and Self-Creation in John Scotus Eriugena', *Journal of Religion* 57, 2: 109–123.

Jones, John N. (1996) 'Sculpting God: The Logic of Dionysian Negative Theology', *The Harvard Theological Review* 89, 4: 355–371.

Putnam, Hilary (1997) 'On Negative Theology', *Faith and Philosophy* 14, 4: 407–422.

Smith, James K. A. (2000) 'Between Predication and Silence: Augustine on How (not) to Speak of God', *Heythrop Journal* XLI, 1: 66–86.

Books

Sells, Michael (1994) *Mystical Languages of Unsaying* (Chicago, IL: University of Chicago Press), Chapter 2, 'The Nothingness of God in John the Scot Eriugena'.

• SECTION B: RELIGIOUS LANGUAGE AS ANALOGICAL

Analogical religious language is a way of speaking positively about the Divine which acknowledges the difference between divinity and humanity and therefore the difficulty of knowing about and giving an exact description of the Divine. Words used analogically are in some sense literally true, but their meaning is stretched in order to encompass the transcendence of the Divine. Thus, if we say that God is good, we mean that God's goodness bears some resemblance to human goodness, but that God is good to a much greater, indeed infinite, degree and cannot be fully understood or described. One of the earliest and most influential accounts of the doctrine of analogy is given by Aquinas.

Univocal and equivocal language

Before Aquinas explains his doctrine of analogy, he considers and dismisses two alternative ways of talking about God – univocal and equivocal language.

Language which is used univocally of God and God's creation means the same when it is applied to God as it does when it is applied to our human world. For example, on this view of language, when we say that God is good, we mean that God is good in exactly the same way in which a human being is good. But Aquinas thought that language cannot be used univocally of God and God's creation because God differs from God's creation. Just as the sun and the heat which it generates are not hot in the same sense, so God and the things which God creates cannot be described in the same way.

Language which is used equivocally of God and God's creation has a different meaning when it refers to God from that which it has when it refers to the human world. But we only understand the meaning of such language when it refers to human beings; we cannot understand its meaning when it is used to describe God. Aquinas rejects this interpretation of religious language too because, if language referred to God and God's creatures only in an equivocal way, there would be no way of gaining knowledge about God and we would be unable to say or prove that God is good, and so on.

Analogical language

Aquinas therefore suggests that words which are applied to both God and God's creatures are used analogically – that is, they are used in different but related senses. Aquinas wrote about his doctrine of analogy in at least three texts – the *Quaestiones Disputatae de Veritate* (*Disputed Questions on Truth*) (1256–1259), the *Summa Contra Gentiles* (1261–1263) and the *Summa Theologica* (1265–1274). These texts are difficult to harmonise, but Aquinas does seem to differentiate between at least two different ways in which language can be used analogically, and these have been very influential in subsequent discussions of religious language.

The analogy of attribution

In the *Summa Contra Gentiles* and the *Summa Theologica* Aquinas says that both God and human beings can be analogously described as 'good' not because the word 'good' applies to both God and human beings in a different but related way (which would imply that 'goodness' exists independently of God), but because God is the cause of goodness in human beings. Although we derive our knowledge of God's goodness from our knowledge of human goodness, God's goodness existed prior to human goodness because God is the source of all perfections and the cause of all creatures.

Objections to the analogy of attribution

If 'God is good' means 'God is the cause of goodness', someone could object that this tells us nothing about the nature of divine goodness. We could, however, respond that this depends upon what we mean by saying that God is the cause of something. For Aquinas, God is an 'efficient cause' (1261–1263, Book I, Chapter 28, Article 7), a term borrowed from Aristotle (c. 384–322 BCE) to mean that God is the agent of change in something which is not God. Efficient causes do not necessarily embody the characteristics of the things or events which they bring about. For example, I could bring about the existence of a knitted sweater without, myself, being a knitted sweater. We could, however, argue that the production of an effect does require certain characteristics to be present in its efficient cause. While I may not resemble a knitted sweater, in order to produce it I must be able to knit and possess the necessary knitting needles and yarn. So perhaps it might be possible to say that, although we have only a limited conception of the true nature of divine goodness, the doctrine of analogy does tell us that God is whatever it is which is able to, and does, produce goodness.

Someone who is a pantheist, a panentheist or perhaps even a classical theist who accepts the doctrine of divine immanence (the belief that God is present everywhere and in everything) might also make use of another of Aristotle's four causes to say that God is the 'material cause' of worldly goodness. This might, in fact, be compatible with Aquinas's teaching that God is the source of all perfections. On this view, 'God is the cause of goodness' would mean that examples of goodness embody or exhibit divine goodness to the extent to which they are good. Alternatively, someone could say, again following Aristotle, that God is the 'formal cause' of goodness. A formal cause is one which provides a thing's structure. Here, God might be said to provide or constitute the plan or pattern in which goodness features and is gradually brought into existence.

The analogy of proportionality

In the *Disputed Questions on Truth*, Aquinas describes the analogy of proportionality, in which two things resemble each other not because one is directly related to the other but because they each have the same relationship to something else. So, 'sight' can be applied both to bodily sight and to understanding because sight has the same relationship to the eye as understanding has to the mind. This means that both God and human beings can be described as 'good' because the relationship between God and divine goodness is the same as that between humankind and human goodness.

Objections to the analogy of proportionality

Perhaps the most significant difficulty with the analogy of proportionality runs as follows. A mathematical proportion must have three known terms for us to be able to find the fourth. For example, if we know that 6 is to 3 as x is to 2, we can find the value of x. Aquinas tries to say that the relationship between humankind and human goodness is the same as that between God and divine goodness and that, since we know the relationship between humankind and human goodness, we can work out the relationship between God and divine goodness. But we cannot do this because we do not know enough about either God or divine goodness. This means that we have two unknown terms, and that the analogy of proportionality therefore fails to help us to understand the nature of divine goodness.

We could, however, argue that we can gain some knowledge of the nature of God and of divine goodness from the scriptures of the world's religions, read in the light of many centuries of human scholarship, and that, although humankind is never likely to produce a definitive account of the nature of God and God's goodness, it might be possible to say something about them by means of Aquinas's analogy of proportionality.

> ## Reflection
> To what extent does the doctrine of analogy help us to talk about the Divine?

Conclusion

In this section, we have considered Aquinas's doctrine of analogy and seen that he thinks that there are two ways in which religious language can be understood as analogical. If we understand God's goodness as an analogy of attribution, we mean to say that God is the cause of the goodness we see around us. It is commonly objected that

'God is good' means much more to the religious believer than 'God is the cause of worldly goodness'. I suggested, however, that, if God is the cause of worldly goodness, this may, in fact, tell us something – if not everything – about God. If God is the 'efficient cause' of goodness, as Aquinas believed, God is whatever it is that is the source of all goodness. But if God is, in some sense, a 'material cause' of goodness, then examples of goodness in our world at least partially 'embody' divine goodness in our world. And if God is, in some sense, a 'formal cause' of goodness, then God provides, or is, the structure, the 'moral rules', perhaps, which enables the creation of worldly goodness.

If we understand God's goodness as an analogy of proportionality, we mean to say that the relationship between God and God's goodness is like – but much greater than – the relationship between humankind and human goodness. It is commonly objected that we do not know enough about either God or God's goodness for an analogy of proportionality to tell us anything about God or God's goodness that we did not already know. I suggested, however, that the terms 'God' and 'God's goodness' are not entirely devoid of content since this is provided, at least to some extent, by the scriptures of the world's religions and the writings of their interpreters across many centuries.

Nevertheless, as Aquinas himself was well aware, not all language about God can be understood analogically. For example, religious believers commonly say 'God is my rock', but God is clearly not rock-like in any literal, even if stretched, sense. This, then, is an example of metaphor, which will be our topic of discussion in the next section of this chapter.

• REFERENCES

Aquinas, Thomas (1952 [1256–1259]) *Quaestiones Disputatae de Veritate* (*Disputed Questions on Truth*) Question 2, Article 11, trans. Robert W. Mulligan (Chicago, IL: Henry Regnery Company), http://dhspriory.org/thomas/QDdeVer.htm.

Aquinas, Thomas (1955–1957 [1261–1263]) *Summa Contra Gentiles* ed. Joseph Kenny, Book I, trans. Anton C. Pegis (New York, NY: Hanover House), http://dhspriory.org/thomas/ContraGentiles.htm, Book I, Chapters 28–34.

Aquinas, Thomas (2016 [1920, 1265–1274]) *The Summa Theologica of St Thomas Aquinas*, trans. Fathers of the English Dominican Province, www.newadvent.org/summa/, First Part, Question 13, Articles 5 and 6.

• FURTHER READING

Encyclopedia articles

Ashworth, E. Jennifer (2013) 'Medieval Theories of Analogy', *Stanford Encyclopedia of Philosophy*, http://plato.stanford.edu/archives/win2013/entries/analogy-medieval.

Hart Weed, Jennifer (n.d.) 'Religious Language', *Internet Encyclopedia of Philosophy*, www.iep.utm.edu/rel-lang/.

Original articles in edited collections

Hughes, Gerard J. (1987) 'Aquinas and the Limits of Agnosticism' in Gerard J.
    Hughes (ed.) *The Philosophical Assessment of Theology: Essays in Honour of Frederick
    C. Copleston* (Tunbridge Wells: Search Press), 37–52.
Ross, James (1998) 'Religious Language' in Brian Davies (ed.) *Philosophy of Religion:
    A Guide to the Subject* (London: Cassell), 106–135.

Articles

Deely, John (2002) 'The Absence of Analogy', *The Review of Metaphysics* 55, 3: 521–550.
Gamwell, Frank (2001) 'Speaking of God After Aquinas', *The Journal of Religion* 81,
    2: 185–210.
McClendon, Jr. James Wm. and Smith, James M. (1973) 'Ian Ramsey's Model of
    Religious Language: A Qualified Appreciation', *Journal of the American Academy
    of Religion* 41, 3: 413–424.
Sherry, Patrick (1976) 'Analogy Today', *Philosophy* 51, 198: 431–446.

Books

Macquarrie, John (1994) *God-Talk: An Examination of the Language and Logic of
    Theology* (London: XPress Reprints), Chapter 10.
Stiver, Dan R. (1996) *The Philosophy of Religious Language: Sign, Symbol and Story*
    (Malden, MA: Blackwell), 14–15, 20–29.
Swinburne, Richard (2016) *The Coherence of Theism* (Oxford: Clarendon Press), 55–75.
White, Roger M. (2010) *Talking About God: The Concept of Analogy and the Problem of
    Religious Language* (Farnham: Ashgate).

• SECTION C: RELIGIOUS LANGUAGE AS METAPHORICAL

As we saw at the end of Section B, not all positive religious language is analogical. For example, a believer who says 'The Lord is my rock' (Psalm 18:2) is clearly not claiming that God is an inanimate physical body of determinate size, shape and location. She is more likely to be claiming that God is unchanging and dependable – that is, something upon which she can depend in even the most difficult of circumstances. This means that at least some religious language may be understood as metaphorical.

Broadly speaking, a metaphor is a word or phrase in which we speak about something – or someone – as if it were something – or someone – which it clearly is not in any literal sense, but with which it shares some characteristics which we wish to highlight. So, for the believer who says 'God is my rock', God is not 'a rock' even in an extended literal sense but, in calling God 'a rock', she highlights in God the characteristics which God shares with rocks – that God is unchanging and therefore dependable.

Reflection

What is the difference between an analogy and a metaphor?

Which of the following are analogies and which are metaphors? Give reasons for your answers.

'The Lord is good' (Psalm 100:5)

'You are the King of Israel' (John 1:49)

'Allah is Mighty, Wise' (Qur'an 8:10)

'Your Maker is your husband' (Isaiah 54:5)

'There is one God, the Father' (I Corinthians 8:6)

The meaning of metaphor

There are a number of theories about the meaning of metaphor. Here are some of the most common:

1 The ornamental or substitution theory of metaphor

According to this theory, metaphor is just a decorative substitution for literal language; it embellishes what we already know, but does not tell us anything which we do not already know. On this view, then, saying 'God is my rock' is simply a decorative substitution for 'God is unchanging; I can always depend upon God'. It is simply a more interesting – and, in this case, at least – a more concise way of talking about God which can easily be translated into literal language.

John Locke (1632–1704) seems to have thought of religious metaphors simply as helpful illustrations using things familiar to them from daily life for those without the time or ability to understand theology – by which he meant manual labourers, and women (1958 [1695]: 76). But while this may be demeaning to a significant pro-portion of humankind, and therefore not a view which would be widely regarded as acceptable today, it could be argued that, even if metaphors can be translated into literal language, they can help to make difficult concepts easier to grasp, thereby helping religious believers to understand better something of the nature of the Divine.

2 The emotive theory of metaphor

This theory of metaphor claims that it is the emotional impact of a metaphor which provides the key to understanding it. So, to return to the 'God is my rock' example, according to this theory, the meaning of the phrase is to be found in the emotion which it sparks – perhaps a feeling of security and comfort in the face of life's difficulties. Understood in this way, metaphor can make a written or spoken text more vibrant, enabling the believer to engage with the Divine at a deeper level.

3 Cognitive theories of metaphor

During the twentieth century, a number of key contributions to our understanding of metaphor claimed that metaphor is not only a decorative literary device or a way of producing an emotion. Since the work of I. A. Richards (1893–1979) (1936) it has been widely accepted that metaphor can also convey understanding (cognition) of something which cannot be described in any other way, while Max Black (1909–1988) (1954–1955) argued that metaphor not only helps us to understand reality but perhaps also, in some sense, creates reality.

Paul Ricoeur (1913–2005) (1978) pointed out that it is a metaphor's literal absurdity, its 'semantic shock', which draws our attention to its 'semantic innovation', the new meaning which the words convey. George Lakoff (2003 [1980]) and Mark Johnson (1981) argued that, in addition to those which provoke 'semantic shock', there are also 'metaphors we live by' – i.e. those which have not yet come to be understood as literal (for example, 'dead' metaphors such as the 'legs' of a chair), but which are nevertheless metaphors in a less striking sense.

Religious metaphors may fall into both categories. An example of a metaphor which gives rise to a semantic shock may be found in Deuteronomy 32:18, where we find a reference to God giving birth to God's people. Metaphors of this kind have been developed by Sallie McFague (1987), who recommends that God should be thought of not as Father, Son and Holy Spirit, but as Mother, Lover and Friend. Many religious metaphors fall into the category of metaphors we live by, however. 'God is my rock' may be said to fall into this category, since the word 'rock' is so commonly applied to both God and human beings that it has long ceased to be surprising.

Ian T. Ramsey (1915–1972) argues (1971 [1966]) that the metaphors, or 'models', of God in the Hebrew Bible/Old Testament may be divided into three categories:

- Those associated with the home and friends (Father, Mother, Husband, Friend);
- Those associated with work (Shepherd, Farmer, Dairymaid, Laundress, Builder, Potter, Fisherman, Tradesman, Physician, Teacher/Scribe, Nurse, Metal worker); and
- Those associated with national or international politics (King, Warrior, Judge).

Ramsey argues that models of the first kind (those associated with the home and friends) are used when talking about God because patterns of behaviour which are commonly associated with parents, spouses and friends, such as reliability and trustworthiness, are similar in some respects to patterns which we see in the natural world, such as the regular occurrence of seed-planting and harvest. So, Ramsey says, we can refer to God as, for example, 'Friend' because we can see features of the natural world which suggest reliability and trustworthiness.

But, just as our relationships with our parents, spouses and friends are, in some sense, 'more' than simply an account of common patterns of behaviour, so models of God which are associated with the home and family also refer to something which is 'more' than just an account of characteristic patterns of behaviour and can, at least sometimes, lead to what Ramsey calls 'cosmic disclosures'. These are situations in which we are somehow able to see another 'dimension' of the Universe and which can happen in any situation, whether this be while sitting at home, participating in a religious ceremony or on a walk in the country. So, to speak of God in terms of the model 'Friend' is not only to refer to the reliability and trustworthiness of natural processes; it is also to experience a 'sense of kinship' (207) with the Universe.

Models of the second type, those associated with work, also tell us about behaviour – for example, Ramsey suggests that the model 'Shepherd' implies that there must have been something about the social behaviour of the Israelites which was similar to the behaviour of sheep, and that it would therefore be appropriate to describe the behaviour of God in terms of the work of a shepherd. Again, such models, normally used to describe human beings, can be occasions of cosmic disclosure. So, both the event (Israel behaving like sheep) and the application of the model of 'Shepherd' to God not only disclose something about the 'character' of God but also, in some sense, reveal the transcendence ('otherness') of God – that is, the knowledge that, although God has some of the characteristics of a human shepherd, God is also, in some sense, very different from, and much greater than, a human shepherd.

Lastly, Ramsey argues that models of the third type, those which are derived from national or international politics, have unlimited potential to disclose a God who is powerful, victorious and just.

Which theory of metaphor?

Some scholars reject both the ornamental or substitution theory and the emotive theory in favour of cognitive theories of metaphor. For example, Janet Martin Soskice (b. 1951) argues that the ornamental theory reduces metaphor to no more than a riddle or word game (1985: 25). She also claims that, if we adopt an emotive theory of metaphor, it is sometimes difficult to say what the emotive content of a metaphor is, and that the emotive theory cannot explain how the same word can have both positive and negative effects. For example, the word 'sharp' in the phrase 'a sharp wit' is being used in a positive sense (Soskice, 1985: 27). This might be contrasted with the use of the same word in the phrase 'a sharp practice', which implies a range of negative connotations. Similarly, we could say that, although 'God is my rock' is usually associated with positive emotions, if we were to interpret the phase as indicating that God is immovable and therefore uncompromising, it might also be associated with negative emotions.

Cognitive theories of metaphor also encounter a range of objections, however, including the following:

1 The problem of meaning

    The meaning of a metaphor is sometimes unclear. Soskice argues that we can learn the meaning of metaphors by examining their use in the Bible (1985: 154–159), but Gerard J. Hughes objects that, although the way in which metaphors are used in the Bible does often restrict their meaning, in most cases there remains a broad range of possible meanings from which to choose (1987: 58).

Reflection

If a Christian can decide what it means to call God 'Father' by looking at the way in which God is portrayed in the Bible, does this imply that a metaphor cannot tell her anything which she does not already know?

2 The problem of inadequacy

All metaphors are, at least in some respects, inadequate. As Ramsey points out, no one who describes God as a physician asks whether God will benefit from a pay increase for consultants (1971 [1966]): 209). Ramsey suggests two responses which may be applied both to the problem of meaning and to the problem of inadequacy: firstly, we must use a wide range of models so that we may harmonise their 'dominant strands' – the aspects of them which we do want to apply to God – and exclude their limitations. Secondly, we must ensure that our talk about God is consistent with 'patterns of events in the world around us' (210).

3 The problem of preferences

Ramsey also notes what he calls the problem of preferences – the question of how we choose between the variety of models available. He suggests that there are two ways in which the use of a model can be justified. Firstly, it can be compared with other models. For example, the model 'Protector' might be considered more wide-ranging than the model 'Laundress'. And a model such as 'Person' may be better than 'Shepherd' or 'Potter' because it can say what is said by the latter, and more. Secondly, in a development of his response to the problem of inadequacy, Ramsey suggests that we should consider the extent to which a model 'fits' the Universe. For example, although the model 'Love' might encompass many other models, it still has to meet the challenge of the existence of evil in the world, and it must still be possible to show that there are situations in the world which can be 'legitimately "interpreted by love"' (214). Ramsey suggests that, whether or not models 'fit' the world is not, strictly speaking, something which we test by means of experience; he argues that the kind of 'fit' we should look for is more like that which a detective seeks between a working theory of a crime and newly-discovered clues.

4 The problem of reference

Lastly, there is the question of what metaphors or models refer to. When we use metaphors or models in the context of religious belief and practice, how do we know that we are referring to something beyond ourselves? And how do we know that each metaphor or model refers to the same thing? Ramsey asks us to imagine drawing a series of regular polygons with an ever-increasing number of sides, all of which have their vertices (a vertex is a point where two straight lines meet) equidistant from a fixed point. At some point in this process, a circle will be disclosed – even if we have to refer to it as x because we do not know about circles. If, in such circumstances, we then wanted to speak about x, talk about polygons would be a reasonable approximation. And, if someone eventually discovered a treatise about circles, it would become clear that there were close similarities between talk about circles and talk about x, so that it would now be reasonable to refer to x as 'circle'. Similarly, Ramsey suggests, repeated cosmic disclosures are gradually revealing to humankind an x which is so all-embracing – something which is experienced across the world by so many people – that it is reasonable for us to think that there is just one x, and that some metaphors or models provide us with better ways of speaking about it than others. This might lead us to talk about x in language which is close to that which a believer uses about God. We would therefore be justified in saying that x is God, and that the metaphors or models are metaphors or models of God, and that cosmic disclosures disclose God.

This may be an imprecise method for conveying understanding, but, as Hughes points out, even in the physical sciences, theories are described in terms of metaphors for which there is no literal translation. Hughes therefore concludes that metaphor can express some theological truths which have no literal equivalent; it may not offer us a precise way of speaking about God, but this does not mean that it cannot refer to God.

Reflection

Is it reasonable to argue that a cosmic disclosure can confirm what a metaphor refers to, or that metaphors and models are our best attempts to describe cosmic disclosures?

How might cosmic disclosures be distinguished from 'spurious or hallucinatory experiences' (Stiver, 1996: 77)?

Conclusion

In this section, we have examined several interpretations of metaphor and model. Broadly speaking, these may be divided into non-cognitive interpretations, which hold that metaphorical language does not add to our knowledge about God, and cognitive interpretations, which claim that metaphor does enable us to say something about God which cannot be communicated in any other way.

Although some may be dismissive of non-cognitive interpretations, the ornamental/substitution theory can help us to grasp difficult concepts, while the emotive theory can help us to engage with the concept of the Divine, even if we cannot always say exactly what emotions have been produced. This may be no more problematic than it is for any kind of aesthetic experience, however. For example, many would agree that music conjures up a range of emotions, some of which may be undisputed. In other cases, however, people will have different experiences of the same piece of music and its performance and will describe this, insofar as they can describe it, in different ways. In such cases, this emotive ambiguity is not usually said to detract from the value of the experience.

Cognitive theories suggest that both our understanding and our emotions may be hinting at something 'beyond' ourselves, an unknown 'x' which we cannot fully understand. So perhaps these theories of metaphor are not mutually exclusive; it may not be necessary to choose just one interpretation of metaphor since each of them may have something to contribute to our understanding of how we can use words which are normally applied to things or phenomena within our human world to that which is, in some sense, greater than any worldly thing or phenomenon. It may therefore be a cumulative theory of metaphor which most effectively enables us to speak of the Divine.

• REFERENCES

Black, Max (1954–1955) 'Metaphor' in *Proceedings of the Aristotelian Society*, N. S. 55, 273–294; reprinted in Mark Johnson (ed.) *Philosophical Perspectives on Metaphor* (Minneapolis, MN: The University of Minnesota, 1981), 63–82.

Hughes, Gerard J. (1987) 'Aquinas and the Limits of Agnosticism' in Gerard J. Hughes (ed.) *The Philosophical Assessment of Theology: Essays in Honour of Frederick C. Copleston* (Tunbridge Wells: Search Press), 52–60.

Johnson, Mark (1981) (ed.) *Philosophical Perspectives on Metaphor* (Minneapolis, MN: The University of Minnesota).

Lakoff, George and Johnson, Mark (2003 [1980]) *Metaphors We Live By* (Chicago, IL: University of Chicago Press).

Locke, John (1958 [1695]) *The Reasonableness of Christianity with A Discourse of Miracles and Part of A Third Letter Concerning Toleration*, ed. I. T. Ramsey (California: Stanford University Press).

McFague, Sallie (1987) *Models of God: Theology for an Ecological, Nuclear Age* (Philadephia, PA: Fortress Press); extract reprinted in John Hick (ed.) *Classical and Contemporary Readings in the Philosophy of Religion* (Englewood Cliffs, NJ: Prentice-Hall, 1990), 433–463.

Ramsey, Ian T. (1966) 'Talking About God' in F. W. Dillistone (ed.) *Myth and Symbol* (London: SPCK); extract reprinted in Ian T. Ramsey (ed.) *Words About God: The Philosophy of Religion* (London: SCM Press, 1971), 202–223.

Richards, I. A. (1936) *The Philosophy of Rhetoric* (Oxford: Oxford University Press), Chapter V, 87–112; reprinted in Mark Johnson (ed.) *Philosophical Perspectives on Metaphor* (Minneapolis, MN: The University of Minnesota, 1981), 48–62.

Ricoeur, Paul (1978) 'The Metaphorical Process as Cognition, Imagination and Feeling', *Critical Inquiry* 5, 1: 143–159; reprinted in Mark Johnson (ed.) *Philosophical Perspectives on Metaphor* (Minneapolis, MN: University of Minnesota Press, 1981), 228–247.

Soskice, Janet Martin (1985) *Metaphor and Religious Language* (Oxford: Clarendon Press, 1985), Chapters 7 and 8.

Stiver, Dan R. (1996) *The Philosophy of Religious Language: Sign, Symbol and Story* (Malden, MA: Blackwell), 74–78, 112–122, 127–133.

• FURTHER READING

Original articles in edited collections

Brümmer, Vincent (2006) 'Metaphorical Thinking' in John R. Hinnells (ed.) *Brümmer on Meaning and the Christian Faith: Collected Writings of Vincent Brümmer* (Farnham: Ashgate), 143–154.

Frankenberry, Nancy (2002) 'Religion as a "Mobile Army of Metaphors"' in Nancy Frankenberry (ed.) *Radical Interpretation in Religion* (Cambridge: Cambridge University Press), 171–187.

Articles

Burgess, Andrew J. (1972) 'Irreducible Religious Metaphors', *Religious Studies* 8, 4: 355–366.

Harrison, Victoria (2007) 'Metaphor, Religious Language and Religious Experience', *Sophia: International Journal for Philosophy of Religion* 46, 2: 127–145.

Insole, C. J. (2002) 'Metaphor and the Impossbility of Failing to Speak About God', *International Journal for Philosophy of Religion* 52, 1: 35–43.

Books

Alston, William P. (1989) *Divine Nature and Human Language: Essays in Philosophical Theology* (Ithaca, NY: Cornell University Press), Essay 1.

Aquinas, Thomas (2016 [1920, 1265–1274]) *The Summa Theologica of St Thomas Aquinas*, trans. Fathers of the English Dominican Province, www.newadvent.org/summa/, First Part, Question 13, Article 3.

Avis, Paul (1999) *God and the Creative Imagination: Metaphor, Symbol and Myth in Religion and Theology* (London: Routledge), Chapter 9.

Hick, John (2005 [1993]) *The Metaphor of God Incarnate* (London: SCM Press).

Ramsey, Ian T. (1957) *Religious Language* (London: SCM Press).

Soskice, Janet (2007) *The Kindness of God: Metaphor, Gender and Religious Language* (New York, NY: Oxford University Press).

Vroom, Hendrik K. (2006) *A Spectrum of Worldviews: An Introduction to Philosophy of Religion in a Pluralistic World*, trans. Morris and Alice Greidanus (Amsterdam and New York: Editions Rodopi B. V.), Chapter 5.

3

religious language: twentieth-century developments

• INTRODUCTION

So far, we have seen that we can talk about the Divine using the negative way (by saying only what the Divine is not), the doctrine of analogy (which claims that the attributes of the Divine are like human attributes, but that the human versions of these attributes are lesser forms of them) or metaphor (by talking about the Divine in terms of something which is not literally applicable [e.g. 'God is my rock'], but which implies some of the attributes of the Divine). Each of these forms of religious language has been in use for many centuries and remains in use today.

In this chapter I will examine two important developments in the study of religious language from the twentieth century.

• SECTION A: RELIGIOUS BELIEF AND LANGUAGE-GAMES

In this section, I will consider the claim, derived from the work of the philosopher Ludwig Wittgenstein (1889–1951) and applied to religious language most notably by D. Z. Phillips (1934–2006), that religious language is a 'language-game' which can only be understood by those who learn its 'grammar' – the rules for its use.

Wittgenstein's language-game theory

In his later philosophy, particularly the *Philosophical Investigations* (published post-humously in 1953), Wittgenstein argues that the meaning of language depends upon the way in which it is used; philosophy does not tell us what we should and should not say but 'leaves everything as it is' (1953: paragraph 124) and simply observes and describes how language is used.

Wittgenstein talks about both 'forms of life' and 'language-games', although in neither case is the meaning of the term unambiguous. By 'form of life', Wittgenstein appears to mean something like 'way of life' – in other words, the actions which are associated with different activities. On this view, a religious form of life might include such things as attending a synagogue, church or mosque, participating in religious ceremonies, and so on. In his use of the term 'language-game', Wittgenstein draws our attention to 'the fact that the speaking of language is part of an activity, or of a form of life' (1953: paragraph 23), although, for Wittgenstein, a language-game such as 'thanking' may be associated with more than one form of life. For example, thanking may be associated both with 'hospitality' in which an appropriate action might be to offer a gift of flowers, and with 'religion' in which an appropriate action might be to kneel or, for Muslims, adopt the position of *sajdah* (head, knees and hands on the floor) and pray (my example). He argues that we cannot judge whether a language-game is meaningful by observing it from the outside; we learn to distinguish between sense and nonsense by using language in various situations throughout our lives.

In using language, we learn its 'grammar' – the rules for its use which establish what can and cannot be said. Like forms of life and language-games, grammar is simply 'given'; the rules of grammar cannot and do not need to be justified. We do not decide the grammar which governs the way in which we talk about material objects; we have to take some things for granted, otherwise we would not be able to make any judgements at all (Wittgenstein, 1969: 211).

Reflection

What is the difference between a form of life and a language-game?

Wittgenstein on religious belief

Wittgenstein never gave a comprehensive philosophical analysis of religious belief, but there are a few shorter writings which have some bearing on any discussion of his view of the grammar of religious language.

In his *Remarks on Frazer's Golden Bough* (1975), written in 1931, Wittgenstein rejects the reductionist explanations of apparently primitive religious ceremonies (that is, explanations which describe such ceremonies in terms which are not recognisably religious) of the anthropologist James George Frazer (1854–1941). He says that the practices described in *The Golden Bough* (subtitled *A Study in Comparative Religion* in its first edition [1890] and amended to *A Study in Magic and Religion* in its second edition [1900]) are not the consequence of erroneous scientific theories, and the participants are not 'stupid'. The ceremonies only appear superstitious if we neglect the role they play in people's lives. Wittgenstein resists strongly the tendency to explain beliefs and practices, and says that the idea that primitive human beings experienced a sense of awe when confronted by natural phenomena because they could not explain them is a stupid superstition of our time. In attempting to explain religious practices, Frazer thinks that the participants commit 'errors' or 'mistakes', but Wittgenstein says that 'none of them was making a mistake except when he was putting forward a theory' (29). We can speak of 'errors' or 'mistakes' only within the context of opinions, hypotheses and explanations. Wittgenstein says that the anthropologist should describe rather than explain; we can only describe, because 'human life is like that' (30).

In his *Lectures and Conversations on Aesthetics, Psychology and Religious Belief* (1966), transcriptions of lectures given between 1938 and 1946, Wittgenstein says that religious beliefs are not true in the sense that they are based on good evidence; even if it could be shown that religious beliefs cannot be doubted, this would not lead him to change his whole life. Rather, the person who says that religious beliefs are true is saying that she lives by them, that they provide a framework for her life. It follows from this that religious belief cannot be justified by means of procedures which are used outside the religious framework; religious belief is an absolute 'rock-bottom' conviction.

D. Z. Phillips on religious belief and language-games

D. Z. Phillips (1934–2006) was, perhaps, the best-known of a group of philosophers who applied Wittgenstein's later philosophy to religious belief. Following Wittgenstein, Phillips argues (1963, 1993) that the purpose of philosophy is not to ask questions about what does or does not exist, but simply to describe what people say and do. So the philosopher of religion who asks questions about the reality of God is not asking *whether* God exists but *how* God exists – she is asking how we are to understand God's reality in the light of what believers say about God and the way in which they put their beliefs into practice.

Phillips argues that religious beliefs and practices are learnt from those who already believe and practice; believers learn to participate in the 'language-game' of belief, and to live the religious 'form of life'. For Phillips, talk about religious belief is a distinctive way of talking with a set of rules for its use which do not apply to other language-games, just as the game of football has a set of rules which do not apply to the game of rugby. But we cannot understand religion simply by analysing its language; we can properly understand the meaning of religious language only by observing and examining the practices with which it is closely allied. So the rules for using a language-game are its grammar, and theology is the grammar of the religious language-game; theology tells us what we can say about, and to, God. But theology may be derived from the experience of God and way of life of the person constructing the theology – i.e. their form of life. Phillips says that, where there is no connection between theology and experience, theology can become simply an academic game. Theology is not derived only from the experience of individuals, however. For Phillips, we cannot choose just *any* idea of God: once we have accepted a theology, we have accepted what can and cannot be said in that religion, and what can and cannot be said does not depend upon the views of any single person.

A child learns a religious language-game by listening to religious stories and watching believers practice their faith and, in so doing, forms an idea of God. But this knowledge of God is not knowledge of an objectively-existing supreme being; it is knowledge of how to use religious concepts. What is regarded as logical in the context of one language-game and form of life may not be regarded as logical in the context of another. So what makes sense in the context of religion may not make sense in the context of science, and vice versa. We therefore need to learn the logical rules which apply in each.

Three objections to the language-game interpretation of religious belief

Objections to the interpretation of religious belief in terms of language-games and forms of life include the following:

1 According to Wittgenstein and his followers, religious belief can only be properly understood by those with faith – that is, from within a religious language-game and form of life – and cannot be criticised from the perspective of any other language-game or form of life, and therefore need not take into account, for example, what scientists say about the origins of the universe, what historians tell us about the events of the early Christian centuries, or our own experience of everyday life.

Phillips admits that, since God's reality is not like the reality of other things, we cannot assess belief in God as if it were like a scientific hypothesis which may or may not be true. But this does not mean that religious believers can say anything they like when talking about their belief. For example, if they were to try to explain away the reality of suffering, or talk about death as if it were a long sleep, we would be able to judge their claims in the light of what we already know about suffering and death and to say that their beliefs fail to take relevant facts into account or distort our understanding (Phillips, 1970). So Phillips argues that religions are not isolated language-games and forms of life which are cut off from all other aspects of life; in fact, they can only be properly understood if we take into account the way in which they relate to other forms of life.

2 Although Wittgenstein and his followers claim simply to describe what religious believers say and do without making any judgement regarding the truth or falsity of the beliefs in question, they are actually recommending a new interpretation of religious belief.

Phillips denies that he is revising or constructing new beliefs, claiming instead that he observes religious beliefs and practices and tries to describe what is really happening, like Wittgenstein, who said: 'I ought to be no more than a mirror in which my reader can see his own thinking with all its deformities so that, helped in this way, he can put it right' (Wittgenstein, 1980: 18). So both Wittgenstein and Phillips aim to help the believer identify and discard beliefs and practices which are not religious but superstitious – in other words, those which are the consequence of fear and constitute a kind of false science. Phillips admits that perhaps only a few people will be sustained by religious belief as described by Wittgenstein and Phillips, although he expects that mistaken interpretations of religious belief are in the process of being replaced by new and better pictures. This does seem to imply that his interpretation of religious belief is, after all, revisionary, but Phillips argues that believers from different historical periods, such as Abraham and Paul, were worshipping the same God, even if there are many differences in their concepts of God, if their beliefs may be seen as part of a common, developing religious tradition.

3 Wittgensteinian interpretations of religious belief are reductionist – that is, they reduce religious belief to something which can no longer be considered religious. For example, if 'God' is simply a word in a language-game, God is no longer the creator of the universe who cares for God's creation.

Phillips denies this charge and argues that, in fact, it is those who accept a more traditional interpretation of religious belief who are guilty of reductionism because, for them, religious beliefs are not beliefs which are accepted for their own sake but a means to a selfish end – a continuing existence of some kind after death.

Conclusion

In this section we have examined the view, derived from the later philosophy of Wittgenstein and developed by Phillips, that talk about God is a language-game. We may observe the way in which religious believers talk about God, and the practices with which their language is associated. If we have grown up surrounded by parents and friends who speak this language and live this form of life, we must choose whether or not to remain within this religious framework and to continue to use it as the framework for our own lives. If we are observers of an unfamiliar language and form of life, we may choose to speak that language and live that form of life in order to test them before deciding whether or not to choose them as the framework for our own lives.

Reflection

Is talk about God a language-game? Consider each of the objections listed above in turn.

• REFERENCES

Frazer, J. G. (1890) *The Golden Bough: A Study in Comparative Religion* (London: Macmillan).

Frazer, J. G. (1900) *The Golden Bough: A Study in Magic and Religion* (London: Macmillan).

Phillips, D. Z. (1963) 'Philosophy, Theology and the Reality of God', *The Philosophical Quarterly* 13, 53: 344–350; reprinted in Brian Davies (ed.) *Philosophy of Religion: A Guide and Anthology* (Oxford: Oxford University Press, 2000), 108–114.

Phillips, D. Z. (1970) *Death and Immortality* (London: Macmillan).

Phillips, D. Z. (1993) *Wittgenstein and Religion* (New York, NY: St Martin's Press).

Wittgenstein, Ludwig (1953) *Philosophical Investigations*, ed. G. E. M. Anscombe and Rush Rhees, trans. G. E. M. Anscombe (Oxford: Basil Blackwell). See especially passages between 232 and 364 (nb. 253–261 and 293).

Wittgenstein, Ludwig (1966) *Lectures and Conversations on Aesthetics, Psychology and Religious Belief*, ed. C. Barrett (Oxford: Blackwell).

Wittgenstein, Ludwig (1969) *On Certainty*, ed. G. E. M. Anscombe and G. H. von Wright, trans. Denis Paul and G. E. M. Anscombe (Oxford: Blackwell).

Wittgenstein, Ludwig (1975) *Remarks on Frazer's Golden Bough*, ed. Rush Rhees, trans. Raymond Hargreaves and Roger White (Oxford: Blackwell).

Wittgenstein, Ludwig (1980) *Culture and Value*, ed. G.H. von Wright in collaboration with Heikki Nyman, trans. Peter Winch (Oxford: Basil Blackwell).

• FURTHER READING

Encyclopedia article

Biletzki, Anat and Matar, Anat (2014) 'Ludwig Wittgenstein', *Stanford Encyclopedia of Philosophy*, www.plato.stanford.edu/archives/spr2014/entries/wittgenstein.

Original articles in edited collections

Hyman, John (2010 [1997]) 'Wittgenstein' in Charles Taliaferro, Paul Draper and Philip L. Quinn (eds) *A Companion to Philosophy of Religion* (Chichester: Wiley-Blackwell, 1999), 176–188.

Moore, G. and Davies, B. (1998) 'Wittgenstein and the Philosophy of Religion' in B. Davies (ed.) *Philosophy of Religion: A Guide to the Subject* (London: Cassell), 27–34.

Neilson, Kai (2013 [2007]) 'The Problem of Religious Language' in Chad Meister and Paul Copan (eds) *The Routledge Companion to Philosophy of Religion* (London: Routledge), 482–486.

Articles

Min, Anselm K. (2008) 'D. Z. Phillips on the Grammar of "God"', *International Journal for Philosophy of Religion* 63, 1: 131–146.

Phillips, D. Z. (2002) 'Propositions, Pictures and Practices', *Ars Disputandi*, 2, 1: 68–74, DOI:10.1080/15665399.2002.10819746, http://dx.doi.org/10.1080/15665399.2002.10819746.

Pihlstrom, Sami (2007) 'Religion and Pseudo-Religion: An Elusive Boundary', *International Journal for Philosophy of Religion* 62, 1: 3–32.

Books

Arrington, Robert L. and Addis, Mark (2004 [2001]) *Wittgenstein and Philosophy of Religion* (London: Routledge).

Clack, Brian R. (1999) *An Introduction to Wittgenstein's Philosophy of Religion* (Edinburgh: Edinburgh University Press).

Kerr, Fergus (1997) *Theology After Wittgenstein* (London: SPCK).

McCutcheon, Felicity (2001) *Religion Within the Limits of Language Alone: Wittgenstein on Philosophy and Religion* (Aldershot: Ashgate).

Stiver, Dan R. (1996) *The Philosophy of Religious Language: Sign, Symbol and Story* (Malden, MA: Blackwell), Chapter 4.

• SECTION B: REALISM AND NON-REALISM IN RELIGIOUS LANGUAGE

From the twentieth century onwards, philosophers of religion have been concerned with the question of whether religious language should be understood as making realist or non-realist claims about religious belief and practice – that is, whether it refers to something which exists independently of human thought, or to ideas created by humankind to embody ideal human values.

Realism and religion

Realism is the view that something exists independently of human perception. Someone can be a global realist (a realist about everything), but it is more common to be a realist about certain aspects of our world. So:

1 A realist about the external world would say that tables and chairs have some kind of existence which is not dependent upon our perceptions of them; they are 'really there', even when we are not looking at them.
2 A realist about morality would say that our actions are right or wrong, regardless of what we think about them; it is not the case that an action is right or wrong simply because human beings – or some of them – decide that it is.
3 A realist about the Divine would say that the Divine exists independently of the human mind, or independently of the community of believers.

There is sometimes a lack of clarity regarding whether a realist is making claims about metaphysics (what exists and the nature of what exists) or epistemology (what and how we can know). Those who accept the latter view commonly say that realism entails, or is equivalent to, acceptance of the correspondence theory of truth, according to which statements are true if they correspond with an objectively-existing reality. A naïve realist would say that language has some kind of direct link with objectively-existing things. But it is now more common to be a critical realist, someone who acknowledges that the way we perceive the world to some extent affects what we see; to put it another way, there is no 'God's-eye view' of reality, no perspectiveless way to see the world. On this view, the link between our language and reality is therefore not straightforward but our statements do nonetheless describe, even if inadequately, an objectively-existing world.

Anti-realism, non-realism and religious language

Anti-realism is sometimes used interchangeably with non-realism, with the latter now the more commonly-used term (e.g. Moore, 2003: 3). Non-realism, then, is the view that our words do not describe something which exists independently of human perception. As with realism, one can be a non-realist about various things. So:

1 A non-realist about the external world would say that there is no more to tables and chairs than our perceptions of them.

2 A non-realist about morality would say that actions are not objectively right or wrong. Our view of what is right and wrong depends on the agreement of the community, not on any external state of affairs.

3 A non-realist about the Divine would say that the Divine has no objective, external existence; the Divine exists within the religious community as a useful idea, and within religious language. The Divine is like a character in a novel, perhaps, not an invisible spirit with whom one can communicate. In the early years of the twenty-first century, this position has come be to known as 'fictionalism' (see, e.g., Eshleman, 2005), although its roots may be traced back at least as far as a paper given by R. B. Braithwaite (1900–1990) in the 1950s (1971 [1955]).

As with realism, it is sometimes unclear whether a non-realist is making claims about metaphysics or about epistemology. A metaphysical non-realist would be claiming that an entity has no existence independently of human perception, whereas an epistemological non-realist would say that we cannot know that an entity has any kind of existence beyond human perception. The latter is sometimes associated with the coherence theory of truth or the pragmatist theory of truth.

According to the coherence theory of truth, statements are true if they cohere with each other – i.e. if they all fit together in a system. So, for non-realists about religious belief, God's attributes cannot conflict with one another. It is worth being aware, however, that the coherence of God's attributes is sometimes regarded as evidence that God exists objectively (e.g. Swinburne, 2016 [1977]), and that lack of coherence is considered to be one of the main reasons why people reject belief in the God of classical theism. By way of clarification perhaps we can say that, for both the realist and the non-realist, if the concept of God is incoherent, belief in this God must be rejected, but scholars can have very different views about what constitutes a coherent concept of God. If the concept is coherent, for the realist, belief remains plausible but requires further argument whereas, for the non-realist, further arguments are unnecessary.

Some non-realists therefore accept a pragmatist theory of truth – the view that true statements are those which work in practice. On this view, someone might accept the beliefs of a religion on the grounds that this is an effective way to promote goodness, kindness and human flourishing. Again, however, it is worth noting that realists, too, may hold a belief because it has positive practical outcomes, although, for the realist, these positive practical outcomes may be taken as indicators that the belief concerns something which exists independently of human perception.

Arguing for realism and non-realism

Whether a realist is making a metaphysical claim or an epistemological one, similar supporting arguments may be used. For example, it may be possible to argue that the Divine exists independently of human perception and/or that our talk about the Divine links up with, no matter how tenuously, some corresponding objectively-existing Reality by appealing to common arguments for the existence of God which claim that an independently-existing Deity provides the best explanation for observable phenomena – the existence or regularity of the world, perhaps. A number of these arguments will be examined in later chapters of this book.

Metaphysical non-realism is difficult to argue for, since it is hard to find arguments which claim to disprove conclusively the existence of an objectively-existing entity. On the basis of the apparent failure of the realist's arguments for an objectively-existing entity, however, the epistemological non-realist might reasonably argue that we have no grounds for claiming to know that there is an objectively-existing entity. Thus, a non-realist is commonly agnostic about what 'really' exists, and simply says that we have no way of knowing the answer to this question. Religion may remain valuable, however, if the following criteria apply to it:

1 Its claims are internally coherent – i.e. if, taken together, they form a coherent system of beliefs, one which does not contain obvious contradictions.
2 Its claims are externally coherent – i.e. they do not contradict human experience, or the claims of other systems of knowledge (that of science, for example) which are generally regarded as true.
3 It promotes goodness, kindness and human flourishing.

Reflection

Can you think of an example of an internally incoherent religious belief-system?

Objections to non-realism

Although the non-realist about religion claims that realist interpretations of religious belief are untenable because, for example, the realist's concept of God is incoherent or the arguments for the existence of God fail to support belief in the realist's God, there are also reasons why someone might reject a non-realist interpretation. For example:

1 If there is no objective truth, there seems to be no justification for rejecting morally objectionable views such as those of Hitler. Don Cupitt (b. 1934) has suggested that such views do not satisfy the requirements of pragmatism, which requires us to choose values which make life worth living (1988: 137), but Hitler could have responded that his values *did* make life worth living for the majority, and that it is impossible to take the needs of everyone into account.

Cupitt has subsequently recognised this difficulty, however, arguing, for example, that it is our 'co-humanity' (2001: 103) which makes some actions more likely to be right and others more likely to be wrong; we do not have a completely free choice. But this seems to imply that it is our physical nature as human beings which determines what makes life worth living – and what does not – and this is not something which we choose, either individually or collectively. For example, I cannot simply choose that it is acceptable to kill someone for pleasure, because killing a person deprives them of the life they would have had and is likely to cause great suffering to them, as well as to their friends and family.

2 If there is no objective truth, on what grounds should we care about the well-being of others? Cupitt describes moral realism as a form of 'servitude or slavery' (2009: 55) and, echoing a famous quotation often attributed to Dostoyevsky, suggests that 'God is dead, and everything is permitted – at least in the sense that morality is only human, and is evolving steadily through our human conversation' (2009: 17). But even if our co-humanity determines what is and is not ethical (which means that not everything is permitted), to what extent can we be truly ethical unless there is some sense in which what is ethical is good for its own sake – that is, just because it is good, and not because we might ultimately derive some direct or indirect benefit from our 'ethical' actions? And yet it would appear that most of humankind, for at least some of the time, does care about other sentient beings for their own sakes – in other words, that goodness is an absolute moral requirement, one which many religious believers would say is imperceptibly linked with the Divine, is the objectively-existing requirement that we do good only because it is good – for goodness' sake. This does not, of course, rule out debates about what this absolute standard of goodness requires of us. Indeed, if truth is nothing but the consensus of opinion, there is no reason why it should ever change. Our conception of what the Divine requires of us changes only because we struggle continually to acquire a better understanding of the nature and application of a goodness which is not dependent on the opinions of individuals or societies.

Wittgenstein and Phillips (see Section A) are sometimes presented as non-realists, on the grounds that they appear to reject many of the claims which are commonly made by theists, but Phillips denies this (e.g. 1993: 35), while refusing to participate in the debate. Towards the end of his life, however, he argued that, although some words and pictures are not representational – some words are not literally true, and some pictures are neither portraits nor diagrams – they still manage to convey 'something real' about the world; pictures can convey 'consciousness of sin', 'despair' or 'salvation', for example (2002: 74). He questions whether the 'something real' which they capture and convey might be described as God and concludes that, '[i]f someone is looking for realism in the philosophy of religion, that could be a good point at which to begin' (74).

Reflection

Why do you think that Phillips is concerned to deny that his view is non-realist? Does it matter whether he is a realist or a non-realist?

Conclusion

In this section we have seen that a realist about the Divine thinks that something with the characteristics of the Divine exists independently of human thought and that religious language, at least to some extent, is talk about an objectively-existing Divinity. By contrast, a non-realist about the Divine thinks either that nothing with the characteristics of the Divine exists independently of human thought, or (a weaker claim) that we do not know whether there is an independently-existing Divinity, and that Divinity exists, as far as we know, only within human thought and language to 'embody' a constellation of ideas which promote human flourishing.

In support of her case, the realist argues that her concept of the Divine is coherent and employs many of the arguments which we will examine in the subsequent chapters of this book, whereas the non-realist argues that the realist's concept of the Divine is incoherent and/or that the arguments which purport to support belief in its existence are unsuccessful. For the non-realist, therefore, the Divine must consist of something other than an objectively-existing Reality. Belief in the existence of the Divine within human thought and language is supported if this belief can be shown to be both internally and externally coherent, and if it promotes goodness, kindness and human flourishing. Without an element of realism, however, it is difficult for the non-realist to explain why some actions are morally wrong, or to justify genuine altruism (acting for the good of the other without any concern for oneself). This may explain the growing popularity (among scholars of religion, but also, perhaps, religious practitioners such as the members of the Sunday Assembly) of forms of religion, or religion-type belief and practice, which require neither belief in the God of classical theism, nor a complete rejection of any kind of realism with regard to religion and the moral beliefs with which religion is usually so closely entwined.

• REFERENCES

Braithwaite, R. B. (1971 [1955]) 'An Empiricist's View of the Nature of Religious Belief' in Basil Mitchell (ed.) *The Philosophy of Religion* (Oxford: Oxford University Press), 72–91.

Cupitt, Don (1988) *The New Christian Ethics* (London: SCM Press).

Cupitt, Don (2001) *Reforming Christianity* (London: SCM Press).

Cupitt, Don (2009) *Jesus and Philosophy* (London: SCM Press).

Eshleman, Andrew (2005) 'Can an Atheist Believe in God?', *Religious Studies* 41, 2: 183–199.

Moore, Andrew (2003) *Realism and Christian Faith* (Cambridge: Cambridge University Press), 3, 73–92.

Phillips, D. Z. (1993) *Wittgenstein and Religion* (New York, NY: St Martin's Press).

Phillips, D. Z. (2002) 'Propositions, Pictures and Practices', *Ars Disputandi* 2, 1: 68–74, DOI:10.1080/15665399.2002.10819746, http://dx.doi.org/10.1080/15665399.2002.10819746.

Swinburne, Richard (2016 [1993, 1977]) *The Coherence of Theism* (Oxford: Clarendon Press).

• FURTHER READING

Encyclopedia articles

Miller, Alexander (2014) 'Realism' *Stanford Encyclopedia of Philosophy*, https://plato.stanford.edu/entries/realism/.

Original articles in edited collections

Trigg, R. (2010 [1997]) 'Theological Realism and Antirealism' in Charles Taliaferro, Paul Draper and Philip L. Quinn (eds) *A Companion to Philosophy of Religion* (Chichester: Wiley-Blackwell, 1999), 651–658.

Articles

Harrison, Victoria (2010) 'Philosophy of Religion, Fictionalism and Religious Diversity', *International Journal for Philosophy of Religion* 68, 1: 43–58.

Insole, Christopher (2002) 'Why Anti-Realism Breaks Up Relationships', *Heythrop Journal* 43, 1: 20–33.

Books

Byrne, Peter (2003) *God and Realism* (Aldershot: Ashgate), 130–136.

Moore, Andrew (2003) *Realism and Christian Faith* (Cambridge: Cambridge University Press), 73–92.

Runzo, J. (ed.) (1993) *Is God Real?* (New York, NY: St Martin's Press).

Scott, Michael and Moore, Andrew (eds) (2007) *Realism and Religion: Philosophical and Theological Perspectives* (Aldershot: Ashgate).

Stiver, Dan (1996) *The Philosophy of Religious Language: Sign, Symbol and Story.* (Malden, MA: Blackwell).

4

personal and impersonal interpretations of the divine

• INTRODUCTION

On even the most cursory glance at the scriptures of the world's religions, it is clear that the Divine is often described in person-like terms. In Hinduism, *Ishvara*, the immanent (within the world) aspect of God described in the Upanishadic literature (part of the Vedas, the foundational scriptures of Hinduism), is a personal God who, in the later (ninth century CE onwards) Bhakti movement, has the six attributes of majesty, omnipotence, glory, beauty, knowledge and dispassion, and may be manifested as Shiva or Vishnu (Sen, 1989; Hick, 2004 [1989]). The portrayal of the Divine as person-like is particularly common in the Abrahamic religions. So, for example, in the Hebrew Bible/ Old Testament, God is said to walk in the Garden of Eden (Genesis 3:8) and to talk with humankind (e.g. Job 38–41). In the New Testament, God speaks to Paul on the Damascus road (Acts 9:4–6) and in the Qur'an, Allah is said to see, and to sit on a throne (57:4). Many believers today would still say that God loves them (e.g. Ephesians 5:29; Qur'an 1:3), and can respond to their prayers (Matthew 7:7–8; Qur'an 11:61).

• IS THE DIVINE 'A PERSON'?

'Person' is a notoriously difficult word to define. Questions about the typical characteristics of personhood and how many of them a person must possess are important in discussions about abortion, euthanasia, disability and the way we treat animals. In these cases, the presence or otherwise of personhood is often thought to determine the rights accorded to the being/s in question. In each of these cases, however, a person must possess a body of some kind. For pantheists and panentheists the totality of the universe may be regarded as divine embodiment (see, for example, Jantzen,

1984). But the teaching that Allah has two hands (Qur'an 38:75) has been commonly interpreted by Muslim scholars as a symbol for divine power, while Abu Abd Allah Muhammad ibn Ali ibn Muhammad ibn Arabi ibn Arabi al-Hatimi at-Tai, known as Ibn Arabi (1165–1240) argued that it is a symbol for the opposites which exist within human beings (Sells, 1994: 86).

Others simply deny divine embodiment. For some (e.g. Thatcher, 1985: 61 and Davies, 2006: 61), this leads to the conclusion that the Divine cannot be thought of as a person. This conclusion is further supported by the fact that the Divine also lacks a number of other characteristics which are commonly said to be possessed by persons. For example, if God is omniscient in the sense that God knows everything which it is possible to know about our past, present and future, God is not capable of abstract thought (Ward, 1992: 261). In addition, the Divine has a number of attributes which persons do not normally have. The Divine is also said to be omnipotent (all-powerful) and perfect, for example. Some scholars have pointed out that this might, in fact, be an advantage for the religious believer because it preserves the idea that the Divine is, in many respects, very different from the created world (Ward, 1992: 264). For example, Giles Fraser notes that:

> The God of Israel is the God of the burning bush, the God who exists in the cloudy mountain-top, whose face cannot be seen. This is not the God who doubles as my best pal, or who fits a snappy one-line definition. The God who has been at the centre of the Church's life for centuries is a God who is disconcertingly inscrutable [impossible to understand], and utterly resistant to cheap certainty.
>
> (2006: 11)

Others suggest that it might be possible to modify the concept of 'person' to enable us to acknowledge that the Divine Person lacks some of the characteristics which persons normally have, and has some characteristics which persons do not normally have. For example, Richard Swinburne (b. 1934) argues that the word 'person', applied to the Divine, is used analogically. God has some of the attributes of personhood – for example, God has beliefs and intentions. But, unlike human persons, God lacks 'thisness'. 'Thisness' is the ultimate quality which makes a human person a person and distinguishes her from other persons, but which cannot be explained in terms of bodily continuity or physical or mental properties such as memories. A human person would still be the same person if her powers were reduced. But, for Swinburne, God is defined in terms of God's properties and God would no longer be God without those properties, or if those properties – power, knowledge and so on – were diminished. For Swinburne, God is 'a supreme form'. The word 'form', too, is used in an analogical sense. For Plato, it referred to a property which may be shared by many things. So, for example, things which are said to be good share the property, or form, of Good or Goodness. For Swinburne, to say that God is a supreme form is to say that God has the role which atheist scientists give to the fundamental laws of physics; God is 'the fundamental principle governing nature' (2016 [1977]: 250). The word is used in an analogical sense, however, because laws of nature do not cause effects. For example, the law of gravity does not cause things to exist; it simply determines how things which already exist move in relation to other things which already exist. But since God is a form who causes things to exist, the word 'form' is being used in an analogical sense.

For Swinburne, then, God lacks the characteristic of 'thisness' which persons normally have, but has some of the characteristics of a 'form' which persons do not normally have. Nevertheless, Swinburne thinks, we can still say that God is a person because God resembles a person (defined by Swinburne as 'a mental substance who is capable of having mental events of some sophistication' [2016: 251 [1977]]) more than God resembles things which are not persons (such as houses, trees or tables).

Swinburne's argument in support of an analogical account of divine personhood is, perhaps, reinforced by the New Zealand government's recent granting of the legal status of personhood to Te Urewera, a former national park, and to the Whanganui River, Te Awa Tapua. In both cases, the legislation recognises the Maori relationship with the land which, if it is understood to be its own person, cannot be regarded as belonging either to the New Zealand government or to the Maori, and is a living entity which possesses its own rights and interests (see Rousseau, 2016; Calderwood, 2016; Ainge Roy, 2017).[1]

Nevertheless, some scholars argue that the Divine cannot be regarded as a person, even in an analogical sense, because the Divine has characteristics such as omniscience, perfection and gender-neutrality which are incompatible with the analogy (Mander, 1997: 411), or because 'personality is a limiting factor and is therefore incompatible with the infinite nature of God' (Legenhausen, 1986: 317).

• IS THE DIVINE 'PERSONAL'?

Some scholars who think that God cannot be thought of as a person, on the grounds that God does not have some attributes which persons normally have and does have some attributes which persons do not normally have, do nonetheless think that God may be described as 'personal' (e.g. Thatcher, 1985: 61; Davies, 2000: 561–563) – in other words, that God does share some of the attributes of human personhood.

Perhaps it would therefore be more appropriate to say that Divine personhood is a metaphor. We have seen that 'God is good' is an analogy because the speaker is claiming that God's goodness resembles human goodness, of which God is the source, but lacks the imperfections which are associated with human goodness – in other words, that 'God is good' is an analogy because the word 'good' is being used in a literal, but extended, sense. By contrast, 'God is my rock' is a metaphor because only some characteristics of a rock are applicable to the Divine. I would suggest that 'God is a person' or 'God is person-like' have more in common with 'God is my rock' than 'God is good'. This is because goodness is a single property, varying degrees of which we can see around us, from which we can infer goodness itself which contains no imperfections. 'Rockness', however, must be defined by listing a range of properties, only some of which may be applicable to the Divine. Similarly, 'personhood' implies a range of properties (some of which are disputed), only some of which may be applicable to the Divine. It may be, however, that some of the attributes implied by the metaphor can be interpreted using analogy. So, if 'rockness' includes the idea of stability, this attribute of 'rockness' may be understood as an analogy for Divine immutability. Likewise, if 'personhood' includes the ideas of agency (the ability to act) and wisdom, these attributes of 'personhood' may be understood as analogies for Divine causality and wisdom.

• GENDER AND THE DIVINE

Within the Abrahamic traditions (Judaism, Christianity and Islam) the Divine (God or Allah) is usually referred to by means of the masculine personal pronoun – that is, as 'he'. Since the Divine is not usually thought to possess attributes which are characteristically male (although some feminist theologians and philosophers of religion would disagree), and in order to avoid the appearance of gender bias, some scholars simply repeat the word 'God' at every reference to the Divine. This becomes cumbersome, however, when it is necessary to refer to the Divine several times in quick succession. Although some languages have a gender-neutral pronoun (for example, in 2015 Sweden added to its official *Svenska Akademiens ordlista* [SAOL] dictionary the word 'hen' to refer to people of unknown gender or inter-gender people), English has no such pronoun in common use (although students at the University of Oxford have recently been told to use the gender-neutral pronoun 'ze' in order to avoid discrimination against transgender people [Bannerman, 2016]).

Since it seems particularly important to find a gender-neutral way to refer to a divine being who is often described in person-like terms but is not generally regarded as masculine, I will often refer to the Divine as 'Xe'. This is derived from 'ze' and pronounced the same, but the 'x' is substituted for the 'z' on the grounds that 'x' is commonly used to stand for something the nature of which we do not fully understand. To avoid unnecessary complexity, however, I will use 'Xe' as a substitute for 'He', but 'God' for 'Him', 'God's' for 'His', and 'Godself' for 'Himself'.

Reflection

Using the conventions described in the previous paragraph, how would you re-write the following sentences?

'When we speak of God as if He were a person, we cannot fully understand what we say. Although we might pray to Him for deeper insight, only God can fully understand the meaning of His own attributes, because only God knows what it is like to be Himself.'

• THE DIVINE AS NON-PERSONAL

Brahman

Although the Upanishadic literature of Hinduism describes *Ishvara*, the immanent aspect of God, it also describes *Brahman*, the transcendent (beyond the world) aspect of God, which is identical with the human Self or universal consciousness (*Atman*).

In the *Mandukya* Upanishad, *Ishvara* is *saguna Brahman*, *Brahman* with attributes, while *nirguna Brahman* is the highest reality which has no attributes and which we are unable fully to understand. As we saw on page 8, it can therefore only be spoken of in negative terms as 'neti, neti' – 'not this, not this'. There are varying interpretations of the Upanishads. The Advaita Vedanta school of philosophy associated with Adi Shankara (dates uncertain, but probably the second half of the eighth century CE) adopts a non-theistic interpretation of *Brahman*, according to which the Divine is a unity without distinctions into which each individual human person will eventually be absorbed. But Ramanuja (1017–1137) argues that it is not possible to think of an object which has no distinctions. Furthermore, the Upanishadic texts do not say that there are no distinctions within *Brahman*, and do say that *Brahman* possesses attributes such as consciousness, knowledge, power and the ability to act (Vroom, 2006: 169).

There are differences of interpretation even within the Advaita Vedanta school, however. *Brahman* is often described as *satchitananda* – as having the attributes of both consciousness and bliss – and Shankara often speaks of oneness with *Brahman* as *satchitananda*, rather than with an Ultimate Reality without attributes (Hick, 2004 [1989]: 281).

Nirvana

As with Hinduism, there are many types of Buddhism, but the concept of *nirvana* features in most of its central forms. The term is commonly understood to refer to the eventual cessation of existence which ends *samsara*, the cycle of birth, suffering, death and rebirth. But John Hick (1922–2012) suggests that it should, rather, be understood to refer to a state of liberation from *samsara*, which is the Ultimate Reality which we experience when we are released from focusing on our own selfish concerns by leaving behind such 'evils' as lust, hatred and illusion (Hick, 2004 [1989]: 285).

Sunyata

While the concept of *nirvana* was important in the earlier Theravada form of Buddhism and developed in the later Mahayana Buddhism, the concept of *sunyata* is a predominantly Mahayana development. The word is difficult to translate. It is normally translated 'Emptiness', but this can be taken to mean that reality has no content. Rather, it means that the world is empty of the selfish evaluations, comparisons and concerns of individuals – either about themselves or about what they regard as their possessions. Everything is as it is in itself. So to say that reality is empty is to say that it is empty from our human point of view because it cannot be fully understood by human thought or described in human language but that it is, nonetheless, full of possibilities. In Zen Buddhism, a state of acceptance of everything as it is, and of ourselves as part of it, may be experienced in every present moment by a person who has achieved a state of enlightenment which enables them to transcend their concerns about themselves. To be able to perceive reality in this way is to be able to perceive Reality itself. This Reality is manifested in everything within our world, but, in itself, has no attributes – not even existence or goodness – and therefore can only be described in negative language. This Reality is thought by some Zen philosophers to have a role which is analogous to that of God in the monotheistic traditions or *Brahman* in the Advaita Vedanta school of Hinduism (Hick, 2004 [1989]: 287–292).

Dao

In early forms of the Chinese philosophies of Confucianism and Daoism we find accounts of the Lord on High (*di*), a personal being who is the source of both life and power, who cares for and is worshipped by his people. The concept of *di* eventually merged with the concept of *tian* (heaven), which was also thought to be the source of life and power, but also infinite. As Chinese thinkers began to focus more on the unity of heaven and humankind, *tian* became gradually less personal and eventually came to be thought of as the Way of Heaven (*tiandao*). The process of depersonalisation was completed in Daoism, but, Chung-Ying Cheng (b. 1935) argues, the idea of divinity remains in the notion of the *dao* as the creative process which generates the totality of the world, including *tian* (Cheng, 1997).

Religious naturalism

Parallels with the teaching of Confucianism and Daoism may be found in contemporary forms of religious naturalism, the view that everything is part of Nature, nothing exists 'beyond' Nature, and that religious meaning may be found in Nature (Stenmark, 2013). Some forms of religious naturalism regard 'God' as a metaphor for the highest human values, which may, therefore, include the metaphor of Divine personhood. Other forms, however, replace the concept of God with that of Nature or the Universe, within which person-like attributes are either less prominent or not present at all.

Reflection

Is it necessary to think of the Divine in terms of personhood?

• CONCLUSION

In this chapter, I have outlined both personal and non-personal conceptions of the Divine. I have suggested that, if the Divine is thought of as, in some sense, personal, Divine personhood must be understood as a metaphor which encompasses a range of properties which may be understood as analogies. This raises the question of which aspects of personhood may be attributed to the Divine. In the next four chapters we will consider whether it is rational to describe the Divine as omnipotent (all-powerful) and omniscient (all-knowing), and capable of acting within the world by means of miracles and answers to the prayers of humankind. As we will see in Chapters 5–8, these attributes of divinity may be interpreted in a variety of ways.

• NOTE

1 I am grateful to an anonymous reviewer for drawing my attention to this meaning of personhood.

• REFERENCES

Ainge Roy, Eleanor (2017) 'New Zealand River Granted Same Legal Rights As Human Being' *The Guardian*, 16 March, www.theguardian.com/world/2017/mar/16/new-zealand-river-granted-same-legal-rights-as-human-being.

Bannerman, Lucy (2016) 'Use Ze Instead of He or She: Oxford Students Get Lesson in Gender Bias', *The Times*, Monday 12 December, 21.

Calderwood, Kathleen (2016) 'Why New Zealand is Granting a River the Same Rights As a Citizen', Sunday Extra, ABC Radio National (Australian Broadcasting Corporation), 6 September, www.abc.net.au/radionational/programs/sundayextra/new-zealand-granting-rivers-and-forests-same-rights-as-citizens/7816456.

Cheng, Chung-Ying (1997) 'Reality and Divinity in Chinese Philosophy' in Eliot Deutsch and Ron Bontekoe (eds) *A Companion to World Philosophies* (Malden, MA: Blackwell), 185–197; reprinted in Andrew Eshleman (ed.) *Readings in Philosophy of Religion: East Meets West* (Malden, MA: Blackwell, 2008), 59–66.

Davies, Brian (2000) 'A Modern Defence of Divine Simplicity' in Brian Davies (ed.) *Philosophy of Religion: A Guide and Anthology* (Oxford: Oxford University Press), 549–564.

Davies, Brian (2006) *The Reality of God and the Problem of Evil* (London: Continuum), 58–62.

Fraser, Giles (2006) 'Atheists' Delusions about God', *Church Times*, 20 October, 11.

Hick, John (2004 [1989]) *An Interpretation of Religion: Human Responses to the Transcendent* (Basingstoke: Palgrave Macmillan), Chapters 15 and 16.

Jantzen, Grace (1984) *God's World, God's Body* (London: Darton, Longman and Todd), see especially Chapter 5.

Legenhausen, Gary (1986) 'Is God a Person?', *Religious Studies* 22, 3–4: 307–323.

Mander, William J. (1997) 'God and Personality', *Heythrop Journal* 38, 4: 401–412.

Rousseau, Bryant (2016) 'In New Zealand, Lands and Rivers Can Be People Too (Legally Speaking)', *New York Times*, 13 July, www.nytimes.com/2016/07/14/world/what-in-the-world/in-new-zealand-lands-and-rivers-can-be-people-legally-speaking.html?_r=0.

Sells, Michael A. (1994) *Mystical Languages of Unsaying* (Chicago, IL: University of Chicago Press).

Sen, Sushanta (1989) 'The Vedic-Upanisadic Concept of *Brahman* (The Highest God)' in Linda Tessier (ed.) *Concepts of the Ultimate* (New York, NY: St Martin's Press), 83–97; reprinted in Andrew Eshleman (ed.) *Readings in Philosophy of Religion: East Meets West* (Malden, MA: Blackwell, 2008), 43–51.

Stenmark, Mikael (2013) 'Religious Naturalism and its Rivals', *Religious Studies* 49, 1: 529–550.

Swinburne, Richard (2016, [1993, 1977]) *The Coherence of Theism* (Oxford: Oxford University Press), Chapter 7, 247–256.

Thatcher, Adrian (1985) 'The Personal God and the God Who is a Person', *Religious Studies* 21, 1: 61–73.

Vroom, Hendrik M. (2006) *A Spectrum of Worldviews: An Introduction to Philosophy of Religion in a Pluralistic World* (Amsterdam: Rodopi), Chapter 7.

Ward, Keith (1992) 'Is God a Person?' in Gijsbert van den Brink, Luco J. van den Bron and Marcel Sarot (eds) *Christian Faith and Philosophical Theology: Essays in Honour of Vincent Brümmer* (Kampen: Kok Pharos), 258–266.

• FURTHER READING

Articles

Burns, Elizabeth (2015) 'Classical and Revisionary Theism on the Divine as Personal: A Rapprochement?', *International Journal for Philosophy of Religion* 78, 2: 151–165. DOI 10.1007/s11153-014-9500-3. First published online 19 December 2014.

Hammond, Guy B. (1964) 'Tillich on the Personal God', *The Journal of Religion* 44, 4: 289–293.

Pailin, David (1976) 'The Humanity of the Theologian and the Personal Nature of God', *Religious Studies* 12, 2: 141–158.

Wynn, Mark (1997) 'Simplicity, Personhood, and Divinity', *International Journal for Philosophy of Religion* 41, 2: 91–103.

Books

Mawson, T. J. (2005) *Belief in God: An Introduction to the Philosophy of Religion* (Oxford: Oxford University Press), 12–20.

Webb, Clement C. J. (1919) *God and Personality* (London: George Allen and Unwin).

5
·divine power

• INTRODUCTION

The God of the Judaeo-Christian tradition is often said to be omnipotent (e.g. Job 42:1–2: 'Then Job answered the Lord: "I know that you can do all things"'; Qur'an 46:33: 'He surely is able to do all things') but it is by no means clear what this means. For some scholars, it means that God is able to bring about any logically possible state of affairs, while others suggest that God can do even what seems to us to be logically impossible – such as making a square circle.

The question of whether, and in what sense, God might be omnipotent is important for at least two reasons:

- God must be all-powerful to enable God to create and be in control of the universe, and respond to human requests for assistance.
- If 'God is omnipotent' means that God can do even what seems to us to be logically impossible, it is difficult to understand why God did not create a world in which human beings freely choose to do what is right on every occasion.

• OMNIPOTENCE DOES NOT INCLUDE THE ABILITY TO PERFORM LOGICALLY IMPOSSIBLE ACTIONS

Al-Ghazali and Aquinas

In *The Incoherence of the Philosophers* (1095), Abu Hamid Muhammad ibn Muhammad al-Ghazali (c1056–1111) claims that the dispute about whether something which is contrary to fact can be an object of power has no substance 'when it is investigated and the gnarl of words is removed' (2007: 256 [1095]). He claims that everything which is possible can be an object of power, but that the impossible is not an object of power. We can only know whether something which is contrary to fact is possible or impossible, however, when we know the meaning of 'possible' and 'impossible'. Al-Ghazali considers a number of examples, including the question of whether, if the motion of a hand normally causes the motion of the ring it wears or the motion of water, it would be possible for God to create the motion of the hand without the motion of the ring, or the motion of the hand in water without the motion of the water. This, he suggests, is absurd because, in order for something to occupy space, that space must first be empty. So if

God causes a hand to move in water, God can only do this if the space into which it moves is empty of water.

The meaning of 'possible' was considered again by Aquinas ([1265–1274]) some 200 years later. He argues that God can do everything which is possible, but that there are two senses of 'possible':

1 Things which are possible in the relative sense are possible for some specified power – a human being, for example. If we were to say that God can do everything which is possible for all created things, this would limit God's power. But if we were to say that God can do everything which it is possible for God to do, this would tell us nothing about God's omnipotence.
2 Things which are possible in the absolute sense are possible if their possibility is implied by their description. For example, 'Socrates is seated' describes a possible state of affairs, whereas 'A man is a donkey' does not. It is in this sense in which, for Aquinas, God can do everything which is possible. God can bring about whatever is possible, and this consists of anything which does not involve a contradiction. Aquinas suggests that it is better to say that contradictory things cannot be done than that God cannot do them.

In his reply to the objection that God cannot change, Aquinas refers us back to a previous argument that God's power is active, not passive. Since God's power is not passive (in other words, God cannot be acted on by another), Xe cannot change. But since God's power *is* active, Xe can still be said to be omnipotent.

His response to a second objection, that God cannot sin, is that God cannot sin because to sin is to fail in doing something, and a God who can do anything which is absolutely possible cannot fail in doing something.

Aquinas also considers whether, if God can give sight to a blind man or raise the dead to life, God can also change the past – whether Xe can make a past event, such as that Socrates ran, not to have been. Aquinas replies that God cannot do such a thing because it implies a contradiction – unlike raising the dead to life, which implies no contradiction. Things which are contradictions cannot be done, even by God.

Lastly, Aquinas considers whether God's actions are determined – whether God could not have acted otherwise. He replies that God's will is the cause of all things, and that there is nothing which makes God's will produce them. Again, he examines the question of whether God's actions are required by God's wisdom and justice, but responds that divine wisdom does not preclude divine freedom.

The paradox of the stone

A number of discussions have revolved around the paradox of the stone, which asks whether God could create a stone which God could not lift. If God could make such a stone, there would then be something which Xe could not do – that is, lift the stone. But if God could not make such a stone, there would still be something which God cannot do – that is, make the stone. George I. Mavrodes (b. 1926) (1963) suggests that the solution to the paradox is, in fact, provided by Aquinas. To say that 'X is able to make a thing too heavy for him to lift' does not seem to involve a contradiction – because a human being could do this. But it does involve a contradiction when X is God – because it would be contradictory for an omnipotent being to make a thing too heavy for that being to lift.

Other scholars, however, are less certain that the paradox can be disposed of simply by claiming that the notion of creating a stone which an omnipotent being cannot lift is incoherent and that we therefore cannot expect God to be able to do this. Further solutions therefore include the following:

Thomas V. Morris (b. 1952) (1991) suggests that God could create an unliftable stone. Either God could create a stone which, once created, no one, not even God, could reasonably expect to be able to move, or God could create an ordinary stone and promise never to lift it. This would be a stone which God cannot lift, but God's inability to lift it would not indicate a lack of the power to do so.

Swinburne's (2016 [1977]) solution to the problem is to say that, in theory, God could make a stone which Xe could not lift but that, in fact, God does not do this. Swinburne admits that, if God actually exercised God's ability to bring about the existence of a stone which is too heavy for God to lift (as Morris allows), Xe would cease to be omnipotent; for Swinburne, omnipotence includes the ability to make Godself no longer omnipotent. But God may remain omnipotent forever because God never exercises God's power to create stones which are too heavy for God to lift.

Reflection

Two of the solutions considered above rely on the claim that God cannot perform a logically impossible action; either it is the creation of the stone which is said to be logically impossible or it is the lifting of the stone which cannot be done. Why might a theist want to say that God cannot perform a logically impossible action?

• OMNIPOTENCE COULD INCLUDE THE ABILITY TO PERFORM LOGICALLY IMPOSSIBLE ACTIONS

We have examined the views of various scholars who think that God cannot perform a logically impossible action. In the Gospel of Matthew, however, Jesus says that '[F]or God all things are possible' (19:26).

Hughes (1995) considers whether God can perform even logically impossible actions by drawing on the arguments of William of Ockham (1287–1347) and René Descartes (1596–1650). For Ockham, God can do whatever is possible – but what is possible depends on God. This means that:

1 God cannot undo the past (because this would involve a contradiction); but
2 God could act in a way which is not in accordance with our causal laws. (Hughes suggests that this amounts to saying that anything is possible for God, for all we know.)

For Descartes, there are some things which God cannot change (those concerned with God's own nature, and causation), but there are others which are only 'contingently necessary' – that is, they depend upon a free decision of God. Hughes says that Descartes is not claiming that God can make contradictions true – merely that God could have created a world in which what we take to be contradictions would not be contradictions.

Hughes concludes that we may not have understood what is and is not possible for God. So, what we take to be contradictory may not be contradictory for God.

• PROCESS THEISM ON DIVINE POWER

Process theologians John B. Cobb (b. 1925) and David Ray Griffin (b. 1939) acknowledge that the Jewish-Christian Bible is unclear about whether God is completely in control of the world and suggest that the Jewish-Christian concept of God has been influenced by ideas of perfection originating in ancient Greek philosophy. Instead, they argue that God does not completely control the world and that God's influence in the world is persuasive, rather than coercive. As such, God provides each worldly agent and situation with an initial impulse to make real the best possibility available, but each agent and situation is free to bring about an alternative outcome. They argue that, although, in the light of Jesus' life, teaching and death, divine power should have been redefined in terms of divine love, controlling power remained an essential part of the concept of divinity. Our own experience, however, coupled with the findings of contemporary psychology, tells us that true love for others is not expressed in an attempt to control them. Instead, we try to persuade them to act in such a way that they will bring about a situation which they will find rewarding (Cobb and Griffin, 2014 [1976]).

• A NON-REALIST INTERPRETATION OF DIVINE POWER

In *Taking Leave of God* (1980), Cupitt begins a still-ongoing process of taking leave of classical theism. This book contains vestiges of classical theism insofar as at least some of the attributes of the God of classical theism are mentioned, although they are substantially re-envisioned. For Cupitt, God is no longer a supernatural being, but the personification of what he refers to as 'the religious requirement' – the requirement that we must become spirit – and God's attributes are therefore 'a kind of projection of its main features as we experience them' (85). With respect to divine power, Cupitt suggests that there is no longer a 'personified absolute Power', but suggests that this is, in fact, liberating because 'the Power over us has become a power within us' (70).

A power within us is rather limited in comparison with the all-encompassing power of an omnipotent God, but if the philosophical difficulties associated with belief in an omnipotent God are considered too great to allow belief in a Divinity of this kind, the idea of a source of power which might help us to maintain a commitment to a religious way of life, to overcome adversity and to work for the common good, might perhaps be an idea which it is better to have than to be without. Divine power understood in this way might enable us to fight the battle against evil and suffering, even if we do not always win it.

> **Reflection**
>
> To what extent do you think Cupitt's re-interpretation of divine omnipotence solves the problems associated with the classical theist's concept of omnipotence?

• CONCLUSION

We have seen that the problems with omnipotence centre round the questions of what we mean by a possible action and whether or not God can perform all such actions. The question is important; a God who is not all-powerful may not be able to fulfil God's promises to human beings, but a God who is all-powerful may be difficult to reconcile with the evil in the world. Common responses suggest that God can do only those things which are logically possible. This sets the scene for some theists to argue that a world in which human beings always make free but perfect choices is a world which is logically impossible, and therefore not one which we could expect an omnipotent God to have been able to create. But this response also 'waters down' omnipotence to the extent that the believer may well question whether such a God is able to assist humankind in times of trouble. One possible solution to this problem, compatible with both classical theism and process theism, might be to think of an electricity supply as a metaphor for divine power. Just as we do not blame the electricity supply if our oven is faulty, so we cannot blame God when we fail to avail ourselves of the resources provided by the Divine.[1] The source of an oven malfunction could, of course, be a power cut, but, as we saw in Chapter 2, not every characteristic of a metaphor will apply to the thing which it is used to describe.

• NOTE

1 I am grateful to Jennifer Knight for this suggestion.

• REFERENCES

Al-Ghazali (2007 [1095]) *The Middle Path in Theology*; extract from 'On Power' in Jon McGinnis and David C. Reisman (eds) *Classical Arabic Philosophy: An Anthology of Sources* (Indianapolis: Hackett Publishing Company, Inc.), 254–265.

Aquinas, Thomas (2016 [1920, 1265–1274]) *Summa Theologica*, First Part, Question 25, www.newadvent.org/summa/1025.htm.

Cobb, John B. and Griffin, David Ray (1976) *Process Theology: An Introductory Exposition* (Louisville, KY: The Westminster Press); extract in Michael Peterson, William Hasker, Bruce Reichenbach and David Basinger (eds) *Philosophy of Religion: Selected Readings* (Oxford: Oxford University Press, 2014 [1996]), 302–308.

Cupitt, Don (1980) *Taking Leave of God* (London: SCM Press).

Hughes, Gerard J. (1995) *The Nature of God* (London: Routledge), Chapter 4.

Mavrodes, George I. (1963) 'Some Puzzles Concerning Omnipotence', *Philosophical Review* 72, 2: 221–223; reprinted in Michael Peterson, William Hasker, Bruce Reichenbach and David Basinger (eds) *Philosophy of Religion: Selected Readings* (Oxford: Oxford University Press, 2014 [1996]), 247–249.

Morris, Thomas V. (1991) *Our Idea of God* (Notre Dame: University of Notre Dame Press), 60–62; reprinted in Michael Peterson, William Hasker, Bruce Reichenbach and David Basinger (eds) *Philosophy of Religion: Selected Readings* (Oxford: Oxford University Press, 2014 [1996]), 247–249.

Swinburne, Richard (2016 [1993, 1977]) *The Coherence of Theism* (Oxford: Oxford University Press), Chapter 9.

• FURTHER READING

Encyclopedia articles

Hoffman, Joshua and Rosenkrantz, Gary S. (2012) 'Omnipotence' *Stanford Encyclopedia of Philosophy*, https://plato.stanford.edu/entries/omnipotence/.

Original articles in edited collections

Hoffman, Joshua and Rosenkrantz, Gary S. (2010 [1997]) 'Omipotence' in Charles Taliaferro, Paul Draper and Philip L. Quinn (eds) *A Companion to Philosophy of Religion* (Chichester: Wiley-Blackwell), 243–250.

Hoffman, Joshua and Rosenkrantz, Gary S. (2013 [2007]) 'Omnipotence' in Chad Meister and Paul Copan (eds) *The Routledge Companion to Philosophy of Religion* (Abingdon: Routledge), 319–328.

Leftow, Brian (2009) 'Omnipotence' in Thomas P. Flint and Michael C. Rea (eds) *The Oxford Handbook of Philosophical Theology* (Oxford: Oxford University Press), 167–198.

Moonan, Lawrence (1998) 'Omnipotence' in Brian Davies (ed.) *Philosophy of Religion: A Guide to the Subject* (London: Cassell), 80–86.

Reprinted articles or book extracts in edited collections

Flint, Thomas P. and Freddoso, Alfred J. (1983) 'Maximal Power' in Alfred J. Freddoso (ed.) *The Existence and Nature of God* (Notre Dame, IN: University of Notre Dame Press), 81–113; reprinted in Thomas V. Morris (ed.) *The Concept of God* (Oxford: Oxford University Press, 1987), 134–167.

Geach, Peter (1973) 'Omnipotence', *Philosophy* 48, 183: 7–20; reprinted in Linda Zagzebski and Timothy D. Miller (eds) *Readings in Philosophy of Religion: Ancient to Contemporary* (Chichester: Wiley-Blackwell, 2009), 213–222.

Kenny, A. (1979) *The God of the Philosophers* (Oxford: Clarendon Press), Chapters 7–9. Part of Chapter 7 reprinted in T. V. Morris (ed.) *The Concept of God* (Oxford: Oxford University Press, 1987), 125–133.

Savage, C. Wade (1967) 'The Paradox of the Stone', *The Philosophical Review* 76, 1: 74–79; reprinted in Eleonore Stump and Michael J. Murray (eds) *Philosophy of Religion: The Big Questions* (Oxford: Blackwell, 1999), 9–12.

Articles

Lore, Andrew (2010) 'Divine Omnipotence and Moral Perfection', *Religious Studies* 46, 4: 525–538.

Oppy, Graham (2005) 'Omnipotence', *Philosophy and Phenomenological Research* 71, 1: 58–84.

Books

Brink, G. van den (1993) *Almighty God* (Kampen: Kok Pharos).

Harrison, Jonathan (1999) *God, Freedom and Immortality* (Aldershot: Ashgate), Chapter 14.

Hoffman, Joshua and Rosenkrantz, Gary S. (2002) *The Divine Attributes* (Oxford: Blackwell), Chapter 8.

Taliaferro, Charles (1998) *Contemporary Philosophy of Religion* (Oxford: Blackwell), Chapter 3.

6

divine wisdom

• INTRODUCTION

Discussions about the nature of divine wisdom and the philosophical problems which are associated with it are usually framed in terms of divine omniscience. On some interpretations, this means that God knows everything there is to know about the past, the present and the future. So, for example, God knows that I had porridge for breakfast last Wednesday, and that I will wear red shoes next Tuesday. Although, at first sight, these might seem rather trivial things for God to be aware of, the motivation for belief in divine omniscience seems to lie both in the way in which God is described in the texts of the world's religions and in the so-called 'perfect being theology' derived from Anselm's (1033–1109) ontological argument for the existence of God (which we will consider in Chapter 13). In the New Testament, the author of the book of Matthew seems to imply that God is aware of every one of the hairs on our heads (Matthew 10:30), and, according to perfect being theology, the Divine must be perfect because, if it were less than perfect, something else would be more perfect – and then that would be divine.

• PROCEDURAL KNOWLEDGE AND KNOWLEDGE BY ACQUAINTANCE

There are several philosophical problems with the idea of divine omniscience. For example, some scholars have questioned whether God can have procedural knowledge or 'knowledge-how', such as how to ride a bicycle, if God does not have a body, or whether God can have knowledge by acquaintance – direct experience of an object, person or state such as envy – if Xe is omnipresent (present everywhere) and morally perfect. It may be that neither of these difficulties are insurmountable, however. In the first case, we can say that, since it is possible for human beings to know how to do something, such as wire an electrical plug, without ever having done so, it is possible that God possesses all God's procedural knowledge without needing a body with which to acquire it. Similarly, it may be that God knows how to do something sinful but does not do so because this would be contrary to God's perfect nature.

Admittedly, it is possible to know how to do something without actually being able to do it. For example, I knew, in theory, how to swim for many years before I was able to do it in practice. The same can apply to riding a bicycle, playing the piano and many other skills which require physical engagement and mastery. Similarly, God might know how to rob a bank, but unless God actually does so, God lacks the knowledge of what it feels like to do such a thing. Perhaps it does not matter if God does not possess knowledge of this kind, however, and if we therefore say that omniscience does not require God to have direct experience of everything which embodied, imperfect beings are able to experience.

• PROPOSITIONAL OR FACTUAL KNOWLEDGE

There is, however, a more significant difficulty with the idea of divine omniscience, namely that, if God knows propositions or facts about the future, this seems to imply that the future is determined (cannot be changed), and that human beings are therefore not free to choose their actions. For example, if God knows that, next Tuesday, I'll be wearing red shoes in order to identify myself to an accomplice in a murder plot, this seems to imply that I am not free to do otherwise. (It also raises the questions of whether God has the power to prevent my actions, or whether God could have created a world in which I did not have the power to act in this way. We considered questions about the nature of divine power in Chapter 5. The question of whether God could have created a world in which I did not have the power to do evil will be examined in Chapter 14.)

The way in which we attempt to address this problem will depend upon whether, and if so how, we think that human beings are free to choose their actions. Broadly speaking, there are three possible ways of thinking about this:

1 Determinism: Human actions are determined by God and are therefore not free.

Al-Ghazali (1095) seems simply to have accepted that human actions are divinely determined. He considers the question of whether, if God knows that Zayd will be killed on Saturday morning, it is possible that Zayd will be alive on Saturday morning, and concludes that it would be possible for Zayd to be alive on Saturday morning if God did not know that Zayd would be killed on Saturday morning, but if God does know this, it is impossible for Zayd to be alive on Saturday morning because this would mean that God's knowledge has been turned into ignorance, which is impossible.

2 Liberty of spontaneity: Human beings are free to act according to their natures – that is, we are free to choose our actions, but our actions are determined by our upbringing, education, and so on.

Antony Flew (1923–2010) (1955) gives the example of a man, Murdo, who freely chooses to marry Mairi, although those who knew them could have predicted the wedding long in advance of its occurrence. On this view, God could know our future free actions as they would be determined by our natures. This is a 'compatibilist' position – in other words, it holds that free will and determinism are compatible.

3 Liberty of indifference: Human actions are not determined in any sense and are therefore free choices in the broadest of senses.

We may decide to reject both 1 and 2 because most religions attempt to teach their followers to live morally better lives and suggest that some kind of punishment will follow failure to do this. If, in fact, our wrong choices are not free choices, then God would be responsible both for our wrong actions and for our unjust punishment. Furthermore, as Boethius (c. 480–524) (523–524) also pointed out, it would seem to render hope hopeless and prayer pointless, since nothing would be able to change a future already determined by divine knowledge.

Option 3, however, raises the question for the theist of how, if human beings make genuinely free choices, God can be genuinely omniscient. In the remainder of this chapter we will consider a number of possible responses.

The omniscience of a timeless God

Boethius

In his treatise *The Consolation of Philosophy* (523–524), composed while awaiting execution for an allegedly treasonable offence, Boethius outlines the problem to 'the Lady Philosophy', who replies that, although it is difficult for us to understand how God could have foreknowledge of free actions, we cannot assume that God can only see future things in the way that we can see them; rather, God can foreknow even things which are not certain to occur.

Expanding upon this, the Lady Philosophy says that, whereas everything which lives within time is continually moving from the past through the present to the future and is unable to see every event of life simultaneously, that which is outside time sees every event simultaneously, including those which, from the perspective of those who live within time, are past or future events. Since God exists beyond time, God's knowledge is knowledge of everything as if it were happening in the present. So God's fore-knowledge of the future is not foreknowledge for God but 'knowledge of a never-passing instant' which 'looks forward on all things as though from the highest peak of the world' (2000: 462 [523–524]).

God's seeing all events does not mean that the events which God sees are determined, any more than our seeing events makes them determined. Just as we see things in our temporal present, so God sees things in God's eternal present. The Lady Philosophy admits that this seems to imply that what God sees will occur must occur, but replies that the same event can be necessary for God, but free in itself. This is because there are two kinds of necessity – simple necessity, as in 'All men are mortal', and conditional necessity, as in 'If I know that a man is walking, it is necessary that he is walking'. In the latter case, the necessity arises not because of a thing's nature but because of the condition – that I know that the man is walking. So human actions may be free in themselves but become necessary only in the conditional sense – the condition being that God knows them, just as a man walking is doing so freely, but if I know that he is walking, his walking is necessary because 'whatever anyone knows cannot be otherwise than as it is known' (463). On this view, then, human freedom is compatible with God's foreknowledge.

But can we alter our intentions? The Lady Philosophy replies that we can do so, but that God will see this. This does not change God's knowledge because God sees all decisions and actions in one simultaneous present. So our future actions do not cause the knowledge of God. And God's knowledge does not determine our actions. We are therefore responsible for them and will be rewarded or punished accordingly.

Aquinas

Aquinas's view of divine omniscience is similar to that of Boethius. He argues that a contingent event (one which may or may not happen) can be seen in two ways – as a present event which can therefore be infallibly known, or as an event which has not yet happened, of which there can be no certain knowledge. For Aquinas, God knows all events in both ways. Although future contingent events happen successively from our point of view, God sees them all at once in God's eternal present. Future contingents are uncertain from our point of view because, to us, they are future contingents, but they are certain for God, who exists beyond time. A man travelling along a road cannot see those who are behind him, but a man who can see the whole road from above sees everyone who is travelling along it (1265–1274).

Unlike Boethius, however, Aquinas is concerned to avoid any suggestion that God's knowledge might depend on something other than God. He therefore argues that God's knowledge is the cause of all things. This was not new, however, since Abu al-Walid Muhammad ibn Ahmad Ibn Rushd (also known as Averroes, the medieval Latin translation of the Hebrew translation of the Arabic Ibn Rushd) (1126–1198) had argued a century earlier in his *Decisive Treatise* (1179) that God's knowledge is a cause rather than an effect of the thing which God knows and attributes this view to the Peripatetic philosophers of ancient Greece (2007: 316 [1179]). Aquinas argues that God's knowledge causes the things which God knows, just as the artist's knowledge is the cause of what he produces. God's knowledge in this sense is called 'knowledge of approbation'. If God's knowledge causes the things which God knows, however, it would seem that, if God knows something, what God knows is determined by God's knowledge.

Seymour Feldman

Seymour Feldman suggests that a solution to the problem of divine omniscience and human freedom may be found in interpretations of the story of the binding of Isaac (Genesis 22) offered by Jewish philosophers and exegetes. In the story, God tells Abraham to take Isaac, his only son, up a mountain, where he must tie him up, kill him and burn him as sacrifice to God. Feldman notes the formula of Rabbi Akiba in the second century that 'Everything is seen, yet freedom is given' (Mishnah, *Pirke Avoth* ['Sayings of the Fathers'] 3:19, quoted in Feldman, 2000: 122 [1985]), and suggests that the application of this formula can be found in most medieval Jewish theology.

The first verse of Genesis 22 usually contains the translation 'God tested Abraham' but, in the Arabic translation of the Bible of Saadya Gaon (882–942), the first major Jewish commentator, the word translated 'test' can mean either 'examine' or 'afflict'. Feldman suggests that the second of these two senses is the correct one, partly because subsequent readers (e.g. Maimonides) seem to have understood it in this way, and partly because Saadia uses the same word in Job 4:2, where it is clear that affliction is meant.

But why would God afflict Abraham? Feldman suggests that the clue is found in the final verse of the chapter, in which, in the usual translation, God says '[N]ow I know that you are a God-fearing man'. In Saadia's version, however, God says 'I have made known to mankind'. So, in Saadia's translation, God is omniscient in the strongest sense and does not learn anything when Abraham shows that he is willing to sacrifice his son. In this interpretation, God enables others to know what they otherwise would not have known, but God's knowledge does not depend, in any sense, on what human beings, in fact, decide to do with their freedom.

So, if we follow Feldman, we might be able to argue that it is possible to derive from the Mishnah and from Saadia an interpretation of divine omniscience which seems to anticipate the arguments of both Boethius and Aquinas and to solve the problems associated with both. In the Mishnah, we are told, in the manner of Boethius, that God sees our free choices but, on Feldman's interpretation of Saadia, God's knowledge does not depend on our free choices.

Reflection

To what extent do you think that Feldman's argument solves the problems associated with the arguments of Boethius and Aquinas? On what grounds might someone object to Feldman's argument?

The omniscience of an everlasting God

We have seen that Boethius and Aquinas hold that God is timeless, and that events which seem to us to be temporal are perceived simultaneously by God. Boethius's argument entails that God's knowledge depends upon free human choices, however, while Aquinas's attempt to avoid this difficulty appears to conflict with human freedom. An alternative interpretation of divine eternity holds that God exists everlastingly within time.

Ibn Rushd (Averroes)

We saw earlier that, for Ibn Rushd, God's knowledge is causal. Unlike Aquinas, however, Ibn Rushd appears to reject the view that God 'knows the created at the time of its creation by means of an eternal knowledge' (2001: 46 [1179]). This, he says, would entail that God's knowledge of created things not existing and of created things existing would be the same knowledge, and this, he thinks, would be absurd because knowledge is a consequence of existence. Since things can exist both potentially and actually, knowledge of the two kinds of existence must be different because the time of existence in each case is different.

Nelson Pike

Nelson Pike (1930–2010) (1965), too, works with the second interpretation of God's eternity, that God exists everlastingly within time, and with the implication that God has always known what will happen in the natural world and which human actions will be performed. He considers the question of whether, if Jones mowed his lawn last Saturday afternoon, God knew that he would do this 80 years before he did so, and Jones could not therefore have done otherwise because this would have made God's belief 80 years ago false.

Pike suggests that, if Jones did have the power to do otherwise, this was not the power to make God's belief false. He examines two possible ways in which Jones' power to do otherwise could be described:

- The power to do something that would have caused God to believe something otherwise than God did 80 years ago.
- The power to cause God not to exist 80 years earlier – because anyone who believed 80 years ago that Jones would mow his lawn would have been wrong, and therefore could not be God.

Pike rejects the first alternative because if God did believe 80 years ago that Jones would mow his lawn on Saturday, Jones did not have the power on Saturday to do something that would have caused God not to hold the belief 80 years ago; no action at a given time can change the fact that a given person held a particular belief at a time prior to the time in question.

Pike also rejects the second alternative. If God existed 80 years ago, Jones could not do something on Saturday which would have brought it about that God did not exist 80 years ago.

This seems to imply that, if Jones did mow his lawn on Saturday and God exists and is omniscient, Jones did not have the power to choose not to mow his lawn.

Pike's argument may be summarised as follows: if someone cannot do something which is logically contradictory (such as cause a person who held a belief at t1 not to hold that belief at t1, or cause a person who existed at t1 not to exist at t1), then it was not within Jones' power to choose not to do something which God knew in advance that he would do.

Pike concludes that there are two possible ways in which the theist could avoid the problem. She could either follow Boethius in claiming that the doctrine of divine omniscience does not require God to hold beliefs about human actions before they are performed, or she could deny any of the assumptions which underpin the argument. For example, she might say that the word 'knowledge' when attributed to God means something other than the meaning it has when it is applied to human beings. This, in fact, was a strategy adopted by Ibn Rushd, who argues that, because God's knowledge is causal, the way in which God knows is not like the way in which human beings know (2007: 317 [1179]).

Omniscience modified

In the remaining part of this chapter, I will consider two further versions of the second strategy suggested by Pike. Swinburne suggests that, while God does know everything about the past and the present, along with those aspects of the future which can be predicted from God's knowledge of the past and present, God does not possess knowledge of future contingent events (events which might or might not happen) because, until the future arrives, there is nothing to be known, even for God. This is a version of what has come to be known as 'Open Theism'. Cupitt and Iris Murdoch (1919–1999) also argue for a limited interpretation of omniscience, suggesting that the Divine is concerned only with morally-relevant knowledge.

Swinburne

Swinburne (2016 [1977]) considers and rejects the following three attempts to show the compatibility of God's omniscience and human freedom:

1 God's beliefs about the future are 'soft facts' – i.e. their truth or falsity depends on events which have not yet occurred. So if God believes in 1974 that Jones will mow his lawn in 1976, if Jones does mow his lawn in 1976, he brings about both that God believes in 1974 that he would mow his lawn in 1976 and that that belief was true.

   Swinburne says that this argument, derived from the work of Alvin Plantinga (b. 1932), simply redefines 'omniscience' so that 'beliefs' are understood in such an analogical sense that it is no longer clear what is meant.

2 Propositions about the future are neither true nor false until that future time is present. Omniscience therefore does not require knowledge of the future because there is, as yet, nothing to know.

   Swinburne suggests that this argument, perhaps originating with Aristotle, also depends upon an analogical use of language. In this case, it is the meaning of 'true' and 'false' which are understood analogically because we normally say that claims about the future are true or false, even though we do not yet know whether they are true or false. Swinburne argues that, even if we adopt these non-standard meanings of the words, it is still possible to claim that God knows all propositions that will be true and therefore that the attempt to side-step the problem by means of analogy, even if acceptable, fails to achieve its objective.

3 God knows what every free agent would do in every possible set of circumstances in which it could be created – in other words, God knows all true counterfactuals of freedom – the free choice/s which would occur in any hypothetical situation. In the light of this knowledge, God decides which creatures to create and in which situations to place them. Since God knows all the possible creatures God could have created and all the choices those creatures would have made in all possible sets of circumstances, God therefore knows the actual choices of creatures in their actual circumstances.

   Swinburne claims that this view, first put forward by Luis de Molina (1535–1600), remains open to the objection which is common to all doctrines of divine foreknowledge – that is, even if the Molinist claims that Jones does not exercise his power in 1976 to make God's belief about him in 1974 false, and that God knows that he will not, God could not know this because such knowledge would depend upon a free choice which Jones has yet to make.

Swinburne therefore concludes that, if human beings have free will, God can be omniscient in what Swinburne calls the strong sense only if God's beliefs about future free choices turn out to be true in every case and this, Swinburne thinks, would be a most extraordinary coincidence.

Swinburne's own view is that omniscience should be understood in 'the weak sense'. This means that God knows:

a All true propositions about the past (e.g. 'Jon killed Ben last Wednesday').
b All propositions which propositions about the past entail (e.g. 'Jon is guilty of murder').
c All logically necessary propositions (e.g. 'A triangle cannot have four angles').

But God does not know the future free choices of either human beings or Godself. God chooses to limit God's knowledge in order to create human beings with free will who are therefore morally responsible for their actions.

Swinburne argues that the Bible implies that God is omniscient only in this limited sense. In the Old Testament, God sometimes has plans for human beings but changes them at their request. For example, in Genesis 18 Abraham asks God not to destroy the righteous along with the wicked of the city of Sodom. Or God may change God's plans because human beings change their behaviour; the book of Jonah tells how God spared Nineveh because it repented, for example. If God changes God's mind, God cannot have fore-known God's own future action, and so God's knowledge cannot be unlimited.

God makes not only absolute promises but conditional promises – that Xe will do something on condition that people act in a particular way. There would be no need for a conditional promise if God already knew how people would act. For example, Jeremiah is told to tell the people of Judah that if they continue in their evil ways then God will destroy both Jerusalem and the Temple. We can assume from this that God does not know whether the people will repent.

Swinburne acknowledges that the New Testament does talk of God's 'foreknowledge', but suggests that this is not always regarded as absolute. Human beings can still cause God to change God's plans. For example, in the Book of Revelation (3:5), Christ, by means of an angel, tells the church of Sardis that those who live a Christian life will not have their names removed from the book of life, God's record of who will be saved, which suggests that if they do not do this, their names will be removed.

Cupitt and Murdoch

We have seen that Swinburne argues that omniscience does not require God to know the future. Both Cupitt and Murdoch limit omniscience still further and suggest that it does not require God to know everything which it is possible to know about the past or the present, either. In *Taking Leave of God* (1980), Cupitt points out that, in the Bible, God's knowledge 'is always intensely practical and ethical; it is knowledge of good and evil and knowledge of what to do ... God is only interested in religiously-relevant knowledge, not knowledge in general' (1980: 86). Secondly, he argues, 'God's knowledge is always ... knowledge of mysteries and secrets. It is always knowledge of things [humankind] do not know, do not want to know, do not want to become publicly known, or do not yet know' (86). The Bible never shows God knowing what everyone knows, or what is obvious. For Cupitt, God is no longer a supernatural being, but the personification of what he refers to as 'the religious requirement' – the requirement that we must become spirit – and God's attributes are therefore 'a kind of projection of its main features as we experience them' (85). So, for Cupitt, the doctrine of divine omniscience means that the religious requirement requires of us:

> complete spiritual integrity ... purity of heart and ... an entire change of life. Nothing can be kept secret or withheld from it. It is precisely what I have most carefully hidden and have kept most deeply buried that the religious requirement insists on bringing to light. I do not begin to be truly religious until I have faced things that I have hidden even from myself and quite forgotten; and in that sense the religious requirement seems to be omniscient, for it searches the heart and knows me better than I know myself. It breaks down barriers to self-knowledge that I have erected as internal defences within myself. For what the religious requirement exposes and brings to light is always bad news. Hence it is spoken of as judging us and condemning us.
>
> (86)

One might expect such a doctrine of the omniscience of the Supreme Good – a description of the Divine which Cupitt uses in *Taking Leave of God* at least twice (110, 117) – to appear in the work of Murdoch, for whom, much more clearly, a version of Plato's Form of the Good offers us the best account we have of what descriptions of God are attempting to refer to. And Murdoch does, indeed, preserve something of the doctrine of divine omniscience; she suggests that:

> We instinctively watch and check ourselves to some extent, but much of our self-awareness is other-awareness, and in this area we exercise ourselves as moral beings in our use of many various skills as we direct our modes of attention. In traditional terms, 'God sees me at every moment' and 'I do not pray just in the morning and the evening, I pray as I breathe'.
>
> (1992: 495)

So Murdoch seems to be translating the doctrine of divine omniscience into a constant watchfulness of the way we attend to and behave towards others. Although the sense of an objectively-existing standard against which we measure ourselves is only implied in this passage, elsewhere in her philosophical works Murdoch develops the idea of a perfect standard which must exist in order to explain our ability to differentiate between different levels of goodness, and our experience, perhaps almost a kind of religious experience (although she would not have put it in those terms), that goodness is not something which human beings create.

While Cupitt might be right to say that the biblical texts which are concerned with divine knowledge all refer to knowledge which is religiously and/or morally relevant, however, there do appear to be at least two exceptions. Perhaps the most significant of these is the passage, part of which was mentioned earlier in this section, in which Jesus says: 'Are not two sparrows sold for a penny? Yet not one of them will fall to the ground outside your Father's care. And even the very hairs of your head are all numbered' (Matthew 10:29–30). Alternative translations for 'care' are given as 'will' or 'knowledge'. The context is Jesus' sending the disciples out into the world to spread his teaching. So the passage seems to be saying that, if God knows about even the death of sparrows or the number of hairs on our heads, how much more will God know and care about the well-being of the disciples?

While this does not necessarily imply divine knowledge of the future, at first sight, it does not seem to refer to morally relevant knowledge, either. But, even in this passage there is a moral undertone, since God knows or is concerned about God's creatures, both non-human and human. So perhaps the idea which is being communicated here is that all creatures are of value, no matter how apparently insignificant they might be. Clearly, divine concern did not prevent suffering, since many of the early Christians were persecuted. Indeed, in verse 28, the disciples are entreated: 'Do not fear those who kill the body but cannot kill the soul'.

A more significant problem appears to affect both Swinburne's and Cupitt's interpretations of divine omniscience, however, in that the Bible does seem to contain passages in which God knows what will happen in the future. Although in Swinburne's examples from Jonah and Jeremiah it could be argued that, in each case, God uses God's detailed knowledge of the past and the present in considering whether to act other than Xe had originally intended, there are also passages in which the future is prophesied, and is not conditional upon free human choices. For example, in Genesis 25:23, Rebekah, mother of Esau and Jacob, is told by God that 'the elder shall serve the younger'. Jacob subsequently persuades Esau to sell him his birthright (29–34), and, with the help of his mother, deceives his father Isaac into giving him the blessing intended for Esau (27:1–40). So here, not only does God seem to know the future; God's knowledge is not morally relevant. In fact, God seems to know in advance that Jacob will perform two immoral actions, and, shortly after they are performed, tells Jacob in a dream that his offspring 'shall be like the dust of the earth' and that he 'shall spread abroad to the west and to the east and to the north and to the south and all the families of the earth shall be blessed in [him] and in [his] offspring' (27:14).

This passage does seem to worry Paul in Romans 9 since he refers to it, noting that Rebekah was given the prophecy about Esau and Jacob 'even before they had been born or had done anything good or bad' (9:11). Paul considers whether this implies that God is responsible for the injustice (14), but replies that this is not the case, since it is for God to choose upon whom Xe will show mercy. Brian Davies (b. 1951) (2006: 96) notes that Paul adds 'who indeed are you, a human being, to argue with God?' (9:20), echoing God's response at the end of the book of Job, and argues that both passages offer support for his view that God is not a moral agent.

There are, as Davies – and many atheists – point out, many biblical passages in which God does not appear to behave in a moral way, but someone who regards the Bible as a collection of documents spanning a number of centuries in which human beings struggle to understand the nature of divine goodness could respond that, where accounts of the nature of divine morality and divine knowledge appear to be contradictory, it is those in which the Divine is portrayed as a force for good, and whose knowledge is relevant to the quest for human goodness, which should prevail.

Reflection

Is there a modified account of omniscience which solves the problems associated with omniscience 'in the strong sense'?

• CONCLUSION

We have seen that a timeless God sees all our actions, including those which, from our perspective, are future but that, for Boethius, if not Aquinas, God does not cause us to act. An everlasting God sees things in succession and, in some accounts at least, does not know our future actions. One might object that this is to lose an important facet of divine omniscience but one might equally argue that, even if God does know the future, suffering still happens. Therefore perhaps there is some other motivation for conceiving of the Divine as omniscient. Cupitt and Murdoch suggest that it might better be conceived as a figurative way of describing the need for complete spiritual integrity. For this reason, I would suggest, divine omniscience is better characterised as divine wisdom, since it is predominantly, and on some interpretations exclusively, concerned with knowledge which has practical moral relevance.

• REFERENCES

Al-Ghazali (2007 [1095]) *The Middle Path in Theology*; extract from 'On Power' in Jon McGinnis and David C. Reisman (eds) *Classical Arabic Philosophy: An Anthology of Sources* (Indianapolis, IN: Hackett Publishing Company, Inc.), 257.

Aquinas, Thomas (2016 [1920, 1265–1274]) *Summa Theologica*, First Part, Question 14, www.newadvent.org/summa/1014.htm.

Averroes (2002 [1179]) *Decisive Treatise and Epistle Dedicatory*, trans. Charles E. Butterworth (Chicago, IL: University of Chicago Press); extracts reprinted in Jon McGinnis and David C. Reisman (eds) *Classical Arabic Philosophy: An Anthology of Sources* (Indianapolis, IN: Hackett Publishing Company, Inc., 2007), 316–317 and (2001 [1179]) *Faith and Reason in Islam: Averroes' Exposition of Religious Arguments*, trans. Ibrahim Najjar (Oxford: Oneworld Publications).

Boethius (1957 [523–524]) *The Consolation of Philosophy*, ed. James T. Buchanan (New York, NY: Frederick Ungar), in Brian Davies (ed.) *Philosophy of Religion: A Guide and Anthology* (Oxford: Oxford University Press, 2000), 456–464.

Cupitt, Don (1980) *Taking Leave of God* (London: SCM Press).

Davies, Brian (2006) *The Reality of God and the Problem of Evil* (London: Continuum).

Feldman, Seymour (1985) 'The Binding of Isaac: A Test-Case of Divine Foreknow-ledge' in Tamar Rudavsky (ed.) *Divine Omniscience and Omnipotence in Medieval Philosophy* (Dordrecht: Kluwer), 105–133; reprinted in Daniel H. Frank, Oliver Leaman and Charles Manekin (eds) *The Jewish Philosophy Reader* (London: Routledge, 2000), 121–123.

Flew, Antony (1955) 'Divine Omnipotence and Human Freedom' in Antony Flew and Alasdair Macintyre (eds) *New Essays in Philosophical Theology* (London: SCM Press), 149–150.

Murdoch, Iris (1992) *Metaphysics as a Guide to Morals* (London: Bloomsbury).

Pike, Nelson (1965) 'Divine Omniscience and Voluntary Action', *Philosophical Review* 74, 1: 27–46; reprinted in Brian Davies (ed.) *Philosophy of Religion: A Guide and Anthology* (Oxford: Oxford University Press, 2000), 465–473.

Swinburne, Richard (2016 [1993, 1977]) *The Coherence of Theism* (Oxford: Oxford University Press), Chapter 10.

• FURTHER READING

Encyclopedia articles

Viney, Donald (2014) 'Process Theism', *Stanford Encyclopedia of Philosophy*, Section 6, https://plato.stanford.edu/entries/process-theism/.

Wierenga, Edward (2013) 'Omniscience', *Stanford Encyclopedia of Philosophy*, https://plato.stanford.edu/entries/omniscience/.

Original articles in edited collections

Mavrodes, George I. (2010 [1997]) 'Omniscience' in Charles Taliaferro, Paul Draper and Philip L. Quinn (eds) *A Companion to Philosophy of Religion* (Chichester: Wiley-Blackwell), 251–257.

Wierenga, Edward (2009) 'Omniscience' in Thomas P. Flint and Michael C. Rea (eds) *The Oxford Handbook of Philosophical Theology* (Oxford: Oxford University Press), 128–144.

Zagzebski, Linda (2010 [1997]) 'Foreknowledge and Human Freedom' in Charles Taliaferro, Paul Draper and Philip L. Quinn (eds) *A Companion to Philosophy of Religion* (Chichester: Wiley-Blackwell), 474–481.

Zagzebski, Linda (2013 [2007]) 'Omniscience' in Chad Meister and Paul Copan (eds) *The Routledge Companion to Philosophy of Religion* (Abingdon: Routledge), 309–318.

Extracts from articles or books in edited collections

Aristotle (1963 [350 BCE]) *De Interpretatione*, Chapter 9, from *Aristotle's Categories and De Interpretatione*, trans. J. L. Akrill (Oxford: Clarendon Press), 50–53;

reprinted in Linda Zagzebski and Timothy D. Miller (eds) *Readings in Philosophy of Religion: Ancient to Contemporary* (Chichester: Wiley-Blackwell, 2009), 241–243.

Hasker, William (1989) *God, Time and Knowledge* (Ithaca, NY: Cornell University Press); extracts reprinted in Chad Meister (ed.) *The Philosophy of Religion Reader* (Abingdon: Routledge, 2008), 146–160.

Articles

Arbour, Benjamin H. (2013) 'Future Freedom and the Fixity of Truth: Closing the Road to Limited Foreknowledge Open Theism', *International Journal for Philosophy of Religion* 73, 3: 189–207.

Laughlin, Peter (2009) 'Divine Necessity and Created Contingence in Aquinas', *Heythrop Journal* 50, 4: 648–657.

Mawson, T. J. (2008) 'Divine Eternity', *International Journal for Philosophy of Religion* 64, 1: 35–50.

Rhoda, Alan R. (2008) 'Generic Open Theism and Some Varieties Thereof', *Religious Studies* 44, 2: 225–234.

Books

Basinger, D. and Cohen, Jeremy (1986) *Predestination and Free Will: Four Views of Divine Sovereignty and Human Freedom* (Downers Grove, IL: InterVarsity Press).

Flint, T. P. (1998) *Divine Providence: The Molinist Account* (Ithaca, NY: Cornell University Press).

Harrison, Jonathan (1999) *God, Freedom and Immortality* (Aldershot: Ashgate), Chapter 16.

Hoffman, Joshua and Rosenkrantz, Gary S. (2002) *The Divine Attributes* (Oxford: Blackwell), Chapter 6.

Hughes, Gerard J. (1995) *The Nature of God* (London: Routledge), Chapter 3.

Molina, Luis de (1988) *On Divine Foreknowledge*, Part IV of the *Concordia*, trans. Alfred J Freddoso (Ithaca, NY: Cornell University Press).

Swinburne, Richard (2016 [1993, 1977]) *The Coherence of Theism* (Oxford: Oxford University Press).

Taliaferro, Charles (1998) *Contemporary Philosophy of Religion* (Oxford: Blackwell), Chapter 5.

7
·divine action

• **INTRODUCTION**

In this chapter, we will consider whether God can use God's powers to perform miracles and whether it is possible for us to understand, even partially, how God acts in our world.

• **CAN GOD PERFORM MIRACLES?**

Isaac Abrabanel (1437–1508) defines a miracle as 'the existence of a thing, or its destruction, without its natural causes and conditions, and which is produced by the intention and will of one who intends and wills' (2000: 278 [1988] [1501]). Abrabanel identifies three kinds of miracle. The first kind are events which could have occurred naturally, such as the plague with which God afflicted Pharaoh in Genesis 12:17. Miracles of the second kind are events which have something in common with natural events but also have a supernatural element. For example, rainfall is a natural event, but the quantity of rain which brought about the Flood described in Genesis 6–9 was supernatural. Miracles of the third kind are events which are opposed to Nature, such as the parting of the Red Sea so that the Israelites could escape from captivity in Egypt (Exodus 14:21–22).

Miracles as violations of laws of nature by a deity

Some two and a half centuries later, David Hume (1711–1776) (1748) described miracles of the third kind as 'violations of laws of nature by a deity' and argued that belief in miracles such as resurrection from the dead is not rational; we should proportion our belief to the available evidence. The available testimony regarding miracles is, however, poor. He argues that, in the whole of history, there has never been a miracle which has been attested by a sufficiently large number of witnesses of good sense, education and learning, with a reputation to lose if they should be found to be telling lies.

Secondly, Hume suggests, human nature loves the fantastic. People enjoy the miraculous accounts of travellers, with descriptions of sea and land monsters. Similarly, religious people, in their enthusiasm to promote a holy cause, may imagine that they see things which are not real. There have been many examples of forged miracles, prophecies and supernatural events, detected either by contrary evidence or by their absurdity.

Thirdly, Hume claims that miracles occur chiefly among 'ignorant and barbarous nations' (1975: 115 [1748]); if they do occur among civilised people, they have been received from 'ignorant and barbarous ancestors' (115). Such people tend to assume that there is a supernatural cause of battles, revolutions, diseases, famine and death, but, Hume suggests, in our more enlightened times, we know that there is nothing mysterious or supernatural involved.

Finally, Hume notes that different religions report different miracles. Therefore, he concludes, no one is justified in believing accounts of miracles. He says that it is impossible that the religions of ancient Rome, Turkey, Siam and China should all be true. Therefore, any miracle from any of these religions discredits the other religions and the miracles which allegedly occur within them.

Comments on Hume's definition of 'miracle'

Some scholars have questioned whether we need to say that a miracle violates a natural law. According to William Lane Craig (b. 1949), there are three main interpretations of natural law:

1 The regularity theory: Laws of nature are not really laws but just 'generalised descriptions of the way things happen in the world' (1998: 153). A natural law merely describes whatever happens in nature. So, if unexpected events occur, these are simply incorporated into the description.
2 The nomic necessity theory: Laws are not only descriptive, they also tell us what can and cannot happen. But they must take into account everything which does happen, and so must be revised if an unexpected event occurs. If a law is inaccurate because God is acting, however, 'the law is neither violated nor revised' (153). On this view, miracles are defined as 'naturally impossible events . . . events which cannot be produced by the natural causes operative at a certain time and place' (154).
3 The causal dispositions theory: Natural laws tell us about the way in which various kinds of things affect other kinds of things – for example, that salt is the kind of thing which dissolves in water. If God acted to prevent salt from dissolving in water, the law would not be violated because salt would still have a disposition to dissolve in water. So a miracle is not a violation of a law of nature but 'an event which results from causal interference with a natural propensity which is so strong that only a supernatural agent could impede it' (154).

Craig argues that none of these interpretations entail that a miracle is a violation of a law of nature. Rather, miracles are 'naturally (or physically) impossible events, events which at certain times and places cannot be produced by the relevant natural cause' (154).

Replies to Hume's objections

Mavrodes (1998) argues that the basis for Hume's arguments lies in the fact that he has never observed a resurrection. But this, Mavrodes argues, is completely irrelevant to the question of whether or not there have been any resurrections in the history of the world because Hume's sample is too small to support any probability judgement about the occurrence, or otherwise, of resurrections. If the number of resurrections is, in fact, very small, the chances of any one person witnessing one are, likewise, very small. Mavrodes argues further that the world is full of unlikely events which do, nonetheless, happen – such as the birth of quintuplets, for example. Hume therefore considers the testimony of others. Mavrodes suggests that Hume concludes that the testimony of others is generally unreliable, however, by first making a judgement about the likelihood of the event reported. Secondly, Hume simply assumes that, since he, personally, has not witnessed a resurrection, the same applies to the remainder of the human race. He offers no evidence for this, when it would appear that there have, in fact, been people who have claimed that they have observed a resurrection – Jesus' disciples, for example.

J. A. Cover (1999) also notes that, apart from the direct evidence provided by testimony, there may also be indirect evidence which is best explained by the hypothesis that an anomalous event occurred, and that this might even be stronger than the direct evidence. So, for example, in the case of Jesus' resurrection, evidence would be provided not just by the testimony of the women who said that they saw him in the Garden of Gethsemane and the disciples who saw him subsequently, but also by the empty tomb, the burial clothes, the initial despondency of Christ's followers being unexpectedly replaced by a cheerful willingness to carry Christ's teaching into the world, and so on.

The question of conflicting truth-claims about religious beliefs will be considered in Chapter 16. For now, suffice it to say that, if believers in different religions claim that the deities of their religions have performed miracles, we need not necessarily conclude that none of the claims is likely to be genuine. We could argue that one group of believers has perceived genuine miracles, while the others are mistaken, or that the world's religions are simply different manifestations of the same Ultimate Reality and therefore that all perceived miracles could be genuine, even if they are interpreted differently by the different religious traditions.

Alternative definitions of 'miracle'

Not all definitions of miracle include the notion of a 'naturally (or physically) impossible event', however. The most common of these alternative definitions have much in common with Abrabanel's first type of miracle and are sometimes called 'coincidence miracles' because they rely on the idea that, although these events may be explicable in terms of laws of nature, they are, nonetheless, occurrences of such extraordinary good fortune that the intervention of a deity is a necessary part of their explanation. Craig cites as examples of this the rockslide which blocks the river Jordan upstream when the Israelites need to cross it (Joshua 3:14–17), and the earthquake which enables Paul and Silas to escape from prison (Acts 15:25–26) (Craig, 1998: 152).

Gareth Moore (1948–2002) (1988) offers two further definitions of 'miracle'. His second definition has some elements in common with Abrabanel's first type of miracle in that a miracle is an extraordinary coincidence which believers consider to have religious significance. As an example of this, Moore tells a story of a stranded explorer who is rescued by a millionaire who is taking a picnic in the desert. The event may be described as a miracle and as arranged by God, but, unlike Abrabanel, Moore suggests that this is not to say that somebody arranged it, because God is not an agent in the way in which human beings are agents.

We might object to both kinds of coincidence miracle, however, that, while beneficial coincidences undoubtedly occur, coincidences which have no effect on the well-being of sentient creatures as well as those which are detrimental are also regular occurrences. We might argue, for example, that every road traffic accident is a detrimental coincidence, and these happen with regrettable frequency.

Moore's first definition has some elements in common with the definition of miracle to which Hume reacts. He describes it as an inexplicable event which believers consider to have religious significance. Moore asks us to imagine an injured child at the foot of a mountain. There is a landslide and a large boulder begins to roll down the mountain. Just before it reaches the child, however, it stops in mid-air and hovers six inches above him. Many tests are carried out, but no cause is ever found. Although the event is regarded as a miracle, and God is said to have saved the boy's life, for Moore, this does not mean that somebody or something held the boulder up, preventing it from crushing the boy. It was a miracle because there was no cause for the boulder not falling on the boy.

Each of these three definitions may be regarded as communicating an understanding of miracle which is so weak that it is difficult to differentiate a miracle understood in one of these three ways from an event which is not a miracle. At best, we might say that any event which is both extraordinary and beneficial might be regarded as a miracle. The nature of its religious significance is, however, far from clear.

Reflection

On what grounds might someone argue that miracles occur?

• SPECIAL AND GENERAL PROVIDENCE

Miracles, no matter how they are understood, are regarded by those who believe in their occurrence as specific examples of divine action. If we think that the Divine is perfectly good and will therefore act, in some sense, providentially towards its creatures, then miracles may be regarded as examples of divine special providence. Even if we do not think that the Divine acts in this way, however, it may be possible to argue that the Divine acts by means of general providence – in other words, that the influence of the Divine may be seen more generally, throughout its creation (see, for example, Wiles, 1986).

• HOW DOES GOD ACT?

If the Divine is able to act in our world, whether by means of some form of special providence or by general providence, this raises the question of how God is able to act in this way. While a pantheist, panentheist or religious naturalist might say that God acts through Nature because God is, in some sense, identical with Nature, if God is thought to be a person or person-like but does not have a body, how might we be able to understand the nature of divine intervention in our world?

J. L. Gaskin (2000) considers whether God's actions are like those of human beings who are allegedly able to perform psychokinetic actions – actions using their minds but not their bodies. Gaskin argues that, even if some people are able to perform actions of this kind, these actions are not analogous to the actions of a disembodied Divinity. He gives two reasons for this:

1 Human beings who claim that they can perform psychokinetic actions have minds which are situated in this-worldly bodies. By contrast, if God can perform actions without using a body, God is a disembodied other-worldly mind.
2 We know that the world changes by means of natural processes, but we do not know how a disembodied mind could operate these natural processes.

Gaskin concludes that human and divine agency are so dissimilar that we cannot say that divine agency is analogous to human agency.

The theist could, however, argue that an effect may be caused by an agent's actions, even when we do not understand how the effect was produced. For example, an oncologist cured my cancer, even though I did not understand how he achieved this. Furthermore, we can say that an effect is likely to have been caused by a particular agent if the effect is of the kind we might expect the agent to produce, given our knowledge of that agent's character and abilities. So, for example, we might look at some of the wonders of nature and conclude that they can only be explained as the consequence of the agency of some powerful and benevolent being. Indeed, al-Ghazali suggests that only divine power can explain why spiders 'weave webs whose marvellous shapes amaze the geometer in their circularity, the parallelism of their sides, and the regularity of their arrangement' (2007: 259 [1095]), or why bees 'shape their hives as hexagons' (259) without knowing that the hexagon is the closest figure with a small number of sides to the circle with respect to the amount of space it can enclose, and also the only figure with a small number of sides which can be fitted together with other figures of the same kind without creating any unoccupied gaps.

Another possible response is to argue that divine agency is a metaphor. There may be insufficient similarities between human and divine agency to enable us to say that divine agency must be understood as an analogy, but there may be enough similarities between the two forms of agency for us to say that divine agency may be understood as a metaphor. So, although we cannot specify how the divine agent acts, we might be able to say that the Divine is whatever it was which brought the universe into existence and provides us with a standard of goodness against which we are required to measure our own actions. Accounts of divine actions and commandments indicate the nature of that moral standard and what it requires of us. So, understood in this way, the Divine makes a difference to humankind because goodness makes a difference to humankind, and this may be regarded as a form of agency in a metaphorical sense.

● CONCLUSION

In this chapter we have examined the question of whether God's actions include miracles. We acknowledged the difficulties associated with various accounts of miracle and suggested that divine action understood as general providence might go some way towards explaining how God can act in our world. We also considered the difficulty of explaining how a disembodied God acts, but suggested several ways in which divine action might be seen as sufficiently like the actions of humankind to be regarded as at least metaphorical.

● REFERENCES

Abrabanel, Isaac (1988 [1501]) *The Works of God*, trans. C. Manekin from *Mif'a lot Elohim* ed. B. Ganut-Dror (Jerusalem: Reuben Mass); extract reprinted in Daniel H. Frank, Oliver Leaman and Charles H. Manekin (eds) *The Jewish Philosophy Reader* (London: Routledge, 2000), 278–279.

Al-Ghazali (2007 [1095]) *The Middle Path in Theology*; extract from 'On Power' in Jon McGinnis and David C. Reisman (eds) *Classical Arabic Philosophy: An Anthology of Sources* (Indianapolis, IN: Hackett Publishing Company, Inc.), 254–265.

Cover, J. A. (1999) 'Miracles and Christian Theism' in Eleanore Stump and Michael J. Murray (eds) *Philosophy of Religion: The Big Questions* (Oxford: Blackwell, 1999), 334–352.

Craig, William Lane (1998) 'Creation, Providence and Miracles' in B. Davies (ed.) *Philosophy of Religion: A Guide to the Subject* (London: Cassell), 136–161.

Gaskin, J. L. (2000) 'Gods, Ghosts and Curious Persons', *Philosophical Writing* 13: 71–80.

Hume, David (1748) *An Enquiry Concerning Human Understanding*, Section X; reprinted in L. A. Selby-Bigge (ed.) *Enquiries Concerning Human Understanding and Concerning the Principles of Morals* (Oxford: Clarendon Press, 1975).

Mavrodes, George I. (1998) 'David Hume and the Probability of Miracles', *International Journal for Philosophy of Religion* 43, 3: 167–182; reprinted in Linda Zagzebski and Timothy D. Miller (eds) *Readings in Philosophy of Religion: Ancient to Contemporary* (Chichester: Wiley-Blackwell, 2009), 583–593.

Moore, Gareth (1988) *Believing in God: A Philosophical Essay* (Edinburgh: T & T Clark), Chapter 7.

Wiles, Maurice (1986) *God's Action in the World* (Eugene, OR: Wipf and Stock).

● FURTHER READING

Encyclopedia articles

McGrew, Timothy (2015 [2010]) 'Miracles', *Stanford Encyclopedia of Philosophy*, http://plato.stanford.edu/archives/win2015/entries/miracles.

Original articles in edited collections

Davis, Stephen T. and Martin, Michael (2004) 'Is it Rational for Christians to Believe in the Resurrection?' in Michael L. Peterson and Raymond J. Vanarragon (eds) *Contemporary Debates in Philosophy of Religion* (Oxford: Blackwell), Chapter 6.

Geivett, R. Douglas (2013 [2007]) 'Miracles' in Chad Meister and Paul Copan (eds) *The Routledge Companion to Philosophy of Religion* (Abingdon: Routledge), 655–665.

Mavrodes, George I. (2005) 'Miracles', in William J. Wainwright (ed.) *The Oxford Handbook of Philosophy of Religion* (Oxford: OUP), Chapter 12.

Murphy, Nancey (2010) 'Divine Action, Emergence and Scientific Explanation' in Peter Harrison (ed.) *The Cambridge Companion to Science and Religion* (Cambridge: Cambridge University Press), 244–259.

Russell, Robert John (2006) 'Quantum Physics and the Theology of Non-Interventionist Objective Divine Action' in Philip Clayton and Zachary Simpson (eds) *The Oxford Handbook of Religion and Science* (Oxford: Oxford University Press), 579–595.

Schlesinger, George N. (2010 [1997]) 'Miracles' in Charles Taliaferro, Paul Draper and Philip P. Quinn (eds) *A Companion to Philosophy of Religion* (Chichester: Wiley-Blackwell), 398–404.

Tracy, Thomas F. (2006) 'Theologies of Divine Action' in Philip Clayton and Zachary Simpson (eds) *The Oxford Handbook of Religion and Science* (Oxford: Oxford University Press), 596–611.

Extracts from articles or books in edited collections

Cobb, John B. and Griffin, David Ray (2014) 'God is Creative-Responsive Love' in Michael Peterson, William Hasker, Bruce Reichenbach and David Basinger (eds) *Philosophy of Religion: Selected Readings* (Oxford: Oxford University Press), 302–308.

Helm, Paul (2014) 'Providence: Risky or Risk-Free?' in Michael Peterson, William Hasker, Bruce Reichenbach and David Basinger (eds) *Philosophy of Religion: Selected Readings* (Oxford: Oxford University Press), 274–282.

Article

Slupik, C. (1995) 'A New Interpretation of Hume's "On Miracles"', *Religious Studies* 31, 4: 517–536.

Books

De Cruz, Helen and De Smedt, Johan (2015) *A Natural History of Natural Theology: The Cognitive Science of Theology and Philosophy of Religion* (Cambridge, MA: The MIT Press), Chapter 8.

Gaskin, J. C. A. (1978) *Hume's Philosophy of Religion* (London: Macmillan).

Harrison, Jonathan (1999) *God, Freedom and Immortality* (Aldershot: Ashgate) Chapter 25.

McGrath, Alister E. (2010 [1999]) *Science and Religion: A New Introduction* (Chichester: Wiley-Blackwell), Chapter 12.

Mackie, J. L. (1992) *The Miracle of Theism: Arguments For and Against the Existence of God* (Oxford: Clarendon Press), Chapter 1.

Polkinghorne, John C. (2005 [1989]) *Science and Providence: God's Interaction with the World* (Philadelphia, PA: Templeton Foundation Press), Chapters 2–4.

Saunders, Nicholas (2002) *Divine Action and Modern Science* (Cambridge: Cambridge University Press).

Sharma, Arvind (1990) *A Hindu Perspective on the Philosophy of Religion* (Basingstoke: Macmillan Press), 16–17.

Swinburne, R. (1970) *The Concept of a Miracle* (London: Macmillan).

Swinburne, Richard (2004) *The Existence of God* (Oxford: Clarendon Press), 277–292.

Trigg, Roger (1998) *Rationality and Religion* (Oxford: Blackwell), 209–215.

Ward, Keith (2007 [1990]) *Divine Action: Examining God's Role in an Open and Emergent Universe* (Philadelphia, PA: Templeton Foundation Press).

Audio

Bragg, Melvyn (2008) 'Miracles', *In Our Time*, BBC Radio 4, first broadcast 25 September 2008, www.bbc.co.uk/programmes/b00dkh78.

8
petitionary prayer

• INTRODUCTION

There are several different kinds of prayer, but most of the philosophical difficulties with the concept of prayer are associated with petitionary prayer, which, broadly speaking, may be defined as making requests to God. There is some overlap in this topic with the topics of the two previous chapters in which we were concerned with questions about what God can know, and whether, and how, God can intervene in our world. As Aquinas recognises, making requests to God seems to imply that God does not know what we need. It also implies that God is able and willing to supply what we need.

• AQUINAS ON PRAYER

Aquinas ([1265–1274]) considers three objections to belief in petitionary prayer:

- Objection 1: Prayer seems to involve making our needs known to God – but 'Your Father knows that you have need of all these things' (Matthew 6:32). It is therefore inappropriate to pray to God.
- Objection 2: Prayer implies that we wish to change God's mind but God's mind is unchangeable.
- Objection 3: It is better to give to someone who does not ask.

Aquinas replies to each of these objections as follows:

- Objection 1: We do not pray to God in order to inform God of our needs and desires, but to remind ourselves of our need for God's help.
- Objection 2: As above, we pray not to change God's mind but in order to obtain what God has provided for us.
- Objection 3: God gives us many things without our asking for them but Xe wants us to ask for some things so that we may confidently depend upon God and recognise that God is the source of all good things.

Eleanore Stump's response

Eleanore Stump (b. 1947) (1979) considers four objections to Aquinas's view of prayer:

1 It seems to imply that our prayers and God's answers to them are determined by God.
2 Why should prayers be part of God's plan as ways of bringing about certain effects?

3 If God is perfect, why should it be necessary for us to ask God to fulfil our desires? Why does Xe not plan the world so that our desires are fulfilled without the need for us to ask?
4 If God cannot change, how can God answer prayer?

Stump assumes that God can change in response to prayer and therefore responds as follows:

- Christianity requires a relationship between God and human beings which is like the love of true friendship.
- Since one of the parties in the relationship is an omniscient, omnipotent, perfectly good person and the other is a fallible, finite, imperfect person, the latter is in danger of becoming completely overwhelmed by the superiority of the former and therefore either dominated or spoiled by association with a person of such greatness.
- Petitionary prayer is a safeguard against these dangers. A person who prays for herself acknowledges that she depends upon God, but her uncertainty regarding the nature of the response serves as a safeguard against excessive pride, which might be the consequence of certainty that God is on her side. Just as a teacher who helps a student only when the student asks for help preserves a healthy teacher–student relationship, so God, in helping human beings only when asked to do so, avoids dominating them, thereby preserving the relationship between Godself and believers.

Stump admits that this view of prayer seems to imply that God does not help those who neither pray for themselves nor are prayed for. She suggests that God will help such people without being asked, but that, since God's usual practice is to give benefits in response to requests, God's primary concern is to enable people to make these requests. For example, in the case of Augustine (354–430), whose mother Monica prayed for him to be saved, it is possible to argue that God would have saved Augustine if Monica had not prayed for him, but not in the same time, by the same process or with the same effect. Stump suggests that, had Monica failed to pray, Augustine might still have been converted to Christianity, but might not have become one of its most powerful authorities.

Stump admits that, in a case such as failure to pray for victims of an earthquake, an adequate answer is much more difficult to find. In a case like this, she suggests, more work on the problem of evil is required – since we might ask why a good God allows earthquakes to happen, and whether God's reasons prevent God from helping those involved.

Nevertheless, Stump argues that there may be some things which will not be received if they are not asked for. She gives as examples the first three requests of the Lord's prayer ('Hallowed be your name. Your kingdom come. Your will be done.'), suggesting that many people must pray for the coming of God's kingdom, a state in which the Earth is populated by people who freely love God, and that God could not bring about God's kingdom without such prayers because it is not possible for God to make human beings freely do anything. So if human beings sometimes fail to pray for a good thing, God might not bring about that good thing, or God might do so, but without the benefit which would have been brought about by means of petitionary prayer.

Reflection

How far does Stump's view avoid the objections to Aquinas's view to which she refers?

In *What Are We Doing When We Pray?* Vincent Brümmer (b. 1932) (2008 [1984]) argues, like both Aquinas and Stump, that prayer plays an important role in maintaining the relationship between God and human beings. Unlike Stump, however, he suggests that God is able to fulfil most of our needs without our asking, but that, if we do not ask, God cannot give in a personal sense.

The problem of unanswered prayer

Brümmer's argument nevertheless fails to address a problem with which Stump concludes her paper – the problem of apparently unanswered prayer. Stump notes that there is nothing in her analysis of prayer which requires that God answer every prayer, and that Christian writings are full of examples of prayers which are not answered. She responds that such cases require us to examine the problem of evil, and that this is outside the scope of her paper.

David Basinger (1995) considers the argument, put forward by Michael J. Murray and Kurt Meyers (1994), that the purpose of prayer is to help the petitioner to learn more about God and thereby to become more like God. If the believer's requests are granted, she learns the nature of things which are in accordance with God's will, while, if her requests are not granted, she learns that her desires are not in accordance with God's will. Basinger responds that:

- When prayers are not answered, this may indeed be because they are not consistent with God's values – but there may be some other reason (such as the overall good of the petitioner or someone else) why God decided not to grant the request.
- The petitioner can learn about God's values only if she does not know before she prays whether her request is consistent with God's values. But if, as some suggest, we can only claim that a prayer has been answered if the 'answer' is compatible with God's values, the petitioner must already know what God's values are.
- While it may be reasonable for God to withhold some things to prevent people being dominated or spoiled, is it reasonable to say that God would withhold more important things – such as protecting a person's life – in order to maintain the relationship between Godself and human beings?

Finally, even if we can find suitable responses to the questions of whether God helps without being asked, and why God sometimes appears not to answer when Xe is asked, there remains the problem of how we can be sure that a prayer has been answered. We noted above the suggestion that some prayers may be incompatible with God's values. So we would not expect an answer to a prayer for vengeance, for example.

But compatibility with divine values alone does not guarantee that an 'answer' has come from God. For example, a person may have recovered from illness without prayer. Nevertheless, Murray and Meyers argue that there are contexts in which it would be reasonable to believe that God caused or failed to cause something which was requested by a petitioner because God wanted things to happen in that way.

Reflection

Can you think of an example of such a context?

• PRAYER AND PANENTHEISM

Another way of addressing the problems associated with petitionary prayer was suggested by Muhammad Iqbal (1877–1938) (2012 [1934]) who develops a concept of prayer in the context of a panentheist idea of Ultimate Reality.

Iqbal argues, first, for the importance of prayer on the grounds that the psychological nature of human beings is such that we carry within us a sense of 'an ideal spectator' (2012 [1934]: 71) to whom we feel an impulse to pray. For Iqbal, however, prayer is not a mystical activity. Rather, prayer is 'a means of spiritual illumination' (72) by which our individual personalities discover how they are related to a larger context. It opens up sources of life which lie within the human ego and 'brings about new power by shaping the human personality' (72). For Iqbal, prayer is 'a necessary complement to the intellectual activity of the observer of Nature' (72), because the scientific observation of Nature keeps us in close contact with the behaviour of Reality, of which we are a part, thereby enabling us to gain a deeper understanding of it. In fact, Iqbal claims, 'all search for knowledge is essentially a form of prayer' (73). The scientist's knowledge may give her a degree of power over Nature, but her observation of it will eventually lead to 'vision of the total-infinite which philosophy seeks but cannot find' (73). Both vision and power are necessary for spiritual expansion; vision without power may lead to an enhanced moral theory without action, while power without vision may be 'destructive and inhuman' (73).

Iqbal argues that all true prayer is not individual but social, since even a hermit who leaves the company of his fellow human beings seeks fellowship with God. He argues that a religious congregation is a group of people who have the same aspiration and 'concentrate themselves on a single object and open up their inner selves to the workings of a single impulse' (73). According to Iqbal, our understanding of human psychology teaches us that association with others opens up our powers of perception, deepens our emotions, and energises our wills to an extent much greater than we can experience as individuals. It is for this reason, Iqbal thinks, that, in Islam, we find both daily congregational prayer and the annual ceremony at the central mosque in Mecca. Although there is no correct form of prayer in Islam, the reason why Muslims pray facing the same way is to enhance their sense of congregational unity and to create and foster their sense of social equality. Indeed, he suggests, a tremendous spiritual revolution would take place 'if the proud aristocratic Brahmin of South India is daily made to stand shoulder to shoulder with the untouchable' (75).

On Iqbal's view, the problem of whether God helps someone for whom no one prays, and the problem of apparently unanswered prayer do not arise. He simply notes that our human minds do not enable us to understand 'the great cosmic forces which work havoc, and at the same time sustain and amplify life' (65). Nevertheless, the Qur'an teaches that the behaviour of humankind and their ability to control natural forces can be improved. He argues that the Qur'an teaches meliorism – that the universe is growing and that humankind can work towards eventual victory over evil. So we pray to improve our own and others' circumstances with the aim of contributing to a positive outcome. There may be people for whom no one prays, but if this is so, it is the responsibility of the human beings who are part of Ultimate Reality to work for positive change.

● THE LANGUAGE OF PRAYER

A view of prayer which has some features in common with that of Iqbal may be found in the work of D. Z. Phillips (1981). For Phillips, prayer is not asking God to make something happen, as if it were a kind of magic. So, prayer for a sick child is not a request for God to heal her because, if no healing takes place, we cannot give an adequate explanation of why God appears to heal some children but not others.

Phillips acknowledges that many religious people do think and act as if they are talking to God when they pray, and he suggests that this belief is not mistaken. The nature of the God to whom they are talking determines the nature of the talk, however. We should therefore not be surprised to find that there are significant differences between the way in which human beings talk to each other and the way in which they talk to God. Just as God's anger is different from that of human beings, so God's speech is different from human speech. In particular, God does not participate in a shared language, which means that words which are applied to God have meanings which are different from those they have when they are applied to human beings. Prayer is therefore not a conversation.

Although, for Phillips, God does not participate in a shared language, God *is* found in the language believers learn when they learn about religion. This shared knowledge of how to use religious concepts is what religion is, and to understand how to use it is to know God. Believers learn the language of prayer by listening to the prayers of others in the context of their religious community. In corporate prayer, the community talks to God but, in doing do, they are also talking to each other. Phillips does not deny the validity of private prayer, but he does think that the meaning of even private prayers depends on the beliefs and practices of the religious community as a whole.

Phillips argues that believers' prayers have a number of possible purposes, including:

1 Telling God about the strength of their desires.
2 Seeking the help which comes from what prayer teaches them. For example, in praying for a friend in danger, they might come to recognise that anxiety may not

enable the danger to be avoided, but that nothing can destroy the value of friendship.

3 Providing others with strength and power. For example, a missionary who knows that he belongs to a praying community and that he is being prayed for might derive strength and power from this during his absence.

4 Creating the power which brings about what believers are praying for. For example, prayer for the world's conversion does not, in itself, bring this about; rather, prayer strengthens believers' ability to testify to and live in accordance with the love of God, and it is this which may bring others to belief.

Finally, Phillips argues that God's answer to prayer must be compatible with what believers already know about the will of God from their religious tradition, as this is understood by their own religious community. For example, in the time of Abraham (b. c. 1800 BCE), when the practice of child sacrifice was not unknown, Abraham might reasonably have thought that God required him to sacrifice his son, but if someone today thought that he had been told by God to sacrifice his son, we would not say that this was the will of God.

• PRAYER AND PRACTICE

We have seen that, for both Iqbal and Phillips, answers to prayer may be expected largely in the actions of believers. A clearer focus on prayer as a religious practice may be found in the work of Keith Ward (b. 1938) (2002).

For Ward, prayer is not petitionary in that it does not involve asking God for things. Rather, prayer might encourage some or all of the following:

1 Attention to the goodness, beauty and wisdom of the world.
2 Reverence for goodness.
3 Appreciation of and gratitude for what we experience.
4 Faith as commitment to the continual possibility of goodness.
5 Examination of our motives and desires.
6 Valuing and helping others.
7 Release from the tyranny of the past.
8 Hope as commitment to positive action for good.
9 Compassion and empathy for others.
10 Reflection on which practical actions we can perform in order to increase goodness in the world.

Conceived in this way, Ward suggests, religious practice is, or should be, 'the formation of the self in virtue' (2002: 210) and avoids philosophical problems of the kind we have been considering in this chapter. Ward suggests that believing in God is undertaking these practices but, if the atheist finds this idea difficult, she could still pray in the manner which Ward recommends. If she were to do this, Ward claims, she would be 'getting to the heart of what prayer to God has always been about, though it has been dressed up in symbols and images which some may now find off-putting' (211).

● CONCLUSION

In this chapter, we have considered four interpretations of what believers do when they pray. The first, which may be broadly termed that of the classical theist and includes the positions of scholars such as Aquinas and Stump, encounters a number of difficulties, including the questions of whether God helps those for whom no one prays, why it would appear that some prayers are not answered, and how we can know that an apparent response is, in fact, an answer to prayer and would not otherwise have happened. The panentheism of Iqbal avoids these difficulties by arguing that we are all part of an Ultimate Reality and that, in our prayers, we seek to understand the nature of this Reality and to work together for the common good. Phillips focuses on prayer as a language in which we talk both to the God and to each other, while Ward focuses on the practical outcomes which might be enabled by the use of religious language. For Phillips, God is found within religious language whereas, for Ward, it is in the practices of religion, and in particular those which are enabled by prayer, in which God is to be found.

This chapter concludes our examination of several key attributes of the Divine. In the next chapter, we will begin to consider whether, once we have ascertained what it might be reasonable to say about the nature of the Divine, there are any arguments which might support belief in its existence.

● REFERENCES

Aquinas, Thomas (2016 [1920, 1265–1274] *Summa Theologica*, Second Part of the Second Part, Question 83, Articles 2, 5, 6, 7 and 17 although Article 2 is the most central, www.newadvent.org/summa.

Basinger, David (1995) 'A Response to Murray and Meyers', *Religious Studies* 31, 4: 475–484.

Brümmer, Vincent (2008 [1984]) *What Are We Doing When We Pray? A Philosophical Inquiry* (London: Routledge).

Iqbal, Muhammad (2012 [1934]) *The Reconstruction of Religious Thought in Islam*, ed. M. Saheed Sheikh with an introduction by Javed Majeed (Stanford, CA: Stanford University Press), 50–75.

Murray, Michael J. and Meyers, Kurt (1994) 'Ask and It Will Be Given to You', *Religious Studies* 30, 3: 311–330.

Phillips, D. Z. (1981) *The Concept of Prayer* (Oxford: Basil Blackwell).

Stump, Eleonore (1979) 'Petitionary Prayer', *American Philosophical Quarterly* 16, 2: 81–91; reprinted in Eleanore Stump and Michael J. Murray (eds) *Philosophy of Religion: The Big Questions* (Oxford: Blackwell, 1999), 353–366.

Ward, Keith (2002) *God: A Guide for the Perplexed* (London: Oneworld), 209–212.

● FURTHER READING

Encyclopedia article

Davison, Scott A. (2012) 'Petitionary Prayer' *Stanford Encyclopedia of Philosophy*, https://plato.stanford.edu/entries/petitionary-prayer/.

Original articles in edited collections

Taliaferro, Charles (2013 [2007]) 'Prayer' in Chad Meister and Paul Copan (eds) *The Routledge Companion to Philosophy of Religion* (Abingdon: Routledge), 677–685.

Extracts from articles or books in edited collections

Abrabanel, Isaac (1494) *Principles of Faith (Rosh Amanah)*, trans. M. Kellner (1982) (Oxford: Littman Library); extract reprinted in Daniel H. Frank, Oliver Leaman and Charles H. Manekin (eds) *The Jewish Philosophy Reader* (London: Routledge, 2000), 108–110.

Heschel, Abraham Joshua (1969) 'On Prayer', *Conservative Judaism* 25, 1: 1–12; reprinted in Daniel H. Frank, Oliver Leaman and Charles H. Manekin (eds) *The Jewish Philosophy Reader* (London: Routledge, 2000), 588–597.

Ibn Paquda, Bachya (late eleventh century) *The Book of Direction to the Duties of the Heart*, trans. M. Mansoor (1973) (Oxford: Littman Library); extract reprinted in Daniel H. Frank, Oliver Leaman and Charles H. Manekin (eds) *The Jewish Philosophy Reader* (London: Routledge, 2000), 105–108.

Kellner, Menachem (1987) 'Heresy and the Nature of Faith in Medieval Jewish Philosophy', *Jewish Quarterly Review* 77, 4: 299–318; reprinted in Daniel H. Frank, Oliver Leaman and Charles H. Manekin (eds) *The Jewish Philosophy Reader* (London: Routledge, 2000), 114–118.

Leaman, Oliver (1995) *Evil and Suffering in Jewish Philosophy* (Cambridge: Cambridge University Press); extract reprinted in Daniel H. Frank, Oliver Leaman and Charles H. Manekin (eds) *The Jewish Philosophy Reader* (London: Routledge, 2000), 110–113.

Articles

Mander, W. J. (2007) 'Theism, Pantheism and Petitionary Prayer', *Religious Studies* 43, 3: 317–331.

Oppenheimer, H. (1970) 'Petitionary Prayer', *Theology* LXXIII, 1: 54–64.

Books

Davison, Scott A. (2017) *Petitionary Prayer: A Philosophical Investigation* (Oxford: Oxford University Press).

Geach, P. (1969) 'Praying for Things to Happen' in his *God and the Soul* (London: Routledge and Kegan Paul), 86–99.

Guessoum, Nidhal (2011) *Islam's Quantum Question: Reconciling Muslim Tradition and Modern Science* (London: I. B. Tauris), 333–335.

Harrison, Jonathan (1999) *God, Freedom and Immortality* (Aldershot: Ashgate), Chapter 26.

Moore, G. (1988) *Believing in God: A Philosophical Essay*. (Edinburgh: T & T Clark), Chapter 6.

Polkinghorne, John C. (2005 [1989]) *Science and Providence: God's Interaction with the World* (West Conshohocken, PA: Templeton Foundation Press), Chapter 6.

Ward, K. (2007 [1990]) *Divine Action* (Philadelphia, PA: Templeton Foundation Press), Chapter 9.

Wiles, M. (1986) *God's Action in the World* (Eugene, OR: Wipf and Stock), Chapter 8.

9

arguments for the existence of the divine: cosmological arguments

• INTRODUCTION

In this and the next four chapters I will examine five of the most common types of argument for the existence of the Divine. Four of these are *a posteriori* arguments, arguments which are based on our experience – of the existence of the world, the apparent order of the world and moral values, as well as allegedly direct experiences of the Divine – and one, the ontological argument, which is *a priori*, based on an analysis of ideas. In each case, I focus on some of the most significant of the many versions of the argument.

• COSMOLOGICAL ARGUMENTS

The cosmological argument is based on the assumption that the existence of the world needs to be explained. The activity of God is said to provide this explanation.

Broadly speaking, there are three forms of this argument:

A God is responsible for the *beginning* of the universe, for bringing it into existence.
B God is responsible for the *continued existence* of the universe.
C Only God provides a *sufficient reason* for the existence of the universe.

In this chapter, I will consider an example or examples of each form of the argument together with objections which apply only to that form of the argument. Objections which apply to cosmological arguments more generally will be considered towards the end of the chapter.

• A. GOD AS THE EXPLANATION FOR THE BEGINNING OF THE UNIVERSE

The *kalam* cosmological argument

The *kalam* cosmological argument originated in the Middle Ages with Abu Yusuf Ya'qub ibn Ishaq al-Kindi (c. 800–c. 870) and al-Ghazali (*kalam* refers to Arabic theology), and has been developed more recently by Craig.

Al-Ghazali's cosmological argument

Al-Ghazali (1097) argues that:

1 Material (physical) objects are either in motion or at rest.

Proof: We know this because anyone who claimed to be able to think of a physical object which was neither in motion nor at rest would be regarded as irrational.

2 Both motion and rest are caused.

Proof: There is nothing in motion which cannot be thought capable of coming to rest, and nothing at rest which cannot be thought capable of motion.

3 If everything is caused by something which is, itself, caused, this implies that there is an infinite causal chain, each link of which depends on the previous link, going back into an infinite past – in other words, that the causal chain of events is an actual infinite, a set of things the number of which cannot increase, any part of which is equal to the whole of it. (This contrasts with a potential infinite, a set of things the number of which can increase and is always finite [a potential infinite grows towards infinity but never gets there], no part of which will ever be equal to the whole of it.)

4 But the number of events in any causal chain of events cannot be an actual infinite.

Proof: If each causal chain stretches back into an infinite past, the present link in the chain would never be reached.

5 The universe is originated and depends upon the Creator.

Craig's cosmological argument

Building on the *kalam* argument of al-Ghazali, Craig (2002) develops a contemporary version of the argument. In outline, he argues that:

1 'Whatever begins to exist has a cause.
2 The universe began to exist.
3 Therefore, the universe has a cause' (2008: 198 [2002]).

The arguments for each of these run as follows:

1 Whatever begins to exist has a cause

Craig claims that this is intuitively obvious, and that we should not try to use the less obvious to prove the obvious. Although J. L. Mackie (1917–1981) (1982) asks what reason we have to accept this premise, appealing for support to Hume's suggestion that we are able to conceive of uncaused objects, even Mackie admits that the causal principle is constantly confirmed by our experience.

2 The universe began to exist

Craig puts forward four arguments in favour of the view that the universe had a beginning – two philosophical and two scientific:

An argument from the impossibility of an actually infinite number of things

Craig argues that:

a There cannot be an actually infinite number of things. As we saw earlier, this means that there cannot be a number of things which cannot increase, any part of which is equal to the whole of it.
b A series of events in time which had no beginning would be an actually infinite number of things.
c Therefore, there cannot be a series of events in time which had no beginning.

Craig supports his argument that there cannot be an actually infinite number of things by appealing to the puzzle of 'Hilbert's Hotel', a hotel with an infinite number of rooms. In this puzzle:

i All the rooms are full.
ii A new guest arrives and all the guests are moved up to the next numbered room, to infinity, thus vacating room 1 for the new guest.
iii This does not appear to make sense because, before the new guest's arrival, all the rooms were full and there are now no more people in the hotel than there were before – in other words, the number of people is infinite in both cases.
iv An infinite number of new guests arrive and all the guests are moved into the room with the number which is the double of the number of their current room, thus vacating all the odd-numbered rooms for the new guests.
v This does not appear to make sense either because, before the arrival of the new guests, all the rooms were full and there are now no more people in the hotel than there were before – in other words, the number of people is infinite in both cases.
vi If the guest in room 1 leaves, or all the guests in odd-numbered rooms leave, the hotel still contains an infinite number of people.
vii But if all the guests except those in rooms 1, 2 and 3 were to leave, the hotel would be almost empty and the infinite would have been converted to finitude, although the same number of guests would have left as when those in the odd-numbered rooms left.

Craig suggests that the absurdities in this puzzle show that an actually infinite number of things cannot exist. Since a series of events in time which had no beginning would be an actually infinite number of things, there cannot be such a thing. Therefore, the universe must have had a beginning.

The argument from the impossibility of forming an actually infinite collection of things by successive addition

Craig argues that:

a The series of events in time is formed by adding one event after another.
b It is not possible to add to an actual infinite; a number which we can add to can only be a potential infinite, not an actual infinite. This is sometimes referred to as 'the impossibility of counting to infinity or the impossibility of traversing the infinite' (202).
c Therefore the series of events in time cannot be an actual infinite.

An argument based on the isotropic expansion of the universe

Craig argues that the so-called 'Big Bang' model of the origin of the universe supports the view that the universe – all matter and energy, along with space and time – came into being out of nothing a finite time ago. He notes that various alternative theories have been proposed, but that none of these have been shown to be superior to the Big Bang theory.

An argument based on the thermodynamic properties of the universe

The Second Law of Thermodynamics (according to which processes which occur within a closed system tend towards a state of equilibrium – that is, a state in which the quantities which specify its properties – e.g. temperature – remain unchanged) suggests that the universe (which is a gigantic closed system because there is nothing outside it) and its processes are gradually running down towards a state of equilibrium, and that it will eventually die. Whether this so-called heat death will occur because the universe will contract into a hot fireball (a 'big crunch') or because it will expand forever, if the universe had always existed we would already have reached this final state.

Even if we accept an oscillating model of the universe, according to which the universe expands and contracts forever, the Second Law of Thermodynamics implies that, if we were to trace the series of oscillations backwards, each oscillation would be smaller than the last until we reached a first and smallest oscillation.

So, Craig claims, on each model, the universe was created a finite time ago and is now winding down. He therefore concludes that the universe's energy was part of its creation.

3 The universe has a cause

Craig claims that it follows from 'whatever begins to exist has a cause' and 'the universe began to exist' that 'the universe has a cause' (209).

Craig suggests that the cause of the universe must have the following characteristics:

a It must transcend space and time because it causes space and time.
b It must be changeless and immaterial because 'timelessness entails changelessness, and changelessness implies immateriality' (209).

c It must be beginningless and uncaused because Ockham's Razor (a philosophical principle developed by William of Ockham) requires that we do not multiply causes without necessity.

d It must be very powerful because it created the universe from nothing.

e It must be personal because there cannot be a scientific explanation for the beginning of the universe because there is nothing which precedes it. The personhood of the cause is also implied by its timelessness and immateriality because only minds or abstract objects can be timeless or immaterial, and abstract objects cannot function as causes. If the cause of the universe were merely 'an impersonal set of necessary and sufficient conditions' (210) – that is, a set of circumstances some of which must exist for an event to occur, and some of which may enable an event to occur – the existence of the universe would be inevitable. Only the existence of a personal agent who chooses to bring the universe into existence explains the beginning of the universe a finite period of time ago.

Craig claims that these philosophical arguments are supported by 'the observed fine-tuning of the universe, which bespeaks intelligent design' (210). He suggests that the fine-tuning of the universe which enables the development and continued existence of intelligent life is best explained by the intelligent design of a personal Creator. This argument will be considered further in the next chapter.

Reflection

In what respects is Craig's argument similar to that of al-Ghazali? In what respects does it differ?

Objections to the *kalam* cosmological argument

The arguments of both al-Ghazali and Craig depend upon the claim that there cannot be an actual infinite. The 'Hilbert's Hotel' example is designed to show that, although we cannot add to or subtract from infinity (because we cannot have more or fewer than the maximum conceivable number of things), we can conceive of a scenario in which it seems rational to do so. If that is the case, the concept of an actual infinite does not make sense and therefore there cannot be an actually infinite causal series.

Craig's second argument for the claim that there cannot be an actual infinite, derived from that of al-Ghazali, makes basically the same point – that we cannot add to an actually infinite series of events in time. If, however, we think of an infinite series of events in time from the timeless perspective of an eternal present, then each event in time is not an addition to a succession of events but merely one point on an infinite temporal spectrum. Clearly this notion, too, is not without its difficulties (it requires a 'God's-eye-view' of the world in order to undermine this argument for believing in the existence of such a God, for example), but it does, at any rate, cast doubt on the claim that there cannot be an actually infinite series of past events and that God is required to explain the existence of the universe.

Craig's argument also depends upon scientific claims about the origins of and future prospects for our world. It is not the work of philosophy to assess the scientific basis of the Big Bang theory of the origins of the universe or the Second Law of Thermodynamics, but the philosopher may legitimately consider the implications of these, should they turn out to be correct. In both cases, however, they describe a process by means of which the universe began its life and is gradually running down, neither of which, arguably, requires a divine explanation.

• B. GOD AS THE EXPLANATION FOR THE CONTINUED EXISTENCE OF THE UNIVERSE

Aquinas's cosmological arguments

Although Aquinas believed that God caused the universe to come into existence, he did not think it possible to provide a philosophical proof for this. He did, however, argue that God is responsible for sustaining the existence of the universe and that every causal chain therefore depends ultimately upon God.

The first three of Aquinas's Five Ways (1265–1274) are usually regarded as forms of the cosmological argument. (The Fourth Way is a form of the moral argument, and the Fifth Way is a version of the design argument.)

The First Way: The Argument from Motion, runs as follows:

1 Some things are in the process of changing.
2 Nothing changes itself. For example, wood requires fire to make it hot.
3 But there cannot be an endless series of things causing change.
4 So there must be a cause of change which is not caused to change by anything else – that is, God.

In short, Aquinas argues that the cause of all changes must ultimately be traced to a first mover, which is God.

We could object to the First Way on the grounds that it is not the case that nothing changes itself. For example, if human beings have free will, there are many ways in which we can change ourselves. I can improve my fitness by going to the gym, for instance. Aquinas could respond, however, that, although I might be able to choose to improve my lung function by running on a treadmill, I am not ultimately responsible for having a physical body which can be changed in this way.

According to the Second Way, sometimes known as the First Cause Argument:

1 The existence of something requires a cause.
2 The existence of everything requires a cause which is not caused to exist by anything else (because if there were no such cause then nothing would exist; something has to start off the causal chain).
3 Some things do exist.
4 Therefore there must be a first cause – that is, God.

In summary, Aquinas argues that the cause of the existence of everything must ultimately be traced to a first cause which was not caused to exist by anything else, and that this cause is God.

Perhaps Aquinas's most significant version of the cosmological argument, however, is the Third Way: The Argument from Contingency, in which he argues as follows:

1 Some things can either exist or not exist.
2 Things which can either exist or not exist did not exist at some time; they cannot have existed forever.
3 If everything were like this, there would have been a time when nothing existed at all.
4 If this were so, there would be nothing existing now (because there must have been something to cause the existence of contingent things [in this context, things which may or may not exist]).
5 So there must be some things which cannot not exist – that is, which exist necessarily.
6 The existence of all necessary things cannot be a brute fact.
7 Therefore there must be something which is both necessary and not caused to exist by anything – that is, God.

Note that, for Aquinas, a necessary thing is a thing which must exist, but may still depend for its existence on another necessary thing. In Aquinas's view, only God is a necessary thing whose existence does not depend on any other thing – either contingent or necessary.

In summary, then, Aquinas argues that the existence of contingent things must be explained by the existence of necessary things, and the existence of necessary things which are, nonetheless, caused to exist by something, must be explained by the existence of something which is both necessary and not caused to exist by anything external to itself. This cause is God.

An objection to Aquinas's Third Way

Perhaps the key objection to Aquinas's Third Way is that, even if the existence of most things is contingent, which means that, in each case, there must have been a time when it did not exist, this does not entail that, without divine intervention, nothing would exist now. This might be the case if all contingent things were non-existent at the same time, but it would not be irrational to suppose that there has been, and continues to be, a sequence of contingent things in which the existence of each member overlaps with that of other members. Aquinas might still argue, however, that divine intervention is the ultimate explanation for the existence of the overlapping sequence of contingent things.

A contemporary version of Aquinas's cosmological Argument from Contingency

Herbert McCabe (1926–2001) (1980) attempts to express Aquinas's arguments in modern terms. McCabe thinks that belief in God, by which he means 'belief in the validity of the kind of radical question to which God would be the answer' is 'part of human flourishing' and that 'one who closes himself off from it is to that extent deficient' (2000: 197 [1980]). The 'radical question to which God would be the answer' is a question about the ultimate existence of everything. We might ask how a dog, Fido, came into existence, and this could be a question about who his parents were, about how he came to be a dog rather than a giraffe (in other words, a question about dogs as a species, rather than an individual dog), about biochemistry, physics, and so on, until we get to the 'ultimate radical question' of how Fido exists rather than nothing – that is, the 'God-question'. Whatever it is that answers this question is what we call 'God'.

Reflection

In what respects do Aquinas's cosmological arguments differ from those of Craig?

• C. GOD AS THE SUFFICIENT REASON FOR THE BEGINNING OF THE UNIVERSE

Richard Taylor (1919–2003) (1991) puts forward a version of the cosmological argument which is based on the principle of sufficient reason, which states that everything has a reason which is sufficient to explain its existence. Taylor asks us to suppose that we have come across a large translucent ball of about our own height in the woods. We would not assume that it had appeared there by itself; we would assume that there was an explanation for its existence. Likewise, since it is possible that the world might not have existed, the principle of sufficient reason requires that there must be a reason not only for the existence of everything in the world but also for the existence of the world itself. This reason is provided by the existence of a self-caused being which 'exists, not contingently or in dependence upon something else, but by its own nature . . . it is a being which is such that it can neither come into being nor perish' (2008: 96 [1991]) – i.e. a necessary being.

Reflection

What does Taylor mean by 'necessary being'? How does his understanding of the term differ from that of Aquinas?

• FURTHER OBJECTIONS TO COSMOLOGICAL ARGUMENTS

At the beginning of this chapter we saw that cosmological arguments rest on the assumption that the existence of the world requires explanation. A key objection to arguments of this kind, therefore, is to claim that the existence of the universe is a 'brute fact' which does not require an explanation. In a famous radio debate with Frederick Copleston (1907–1994), Russell said: 'I should say that the universe is just there, and that's all' (1990: 232 [1948]). Mackie argues that, although it might be intellectually satisfying to claim that there is some explanation for the totality of everything which exists, 'we have no right to assume that the universe will comply with our intellectual preferences' (1982: 86–87). In a similar vein, Paul Edwards (1923–2004) (1959) suggests that, although it might be possible to explain why there are five Inuit standing on the corner of Sixth Avenue and 50th Street by explaining how each person came to be there, it would be absurd to ask for an explanation of why the group as a whole is in New York.

We might, however, respond that, although we could find out the reason why each individual Inuk came to be standing with others in New York, the fact that they are all far from their home and standing in the same place at the same time suggests that we are likely to find that they all have a common reason for being there. McCabe argues that to say that the universe is just there is as arbitrary as it is to say that dogs are just there. Although, from Charles Darwin (1809–1882), we know how dogs come about, it is not irrational to ask how the universe has come about just because we do not know the answer.

Secondly, it may be objected that the word 'cause', when applied to the universe, means something different from its normal use (that is, it refers to creation *ex nihilo* – out of nothing – rather than the transformation of pre-existing materials). In other words, we cannot infer from the fact that things within the universe have causes that the universe as a whole has a cause, because causes within the universe transform pre-existing materials, whereas the kind of cause to which the cosmological argument points creates the universe from nothing.

Craig's response to this objection is that, in both cases, the word 'cause' refers to something which brings about or produces effects. It is therefore legitimate to use the word 'cause' to refer to divine activity, because both divine and human causal activity have some features in common.

Thirdly, it may be objected that, if everything is caused, the cause of the universe must also have been caused.

Craig responds that only things which begin to exist are caused. Something which has no beginning has no cause. On this view, then, it is the existence of God, rather than that of the universe, which is the brute fact.

Reflection

Craig's argument that only things which began to exist are caused might not be helpful to the defender of Aquinas or Taylor. Why is this? How might his response be reformulated in order to avoid the objection?

• ALTERNATIVE ACCOUNTS OF CREATION

So far in this chapter we have considered arguments for the existence of a God who is the first cause and/or sustainer of the existence of the universe. Not all religions or interpretations of religion require belief in a God of this kind, however. For example, Sushanta Sen argues that, according to the *Chāndogya* Upanishad (VI.2.1–2), one of the principal Upanishads, the theory of creation out of nothing should be rejected on the grounds that 'an existent entity can never be produced out of nothing' (2008: 50 [1989]). This is based on a view of causation according to which an effect can only be produced if it already exists in some form in its cause, just as one can only produce oil by crushing seeds if the oil is already present in the seeds.

According to Sen, on the Upanishadic Hindu view, God created the world from God's inner nature. Normally, there is a distinction between a material cause – e.g. the clay from which a pot is made – and an efficient cause – e.g. the potter who makes the pot. In the case of the creation of the world, however, God is both the material cause and the efficient cause; 'God is both the creator and the stuff of the world at the same time' (51). This means that, after creating the universe, God continues to be involved in every part of it.

On this view, both God and the universe are eternal – that is, without beginning or end. Although the universe is periodically reabsorbed into God and projected outwards again, this does not mean that there are times when the universe does not exist. At the point of reabsorption, what has been reabsorbed continues to exist in an 'unmanifested' form. And it is not the case that the whole universe is reabsorbed at the same time; although one solar system may be disintegrating, many others will continue to be manifested. So although individual worlds may begin and end, this applies only to one cycle; creation as a whole is without beginning or end.

Reflection

To what extent does Sen's understanding of creation avoid the objections to creation *ex nihilo* which we considered above?

• CONCLUSION

In this chapter, we have seen that the success, or otherwise, of the cosmological argument depends upon our willingness to grant that the beginning and/or continued existence of the universe requires an explanation, and to accept both that God is its cause in an analogical sense and that God requires no cause. We concluded with a brief examination of one Hindu account of creation and saw that, on this view, God is, in some sense, identified with the universe which God creates from God's own Being. The latter view might, to some extent, contribute to an effective answer to the questions raised by the former, enabling us to say not so much that the Big Bang was the means by which the God of the classical theist created the universe, but that whatever caused the Big Bang is what we mean by 'God'. This gives us a more limited conception of what God might be like, however, for which reason we turn in the next chapter to the teleological or design argument, which attempts to prove that the apparent design which we see in our universe ultimately requires a divine explanation.

• REFERENCES

Al-Ghazali, Abu Hamid (1097) *The Jerusalem Tract*, trans. and ed. A. L. Tibawi, *The Islamic Quarterly* 9 (1965), 3–4: 62–122, 98–99; reprinted in Linda Zagzebski and Timothy D. Miller (eds) *Readings in Philosophy of Religion: Ancient to Contemporary* (Chichester: Wiley-Blackwell, 2009), 66–67.

Aquinas, Thomas (2016 [1920, 1265–1274]) *The Summa Theologica of St Thomas Aquinas*, trans. Fathers of the English Dominican Province, www.newadvent.org/summa/ Part I, Question 2, Article 3.

Craig, William Lane (2002) 'the Kalām Cosmological Argument' in William Lane Craig (ed.) *Philosophy of Religion: A Reader and Guide* (Edinburgh: Edinburgh University Press), 92–113; reprinted in Chad Meister (ed.) *The Philosophy of Religion Reader* (Abingdon: Routledge, 2008), 197–214.

Edwards, Paul (1959) 'A Critique of the Cosmological Argument' in Hector Hawton (ed.) *The Rationalist Annual* (London: Pemberton Publishing Company), 63–77; reprinted in Brian Davies (ed.) *Philosophy of Religion: A Guide and Anthology* (Oxford: Oxford University Press, 2000), 202–212.

McCabe, Herbert (1980) 'God: I – Creation', *New Blackfriars* 61, 724: 408–415; reprinted in Brian Davies (ed.) *Philosophy of Religion: A Guide and Anthology* (Oxford: Oxford University Press, 2000), 196–201.

Mackie, J. L. (1982) *The Miracle of Theism: Arguments For and Against the Existence of God* (Oxford: Clarendon), Chapter 5.

Russell, Bertrand, and Copleston, F. C. (1948) The Third Programme of the British Broadcasting Corporation, edited portion available at www.youtube.com/watch?v=hXPdpEJk78E; transcript first published in *Humanitas* (Manchester, 1948) reprinted in John Hick (ed.) *Classical and Contemporary Readings* (Englewood Cliffs, NJ: Prentice Hall, 1990), 227–234.

Sen, Sushanta (1989) 'The Vedic-Upanisadic Concept of *Brahman* (The Highest God)' in Linda Tessier (ed.) (1989) *Concepts of the Ultimate* (New York, NY: St Martin's Press), 83–97; reprinted in Andrew Eshleman (ed.) *Readings in Philosophy of Religion: East Meets West* (Oxford: Blackwell, 2008), 43–51.

Taylor, Richard (1991) 'A Cosmological Argument for God's Existence' in Richard Taylor *Metaphysics*, 4th edn (Englewood Cliffs, NJ: Prentice Hall), 100–107; reprinted in Andrew Eshleman (ed.) *Readings in Philosophy of Religion* (Oxford: Blackwell, 2008), 91–96.

• FURTHER READING

Encyclopedia article

Reichenbach, Bruce (2016) 'Cosmological Arguments', *Stanford Encyclopedia of Philosophy*, https://plato.stanford.edu/entries/cosmological-argument/.

Original articles in edited collections

Oderberg, David S. (2013 [2007]) 'The Cosmological Argument' in Chad Meister and Paul Copan (eds) *The Routledge Companion to Philosophy of Religion* (Abingdon: Routledge), 401–410.

Pruss, Alexander R. and Gale, Richard M. (2005) 'Cosmological and Design Arguments' in William J. Wainwright (ed.) *The Oxford Handbook of Philosophy of Religion* (Oxford: OUP), Chapter 5.

Shihadeh, Ayman (2008) 'The Existence of God' in Tim Winter (ed.) *The Cambridge Companion to Classical Islamic Theology* (Cambridge: Cambridge University Press), 204–214.

Stoeger, William R. (2010) 'God, Physics and the Big Bang' in Peter Harrison (ed.) *The Cambridge Companion to Science and Religion* (Cambridge: Cambridge University Press), 173–183.

Extract from book in edited collection

al-Muqammiṣ, Dāwūd (1989) *Dāwūd ibn Marwān al-Muqammiṣ's Twenty Chapters*, ed. and trans. S. Strousma (Leiden: E. J. Brill); extract reprinted in Chapter 7 in Daniel H. Frank, Oliver Leaman and Charles H. Manekin (eds) *The Jewish Philosophy Reader* (London: Routledge, 2000), 168–171.

Articles

Craig, William Lane, various articles on arguments for God's existence, including the kalām argument, may be found at http://leaderu.com.

Gale, Richard M. and Pruss, Alexander (1999) 'A New Cosmological Argument', *Religious Studies* 35, 4: 461–476.

Books

Craig, William Lane (2001) *The Cosmological Argument from Plato to Leibniz* (Eugene, OR: Wipf and Stock).

Davis, Stephen T. (1997) *God, Reason and Theistic Proofs* (Edinburgh: Edinburgh University Press), Chapter 4.

Evans, C. Stephen (2010) *Natural Signs and Knowledge of God: A New Look at Theistic Arguments* (Oxford: OUP), Chapter 3.

Goldschmidt, Tyron (ed.) (2014) *The Puzzle of Existence: Why is There Something Rather than Nothing?* (New York and Abingdon: Routledge).

Guessoum, Nidhal (2011) *Islam's Quantum Question: Reconciling Muslim Tradition and Modern Science* (London: I. B. Tauris), Chapter 6.

Haldane, J. J. (1996) 'The Cause of Things' in J. J. C. Smart and J. J. Haldane (eds) *Atheism and Theism* (Oxford: Blackwell), 129–140.

Sharma, Arvind (1990) *A Hindu Perspective on the Philosophy of Religion* (Basingstoke: Macmillan Press), 1–4, 12–13.

Sweetman, Brendan (2010) *Religion and Science: An Introduction* (New York, NY: Continuum), 171–185.

Swinburne, Richard (2004 [1979]) *The Existence of God* (Oxford: Clarendon Press), Chapter 7.

Taliaferro, Charles (1998) *Contemporary Philosophy of Religion* (Oxford: Blackwell), 353–365.

Yaran, Cafer S. (2003) *Islamic Thought on the Existence of God: Contributions and Contrasts with Contemporary Western Philosophy of Religion* (Washington: The Council for Research in Values and Philosophy), Chapters 5 and 6.

Web resources

Craig, William Lane (1991) 'The Existence of God and the Beginning of the Universe', Truth: A Journal of Modern Thought 3 (1991): 85–96. Available on Craig's website at: www.reasonablefaith.org/the-existence-of-god-and-the-beginning-of-the-universe.

10

arguments for the existence of the divine: design arguments

• INTRODUCTION

In the previous chapter we saw that cosmological arguments claim that the existence of God explains the existence of our world or some aspect of it. By contrast, the design or teleological (from the Greek *telos*, meaning 'purpose', 'end' or 'design') argument claims that the existence of God explains the apparent design of the world or some aspect of it.

Note that the argument is now usually referred to as an argument 'to' or 'for' design, rather than an argument 'from' design. Mackie (1982: 133) claims that an argument from design already assumes that the world has been designed, and that it is therefore more accurate to say that it is an argument from the appearance of design to, or for, design.

• DESIGN IN THE SENSE OF PURPOSE

The design argument can be traced back as far as Heraclitus (500 BCE). A version of the argument was offered by the Indian Nyaya (logical-atomist) school (100–1000 CE), who argued that the order in the world is like that of both human artefacts and the human body, and therefore requires a divine explanation (Collins, 2013).

But it is William Paley (1743–1805) who gives us perhaps the most famous version of the argument in his *Natural Theology, or Evidences of the Existence and Attributes of the Deity Collected from the Appearance of Nature* (1802). Paley says that if he found a stone on a heath, he would be justified in saying that it might always have been there. But, he says, if he found a watch on the ground and someone asked how it came to be there, he would not be justified in saying that it had always been there. In this case, he argues, we would conclude that the watch had been put together for a purpose and that it must therefore have had a maker.

Paley claims that we would come to this conclusion even if we had never seen a watch made, if we had never known an artist who could make one, if we could not make one ourselves or even understand how it was made, if the watch sometimes went wrong, or if there were some parts of the watch whose purpose we were unable to determine.

We would not think that it was just one of a number of possible combinations of physical matter, that it contained within itself a principle which organised its various parts, that the mechanism was just a trick to make us think that the watch was designed, or that the design was the result of the laws of nature.

Indeed, Paley claims, we would still think that the watch had been designed, even if we knew nothing at all about it.

Similarly, Paley suggests, the natural world contains many examples of apparent design. For example, a bird's wings are made in such a way that it is able to fly, and the fins of a fish enable it to swim. Paley concludes that there must have been a designer of the world, the designer must have been a person, and that person is God.

• OBJECTIONS TO THE ARGUMENT FOR DESIGN IN THE SENSE OF PURPOSE

The classic critique of the argument for design is found in Hume's *An Enquiry Concerning Human Understanding* (1748) (Section XI) and in his *Dialogues Concerning Natural Religion* (1779), both of which were published some years before Paley's statement of the argument in his *Natural Theology*. Hume's key objections include the following:

1 If the argument works, it proves only the existence of a design-producing being and not a being with any of the other attributes which God is commonly said to possess, including the ability to act by choice, because we can only ascribe to a cause the qualities which it needs to produce an effect.

In Chapter 9 we noted that cosmological arguments, even if successful, do not prove the existence of a deity with the full range of attributes which are commonly ascribed to God. With respect to arguments for design, Swinburne (1968) acknowledges that these arguments do not support belief in a God who is good, omnipotent and omniscient. He rejects Hume's claim that we can only ascribe to a cause the qualities which are needed to produce an effect, however, on the grounds that this principle, if universally adopted, would require us to abandon science because scientists commonly argue that the causes of effects have characteristics in addition to those required to produce effects. If this were not the case, scientists would be able to tell us only that the cause of E is something with E-producing characteristics. On this basis, Swinburne thinks it reasonable to preserve God's freedom of choice.

2 Hume claims that we cannot infer from the fact that things in the universe have causes that the universe as a whole has a cause, unless we have experience of other universes and other causes.

Again, we noted a parallel objection to cosmological arguments in Chapter 9. Swinburne responds that, in science, it is reasonable to infer that the relationship between observable As and Bs is similar to that of unobservable A*s and B*s when the unobservable A*s and B*s are similar to the observable As and Bs.

3 Hume argues that the universe is unique; therefore, we cannot reach conclusions about the cause of an object which is the only one of its kind.

Swinburne again appeals to science, arguing that, although the universe and the human race are, as far as we know, unique, cosmologists and anthropologists are nevertheless able to reach well-tested conclusions about them. Thus, he argues, it is not unreasonable to ask questions about the origin of something unique.

Indeed, as we saw earlier, Paley uses a similar argument. He says that we would assume that a watch was designed even if we had never seen one before. The existence of watches points to the existence of watchmakers because watches exhibit regularity.

4 If the world was designed, who designed the designer?

Yet again, we noted a parallel version of this objection in the chapter on cosmological arguments. Swinburne suggests that the existence of the designer does not need to be explained. He notes that scientists have always postulated (put forward as a hypothesis for testing by means of argument) entities to explain effects (282). We might note here the very recent (at the time of writing, three days ago) announcement of the discovery of gravitational waves, predicted by Albert Einstein in 1916.

Not all religious believers would accept that apparent order is explained by a divine designer, however. For example, the classical Sankhya school of Hindu thought held that the existence of *prakrti*, matter, explains the apparent order in the world; in other words, the universe made itself (Sharma, 1990: 5; see also Ruzsa, 2015). On this view, it is not God but the apparent orderliness of the world which is the 'brute fact' requiring no further explanation.

5 Why should there be only one designer? It takes many people to build a house or a ship, for example.

Swinburne argues that, although order is often produced by groups of human beings, this does not imply that every instance of order must be produced by a group. As Swinburne points out, Hume is aware of 'the obvious counter-objection' which is supplied by Ockham's razor. Applied to the design argument, it leads to the conclusion that there is no reason to say that there is more than one God. Hume thinks that this does not apply to his argument, however, because we do not know whether there is a God with enough power to order the whole universe. Swinburne argues that it does, in fact, apply, whether or not we have such knowledge. Further, he suggests that, if the universe were ordered by several deities, we would expect to see signs of the work of different deities in different parts of the universe. For example, there might be an inverse square law of gravity in one place, and a law just short of being an inverse square law in another.

6 Hume argues that the universe could be the result of chance – that is, that there are periods of chaos and order and we are currently living in a period of order.

Swinburne responds that, even if the universe is the result of chance, we still need to explain the present order. He suggests that the view that the universe is the result of chance becomes less plausible as time progresses and order remains.

Darwin, design and irreducible complexity

Since the publication of Darwin's *The Origin of Species by Means of Natural Selection* in 1859, some scholars (e.g. Richard Dawkins (b. 1941)) have argued that we no longer need God to explain the way in which the natural world seems to be so admirably suited to its purposes. According to Darwin, the current state of the universe is merely the result of the struggle for survival; those organisms which were unable to adapt to their environments simply did not survive. According to Dawkins (1995), we are obsessed with purpose. If we were to attempt to explain the purpose of cheetahs, we would have to conclude that they are designed in order to kill antelopes. In fact, the only utility function which we can see in the natural world is the maximisation of DNA survival. As long as DNA is passed on to the next generation, any suffering which results is not important.

Plantinga (2011) argues that the doctrine of creation is not incompatible with Darwinism, however, since:

> God could have caused the right mutations to arise at the right time; he could have preserved populations from perils of various sorts, and so on; and in this way he could have seen to it that there come to be creatures of the kind he intends.
>
> (2011: 11)

But what is not compatible with the Christian belief in creation is the claim that the process of evolution is unguided. This is Dawkins' claim. He supports it by arguing that it is possible that unguided natural selection could have produced wonders such as the mammalian eye, the wing or the bat's sonar. Plantinga claims that his argument is weak for two reasons:

1 There is 'no *guarantee* that there is a not-too-improbable path through organic space from some early population of unicellular organisms to human beings, or, for that matter, to fruit flies' (22).
2 Biologists disagree about whether there is a Darwinian series for the eye and other forms of life. For example, Michael Behe (b. 1952) thinks that it is very unlikely that there is such a series.

Behe (2000) notes Darwin's hypothesis that the eye evolved from a light-sensitive spot, but asks where that spot came from. According to Behe, recent science has shown that what Darwin thought of as a simple starting point is, in fact, extremely complex. Behe argues that it is irreducibly complex – in other words, that it is a system which would fail to function if one of its components were removed – and therefore that it must have been designed. Likewise, the bacterial flagellum, which enables some bacteria to swim, requires about forty different proteins to function. Without a range of parts, it fails to work and is therefore also irreducibly complex.

Plantinga suggests that, at best, what Dawkins shows is that we cannot prove that there is not a Darwinian explanation for every aspect of our universe and that it is therefore possible that the world developed without design. Later in the same book, however, Plantinga appears to agree with Paul Draper (b. 1957) that Behe fails to show that the systems which he says are irreducibly complex are, in fact, irreducibly complex (Plantinga 2011: 229). He also notes Behe's own admission that, even if he is right about irreducible complexity, an argument for an intelligent designer is not an argument for the existence of a benevolent God since, in addition to the Christian God, the designer might just as well be 'an angel fallen or not; Plato's demiurge; some mystical new-age force; space aliens from Alpha Centauri; time travellers; or some utterly unknown intelligent being' (Behe, 2003: 277, quoted in Plantinga, 2011: 236).

Plantinga argues, instead, for 'design discourse'. He observes that small children have beliefs about their parents' mental states long before they are able to make inductive inferences (come to probable conclusions) on the basis of evidence, which suggests that the capacity for forming beliefs in this way is part of the cognitive equipment with which we are born; we are 'hard-wired' to form these beliefs in certain circumstances. Paley's design argument is therefore not analogical, inductive nor an inference to the best explanation. In fact, according to Plantinga, it is not an argument at all; it is more like perception than inference because there is 'an immediate and direct impression' (2011: 245). Paley is 'directing our attention to the way we are inclined to form design beliefs in certain circumstances' (247), and trying to put us in a situation in which we form design beliefs. It is this activity which Plantinga refers to as 'design discourse'. He suggests that, since we form beliefs about the mental states of others in this basic way, it is reasonable to suppose that we form beliefs about the design of the world in a similar manner.

Plantinga acknowledges that a basic belief of this kind may be subject to defeaters (evidence and/or arguments which suggest that a belief should be rejected) – either a rebutting defeater which eliminates the belief or an undercutting defeater which makes it less likely. Behe has therefore produced not a design argument but several sets of design discourses for which, Plantinga claims, there are no strong defeaters.[1] He therefore concludes that design discourses support one important part of theistic belief – the belief that the universe was designed – but that it is not clear how far they support theism in its entirety.

Reflection

On the grounds that it is the philosopher's job to tell the truth, Plantinga regrets that he is unable to offer more than 'a wet noodle conclusion' (264). Is he right to describe his conclusion in this way?

• THE 'LAWS OF PHYSICS' ARGUMENT AS A RESPONSE TO OBJECTIONS TO DESIGN IN THE SENSE OF PURPOSE

Swinburne identifies two objections raised by Hume to which someone who argues for design in the sense of purpose, characterised by Swinburne as 'regularities of co-presence', does not have an adequate answer:

1 The argument makes God too anthropomorphic. For someone who accepts it, this world:

> for aught he knows, is very faulty and imperfect, compared to a superior standard; and was only the first rude essay of some infant Deity, who afterwards abandoned it, ashamed of his lame performance; it is the work only of some dependent, inferior Deity; and is the object of derision to his superiors: it is the production of old age and dotage in some superannuated Deity; and ever since his death, has run on at adventures, from the first impulse and active force, which it received from him. . .
> (Hume, 2000: 266 [1779])

Swinburne suggests that this objection would apply to an argument based on regularities of co-presence because an embodied God could have designed the world and then left it to its own devices and an argument from analogy would offer greater support for belief in the existence of an embodied God.

But Swinburne notes that all analogies break down at some point. So, in saying that the relationship between A and B is analogous to that between A* and B*, we need not claim that B* is like B in every respect. For God to account for the regularities in the universe, God must be free, rational and powerful, but we do not need to say that God, like humankind, is embodied and therefore vulnerable to the kind of objections raised by Hume. Swinburne argues that an embodied God could control only God's body and not the scientific laws which operate in the rest of the universe – 'regularities of succession', sometimes called by others (e.g. Sweetman, 2010: 152–158) the 'laws of physics' argument. Since we need God to explain the continuing operation of these scientific laws, Swinburne argues, Xe cannot have a body, and if God cannot have a body, God cannot have designed the world and then left it to its own devices.

Swinburne is considering questions about the existence – or otherwise – of the God of classical theism, however. A person who adopted some version of pantheism, panentheism or religious naturalism might argue that God can control the scientific laws which operate throughout the universe because, in each case, God is identical with the universe, although in the case of panentheism, God may be also 'the soul of the universe, providing the unity that makes it a *universe*' (Griffin, 2014: 80). Griffin argues that, for the process panentheist, the universe may be seen as designed in two senses: firstly, the aim of the evolutionary process is to increase the richness of the experience of the life-forms of the universe; and, secondly, the fact that the universe is able to bring about life-forms presupposes a cosmological order which could be described in terms of design.

Griffin argues that there is a metaphysical principle over which the Divine has no control which entails that increasing the capacity for richness of experience is impossible without also increasing freedom and the power to affect other beings. This means that any being with our human capacity to experience and create good would also have the same capacity to experience and bring about evil.

A panentheist could, however, argue that God the 'world-soul' is something akin to Plato's Form of the Good and requires humankind to strive for the maximisation of goodness. Although the multitude of ways in which we both experience and perpetrate evil may be the 'price' we must pay in order to be the kind of creatures who can also experience and promote goodness in a multitude of ways, as part of the universe, which is part of God, we have the opportunity to grow and develop in such a way that, throughout time, we can very gradually 'tip the balance' in favour of a universe which contains more good than evil.

2 Why can we not regard the universe as a living organism which grows and reproduces in a regular manner, rather than as something like a machine or artefact?

Here again, Swinburne thinks that Hume's objection would apply to an argument based on regularities of co-presence – individual instances of apparently 'good design' – but not to an argument based on regularities of succession because, even if the universe is a living organism, we could still say that the regularity of this organism requires explanation.

Again, the pantheist, panentheist or religious naturalist could say that the Divine may be identified with a universe understood as something like a living organism which grows and reproduces in a regular manner, and is therefore its 'ultimate explanation', or the 'brute fact' which requires no explanation. For the panentheist, however, the 'world-soul' which is also God might also be said to provide an explanation analogous to that for which Swinburne argues.

Reflection

Is Swinburne right to argue that Hume's objections are fatal only to arguments for regularities of co-presence?

Must a defender of an argument for design hold that the Divine is not embodied?

• THE 'FINE-TUNING' OR 'ANTHROPIC' ARGUMENT

Even if the argument from alleged irreducible complexity remains inconclusive, it might be argued that objections to the design argument based on the theory of evolution represent a threat only to arguments based on what Swinburne calls 'regularities of co-presence' – that is, to analogical arguments of the kind made famous by Paley. We have already seen that Swinburne recommends, instead, versions of the argument based on 'regularities of succession' – i.e. arguments based on the regular way in which the universe functions – sometimes referred to by others as the 'laws of physics' argument.

More recently, others, along with Swinburne himself, have developed so-called 'fine-tuning' versions of the argument which appeal to current work in cosmology, astronomy and astrophysics to claim that, if the world had been different in some significant respects, sometimes by even a very small degree, conditions adequate for the support of intelligent life would not have existed.

Scholars who develop arguments of this kind typically offer many examples of the way in which our world seems to have been 'fine-tuned' to support the emergence and continuation of human life. It is because these arguments focus on the conditions which are necessary for human life that they are sometimes called 'anthropic' (from the Greek 'anthropos', 'human being'). Examples of apparent 'fine-tuning' include the following:

1 A reduction in the rate of expansion of the Big Bang of one part in a hundred thousand million millions would have caused the universe to recollapse, whereas an increase of the same magnitude would have produced a universe different from the one which currently exists.
2 The strong nuclear force which exists in the nucleus of atoms enables atoms to resist the force of repulsion which exists in the protons of atoms. If this force had been marginally stronger, the universe would have been dominated by helium atoms and there would have been no hydrogen atoms and therefore no water or life. If the strong force had been increased by even 1%, nearly all carbon would have been burned into oxygen, and an increase of 2% would have prevented the formation of protons from quarks, and therefore atoms. On the other hand, if it had been 5% weaker, this would have resulted in a universe composed entirely of hydrogen (Sweetman, 2010: 160).

Proponents of this argument claim not only that the probability of each condition being such that it was able to support the emergence and continuation of human life was extrmely low but also that the probability of all of these conditions occurring together was even lower and that only a divine designer could constitute an adequate explanation.

• OBJECTIONS TO THE FINE-TUNING ARGUMENT

A common objection to the fine-tuning argument is the so-called multiverse objection – that if there are many universes, it is likely that at least one of them is fine-tuned, and human beings could only exist in one that *is* fine-tuned.

Plantinga responds that, even if there are many universes, in one of which someone playing poker deals himself all the aces and a wild card, the probability that I am dealing honestly if I deal myself all the aces and a wild card remains low. Thus, if there is no God, the probability that *this* universe is fine-tuned for life remains low.

Swinburne (2004 [1979]) makes a similar point by means of an analogy with a card-shuffling machine. In this story, a captor tells his victim that he will only survive if the card-shuffling machine produces the ace of hearts from each of ten packs of cards. The machine does produce ten aces of hearts and the victim survives. The victim seeks an explanation, but the captor remarks that no explanation is required since in any other scenario the victim would not have survived to see anything at all. Swinburne concludes, however, that the victim is right; even though he would not have seen anything if the machine had failed to produce ten aces of hearts, what has happened remains extraordinary and therefore requires an explanation.

Plantinga does acknowledge, however, that 'whether theism is a good explanation of the phenomena depends in part on the antecedent [prior] probability of theism'. He therefore concludes that the fine-tuning argument offers 'some slight support for theism' (224). Again, he admits that this is not a very exciting conclusion, but suggests that 'it does have the virtue of being correct' (224).

• CONCLUSION

In this chapter, we have examined design arguments based on an alleged analogy between the designed artefacts produced by humankind and the apparent design of our universe (Paley), an argument from irreducible complexity (Behe), an argument from the laws of physics (Swinburne) and fine-tuning or anthropic arguments. In each case the argument, if successful, supports belief in a design-producing entity. Taken together with the cosmological argument, we might now say that the Divine is that which is responsible for – or is – both the creation and apparent order of the universe, although, given the preponderance of evil both experienced and perpetrated by created beings, it may be constrained at least to some extent by principles over which it has little ongoing control.

• NOTE

1 A case against the teaching of intelligent design in schools – *Kitzmiller et al.* v *Dover* – at which Behe was an expert witness was, however, upheld in 2005 (see Goodstein, 2005). I am grateful to an anonymous reviewer for drawing this to my attention.

• REFERENCES

Behe, Michael (2000) 'Evidence for Design at the Foundation of Life' in Michael J. Behe, William A. Dembski and Stephen C. Meyer (eds) *Science and Evidence for Design in the Universe: The Proceedings of the Wethersfield Institute* Volume 9 (San Francisco, CA: Ignatius Press), 113–129; reprinted in Chad Meister (ed.) *The Philosophy of Religion Reader* (New York, NY: Routledge, 2008), 256–266.

Behe, Michael (2003) 'The Modern Intelligent Design Hypothesis' in Neil Manson (ed.) *God and Design* (London and New York: Routledge).

Collins, Robin (2013 [2007]) 'The Teleological Argument' in Chad Meister and Paul Copan (eds) *The Routledge Companion to Philosophy of Religion* (London: Routledge), 411–421; revised version reprinted in Chad Meister (ed.) *The Philosophy of Religion Reader* (New York, NY: Routledge, 2008), 267–278.

Dawkins, Richard (1995) *River Out of Eden: A Darwinian View of Life* (New York, NY: Basic Books), Chapter 4, 95–98, 102–106, 120–122, 131–133; reprinted in Eleonore

Stump and Michael J. Murray (eds) *Philosophy of Religion: The Big Questions* (Oxford: Blackwell, 1999), 109–113.

Goodstein, Laurie (2005) 'Judge Rejects Teaching Intelligent Design', *New York Times*, 21 December, www.nytimes.com/2005/12/21/education/judge-rejects-teaching-intelligent-design.html?_r=0.

Griffin, David Ray (2014) *Panentheism and Scientific Naturalism* (Claremont, CA: Process Century Press), Chapter 3.

Hume, David (1748) *An Enquiry Concerning Human Understanding*, Section X; reprinted in L. A. Selby-Bigge (ed.) *Enquiries Concerning Human Understanding and Concerning the Principles of Morals* (Oxford: Clarendon Press, 1975), 109–131.

Hume, David (1779) *Dialogues Concerning Natural Religion*; extract reprinted in Brian Davies (ed.) *Philosophy of Religion: A Guide and Anthology* (Oxford: Oxford University Press, 2000), 260–270.

Mackie, J. L. (1982) *The Miracle of Theism: Arguments For and Against the Existence of God* (Oxford: Clarendon), Chapter 5.

Paley, William (1802) *Natural Theology, or Evidences of the Existence and Attributes of the Deity Collected from the Appearance of Nature*; reprinted in E. D. Klemke (ed.) *To Believe or Not to Believe: Readings in the Philosophy of Religion* (Orlando, FL: Harcourt Brace Jovanovich College Publishers, 1992), 32–39.

Plantinga, Alvin (2011) *Where the Conflict Really Lies: Science, Religion and Naturalism* (Oxford: OUP).

Ruzsa, Ferenc, 'Sankhya', *Internet Encyclopedia of Philosophy*, www.iep.utm.edu/sankhya/, accessed 12 January 2015.

Sharma, Arvind (1990) *A Hindu Perspective on the Philosophy of Religion* (Basingstoke: Macmillan Press).

Sweetman, Brendan (2010) *Religion and Science: An Introduction* (New York, NY: Continuum), Chapters 4 and 6.

Swinburne, Richard (1968) 'The Argument of Design' *Philosophy* 43: 199–212; reprinted in Brian Davies (ed.) *Philosophy of Religion: A Guide and Anthology* (Oxford: OUP, 2000), 274–285.

Swinburne, Richard (2004 [1979]) *The Existence of God* (Oxford: Clarendon Press), Chapter 8 and 346–349.

• FURTHER READING

Encyclopedia article

Koperski, Jeffrey (2015) 'Teleological Arguments for God's Existence', *Stanford Encyclopedia of Philosophy*, https://plato.stanford.edu/entries/teleological-arguments/.

Original articles in edited collections

Demski, William A. (2006) 'In Defence of Intelligent Design' in Philip Clayton and Zachary Simpson (eds) *The Oxford Handbook of Religion and Science* (Oxford: Oxford University Press), 715–731.

Haught, John F. (2006) 'God and Evolution' in Philip Clayton and Zachary Simpson (eds) *The Oxford Handbook of Religion and Science* (Oxford: Oxford University Press), 697–712.

McGrath, Alister E. (2006) 'Darwinism' in Philip Clayton and Zachary Simpson (eds) *The Oxford Handbook of Religion and Science* (Oxford: Oxford University Press), 681–696.

Pennock, Robert T. (2006) 'The Pre-Modern Sins of Intelligent Design' in Philip Clayton and Zachary Simpson (eds) *The Oxford Handbook of Religion and Science* (Oxford: Oxford University Press), 732–748.

Pruss, Alexander R. and Gale, Richard M. (2005) 'Cosmological and Design Arguments' in William J. Wainwright (ed.) *The Oxford Handbook of Philosophy of Religion* (Oxford: OUP), Chapter 5.

Shihadeh, Ayman (2008) 'The Existence of God' in Tim Winter (ed.) *The Cambridge Companion to Classical Islamic Theology* (Cambridge: Cambridge University Press), 201–204.

Wynn, Mark (1998) 'Design Arguments' in B. Davies (ed.) *Philosophy of Religion: A Guide to the Subject* (London: Cassell), 59–64.

Articles

Brown, C. Mackenzie (2008) 'The Design Argument in Classical Hindu Thought', *International Journal of Hindu Studies* 12, 2: 103–151.

Books

Averroes (Ibn Rushd) (2001 [1179]) *Faith and Reason in Islam: Averroes' Exposition of Religious Arguments*, trans. Ibrahim Najjar (Oxford: Oneworld Publications), Chapter 1, 16–44 and 78–91.

Evans, C. Stephen (2010) *Natural Signs and Knowledge of God: A New Look at Theistic Arguments* (Oxford: Oxford University Press), Chapter 4.

Davis, Stephen T. (1997) *God, Reason and Theistic Proofs* (Edinburgh: Edinburgh University Press), Chapter 6.

Dembski, William A. and Ruse, Michael (eds) (2006) *Debating Design: From Darwin to DNA* (Cambridge: Cambridge University Press).

Evans, C. Stephen (2010) *Natural Signs and Knowledge of God: A New Look at Theistic Arguments* (Oxford: OUP), Chapter 4.

Guessoum, Nidhal (2012) *Islam's Quantum Question: Reconciling Muslim Tradition and Modern Science* (London: I. B. Tauris), Chapter 7, 219–242.

Harrison, Jonathan (1999) *God, Freedom and Immortality* (Aldershot: Ashgate), Chapter 7.

McGrath, Alister (2005) *Dawkins' God: Genes, Memes, and the Meaning of Life.* (Oxford: Blackwell).

Shanks, Niall (2004) *God, the Devil, and Darwin: A Critique of Intelligent Design Theory* (Oxford: Oxford University Press).

Taliaferro, Charles (1998) *Contemporary Philosophy of Religion* (Oxford: Blackwell), 365–369.

Yaran, Cafer S. (2003) *Islamic Thought on the Existence of God: Contributions and Contrasts with Contemporary Western Philosophy of Religion* (Washington: The Council for Research in Values and Philosophy), Chapters 2–4.

Young, Matt and Edis, Taner (eds) (2004) *Why Intelligent Design Fails: A Scientific Critique of the New Creationism* (New Brunswick, NJ: Rutgers University Press).

11

arguments for the existence of the divine: moral arguments

• INTRODUCTION

There are various forms of moral argument but, broadly speaking, they argue that the Divine either guarantees or explains morality. Moral arguments for the existence of the Divine therefore include the following:

1 God must exist in order to guarantee that moral behaviour is appropriately rewarded.
2 The existence of objective moral laws requires the existence of a divine lawgiver.

• GOD GUARANTEES MORALITY: KANT'S MORAL ARGUMENT

Immanuel Kant (1724–1804) (1788) argues as follows:

1 The highest good for humankind has two components; morality, and happiness which is in proportion to virtue.
2 Since it is our duty to promote the highest good, it must be possible.
3 But it is clear that human beings do not achieve happiness in proportion to their virtue in this life.
4 It is therefore necessary to postulate the existence of a God who guarantees an immortal life in which this will be achieved.
5 Immortality, freedom (to choose our moral actions and therefore to be responsible for them), and God's existence are therefore the three postulates of practical reason; the intention to promote the highest good presupposes that it must be possible, and immortality, freedom and God's existence are the conditions which make it possible.
6 Religion is therefore 'the recognition of all duties as divine commands . . . because we can hope for the highest good only from a morally perfect (holy and beneficient) and

omnipotent will; and, therefore, we can hope to attain it only through harmony with this will' (2000: 641 [1985, 1788]).

7 We should, however, be motivated to obey the moral law by duty, not by the hope of happiness.

Objections to Kant's moral argument

Mackie (1982) raises two possible objections to Kant's moral argument:

1 Why should we conclude from 'we ought to seek the highest good' that 'the highest good must therefore be possible'? Mackie notes that, even if, as Kant argues elsewhere, the fact that we ought to do something implies that we can do something, the suggestion that we ought to seek to promote the highest good implies only that we can seek to promote it, and that we can to some extent actually promote it; it does not entail that it is possible fully to realise the highest good. For example, we could say that we ought to try to improve the condition of human life, provided that some improvement is possible. But this does not mean that we can make it perfect. Even for the possibility of full realization we would only need a possible all-good and all-powerful Governor. But although we can hope for full realisation of the highest good, we cannot claim that even possible realisation is necessary for moral thought in general.

2 Kant says that we should not obey moral laws through fear of punishment; we should obey them because it is our duty to do so. He also says that it is appropriate that happiness should be proportional to morality – in other words, that happiness is a reward for morality. But is he not contradicting himself? Surely he should say that morality leads only to the happiness brought about by our consciousness of doing what is right.

We could, perhaps, try to respond to the second of Mackie's objections by arguing that Kant is not contradicting himself in saying both that we should obey moral laws because it is our duty to do so and that happiness is a reward for morality because, although our own happiness should not be our motivation for obeying moral laws, it *is* moral to desire and promote a system in which every person, including ourselves, is appropriately rewarded for their efforts.

Mackie's first objection, that although it might be desirable for every person to receive an appropriate reward for their moral efforts, this does not entail that they will, in fact, do so, seems difficult to counter, however. We therefore turn to another form of the moral argument in the hope that it will prove to be more promising.

• GOD EXPLAINS MORALITY: THE MORAL ARGUMENT OF H. P. OWEN

H. P. Owen (1926–1996) (1965) argues that God is the ultimate source of our sense that morality makes certain claims upon us. He offers five arguments for this:

1 We feel constrained by moral claims but can give no explanation of them. When we feel a sense of obligation, this is usually to a person. When we are commanded to do

something there is a commander. So, if we feel constrained by moral claims, this implies a personal source for their authority.

Owen considers three objections:

a Why must language mirror facts? It is invalid to argue that because the existence of law suggests that there must be a lawgiver, the existence of morality suggests that there must be a divine Lawgiver.

Owen replies that an analogy is being used to unify the facts to which the terms refer. Since, in our world, claims imply a claimant and laws imply a lawgiver, the same must be implied in the supra-human order if morality is to be consistent.

b Belief in a divine lawgiver is a human projection of an authoritarian 'father-image'.

Owen replies that the concept of a divine Lawgiver may, indeed, be derived from examples of authoritarian human fathers, but that it is also possible that the authority of human fathers is derived from that of the divine Father.

c The personality of the source of laws does not make them valid. There are object-ive norms to which God must subscribe.

This objection represents the second of the two 'horns' of the Euthyphro Dilemma. The dilemma originated in Plato's dialogue *Euthyphro* (c. 399–395 BCE), in which Socrates questions whether goodness is what the gods love, in which case goodness is whatever the gods command and therefore arbitrary (the first horn of the dilemma), or whether goodness exists independently of the gods, in which case the gods themselves are subject to something external to themselves (the second horn of the dilemma). Since Owen does not accept that God is subject to standards of morality which exist independently of God, he replies that although human commands might be morally invalid, God's commands are always right because God *is* righteousness and truth.

But Owen admits that the argument works only for those who seek an ultimate explanation of facts which are not considered to be self-explanatory.

2 Moral laws require obedience. Since we value the personal more than the impersonal, it is contradictory to say that impersonal claims are entitled to allegiance. It is there-fore better to say that moral claims are rooted in God's personality.
3 Belief in human dignity and unconditional service to others is defensible only upon religious grounds. No one is virtuous in every respect, and, even if they were, they still would not possess their virtues to an infinite degree. But even the agnostic feels compelled to treat all humankind as ends in themselves, regardless of their moral condition. We must therefore conclude that 'human persons exert their distinctive claim on account of their relation to a moral Absolute' (2000: 650 [1965]). The worth of human beings is derived from the 'fact that they are created, loved, and destined for eternal life by God. The value we attach to them is the value bestowed on them by God' (650–651).

4 We speak of responsibility when there are no human persons to whom we are responsible – e.g. a person who wastes his talent is said to be irresponsible. But we can only be responsible to a personal 'other'. And guilt suggests that there is an intelligent being before whom we feel ashamed.
5 Our sense of moral failure can only be addressed by supernatural aid which is given through Christ; this is the gospel proclaimed in the New Testament.

Owen notes that the argument to a divine Lawgiver has been criticised by W. G. Maclagan, who objects on two grounds:

1 The idea of a divine Lawgiver is meaningless. Drawing on the Euthyphro Dilemma, he argues that, if an action is right because God commands it, this is morally disastrous because this would seem to entail that God could command even actions which we consider to be immoral. But if God commands an action because it is right, this is theologically disastrous because this seems to imply that there is a standard of goodness which exists independently of God. But Maclagan also rejects Owen's solution to the dilemma – the claim that moral distinctions are neither the product of God's will nor independent of God but are constitutive of God's understanding – on the grounds that what we know and our knowing it are not the same thing.

   Owen responds that divine and human understanding differ; to say that God knows what is absolutely good is to say that God knows Godself because God *is* goodness.

2 There is no need to suppose that there is a divine Lawgiver; to describe morality as a 'law' is just an inadequate metaphor.

Owen offers three replies:

a The 'law' metaphor is inevitable; even as children we are aware that 'Thou shalt' is distinct from our parents' will and our own desires. Kant speaks of the 'categorical imperative', and Maclagan himself refers to 'the moral demand'.
b As the metaphor of law is inevitable, it is better to have it 'whole than maimed' (654) – in other words, to understand that the moral 'law' is derived from the will of God.
c Even if we discard the metaphor, we still have to explain the 'pressure' of moral claims (654). Maclagan simply says that the moral demand presupposes an order of values about which nothing more may be said.

Owen concludes by stressing five points:

1 Although morality is derived from God's will, the believer may not be aware of this every time he or she makes a moral judgement.
2 Actions which are identified with God's will are also right in purely moral terms, but this is because God is present in all human beings, which enables us to identify actions which are in accordance with divine will.
3 Morality is God's will because God is love, and God's will reflects God's character. It is because God is love that Xe wills us to act morally, and God's love shows us how we should behave.

4 Morality 'is fulfilled in the belief that the whole life of duty is a debt of gratitude to God for his great love in creating us to share in his perfection' (657).
5 Faith enables us to identify the form and content of the moral law with God's will and character.

Objections to Owen's moral argument

As we saw earlier, Owen claims that we often feel a sense of responsibility or guilt, even when there is no human person to whom we are responsible, and that this suggests that there is an intelligent being to whom we feel responsible and before whom we sometimes feel ashamed. Mackie (1982) objects to a similar argument from conscience developed by John Henry Newman (1801–1890) on the following grounds:

1 If the argument works, it does not prove the existence of a God who has all the attributes traditionally ascribed to God.
2 If conscience tells us what we must and must not do, we do not need any supernatural person who commands or forbids certain actions; conscience is merely a fact about the world which needs no further explanation. If we feel guilty when we disobey our conscience, this is simply the feeling which our conscience tells us we should experience when we do something which it regards as morally wrong.
3 Conscience could simply be the influence of other people – parents, friends, traditions or the institutions of society, or part of society (such as the Church). According to this objection, conscience comes from something beyond ourselves, but its sources are human, not divine.

Reflection

Would it be reasonable to respond that, even if we have been conditioned by the influence of other people to feel guilty in certain circumstances, there must have been an original source of the moral values of those who influenced us?

We also saw above that Owen attempts to side-step the Euthyphro Dilemma by arguing that God *is* goodness. But how do we know that God is good? Kai Neilsen (b. 1926) (1973) questions whether this might be understood as a synthetic statement – that is, one which is not merely true by definition but tells us something new about the world. He suggests that, to give an affirmative answer, we would have to claim that God exhibits goodness and love. But the suffering which we see in places such as children's hospitals and concentration camps suggests that God does not exhibit goodness and love. And even if Xe does exhibit goodness and love, we have to use our own logically independent moral criteria to make this judgement. Thus, Neilsen argues, morality cannot be based on belief in God; we require a definition of goodness which is not derived from any claim about the existence and nature of a deity (2000: 672 [1973]).

Neilsen therefore considers whether the statement 'God is good' might, instead, be regarded as analytic – that is, a statement which is made true by the definitions of the words of which it is comprised. Neilsen argues that 'God' does not have the same meaning as 'good'; 'that was good of you' does not mean 'that was God of you' (672), and to say that God is good is not to say that God is God. For Neilsen, we may still say that God is good on the grounds that goodness partially defines divinity, just as we may say 'puppies are young' or 'triangles are three-sided'; in each case, the predicate partially defines the subject. But this does not mean that we can have no understanding of 'good' without an understanding of God because, just as 'young' or 'three-sided' can be understood without reference to puppies or triangles, so 'good' can be understood without reference to God. So, Neilsen suggests, morality without religion is possible, although religion could not exist if we had no conception of morality – because we could make no sense of 'God is good' without an independent understanding of morality.

Neilsen concludes that, whether the statement 'God is good' is synthetic or analytic, the concept of good is distinct from the concept of God; we could know how to use 'good' without knowing how to use 'God'. But we could not know how to use 'God' without knowing how to use 'good'.

Reflection

What, in your view, is the theist's best response to the Euthyphro Dilemma?

• CONCLUSION

We have examined Kant's moral argument which maintains that only God's existence can guarantee that happiness is proportioned to virtue, and Owen's argument that the existence of a divine lawgiver is needed to explain the existence of the moral law. It could, however, be objected that Kant's argument is simply the result of wishful thinking. Owen's argument seems more promising, but arguably falters in its attempt to address the Euthyphro Dilemma. If the main stumbling block is the claim that 'God' is not equivalent to 'Good', however, we could respond that, even if God is 'more than' Good, as many versions of theism would claim, this does not entail that the 'being' of God cannot encompass goodness. Indeed, as we will see in Chapter 13, if God is the greatest conceivable being, this includes goodness, and many other 'great-making' qualities besides.

• REFERENCES

Kant, Immanuel (1985 [1788]) *Critique of Practical Reason*, trans. Lewis White Beck (London: Macmillan); extracts reprinted in Brian Davies (ed.) *Philosophy of Religion: A Guide and Anthology* (Oxford: Oxford University Press, 2000), 639–645.

Mackie, J. L. (1982) *The Miracle of Theism: Arguments for and Against the Existence of God* (Oxford: Clarendon Press), Chapter 6.

Neilsen, Kai (1973) *Ethics Without God* (Prometheus Books); extracts reprinted in Brian Davies (ed.) *Philosophy of Religion: A Guide and Anthology* (Oxford: Oxford University Press, 2000), 668–682.

Owen, H. P. (1965) *The Moral Argument for Christian Theism* (London: George Allen and Unwin); edited extract reprinted in Brian Davies (ed.) *Philosophy of Religion: A Guide and Anthology* (Oxford: Oxford University Press, 2000), 646–658.

• FURTHER READING

Encyclopedia articles

Evans, C. Stephen (2014) 'Moral Arguments for the Existence of God', *Stanford Encyclopedia of Philosophy*, https://plato.stanford.edu/entries/moral-arguments-god/.

Original articles in edited collections

Copan, Paul (2013 [2007]) 'The Moral Argument' in Chad Meister and Paul Copan (eds) *The Routledge Companion to Philosophy of Religion* (Abingdon: Routledge), 422–432.

Evans, C. Stephen (2010 [1997]) 'Moral Arguments' in Charles Taliaferro, Paul Draper and Philip L. Quinn (eds) *A Companion to Philosophy of Religion* (Chichester: Blackwell), 385–391.

Books

Byrne, Peter (1998) *The Moral Interpretation of Religion* (Edinburgh: Edinburgh University Press).

Evans, C. Stephen (2010) *Natural Signs and Knowledge of God: A New Look at Theistic Arguments* (Oxford: OUP), Chapter 5.

Harrison, Jonathan (1999) *God, Freedom and Immortality* (Aldershot: Ashgate), Chapter 8.

Mackie, J. L. (1982) *The Miracle of Theism: Arguments for and Against the Existence of God* (Oxford: Clarendon Press), Chapter 6.

Sorley, W. R. (1918) *Moral Values and the Idea of God* (Cambridge: Cambridge University Press).

Swinburne, Richard (2004) *The Existence of God* (Oxford: Clarendon Press), 212–218.

Taliaferro, Charles (1998) *Contemporary Philosophy of Religion* (Oxford: Blackwell), 370–374.

Wynn, Mark (1999) *God and Goodness: A Natural Theological Perspective* (Abingdon: Routledge).

12

arguments for the existence of the divine: arguments from religious experience

• INTRODUCTION

In the three preceding chapters, we examined three arguments which infer God's existence from some aspect of the world. In this chapter, we will consider the claim that it is possible to have more specific experiences of God or God's effects, and that such experiences constitute evidence for God's existence.

• THE NATURE OF RELIGIOUS EXPERIENCE

Types of religious experience

Swinburne (2004 [1979]) identifies five kinds of religious experience: two public and three private.

The two types of public experience are:

- Those in which God, or God's action, is identified in a public object or scene – such as the night sky.
- Those which occur as a result of unusual public events – e.g. the appearance of the risen Jesus to his disciples (Luke 24:36–49).

The three types of private experience are:

- Those which an individual can describe using normal language – e.g. Joseph's dream that an angel appeared and spoke to him (Matthew 1:20f.).
- Sensations which cannot be described in normal language – e.g. mystical experiences.
- Those in which the individual has no sensations, but is directly aware of God. Swinburne does not describe these as mystical experiences, but others – e.g. William Alston (1921–2009) – do so.

The characteristics of mystical experience

William James (1842–1910) (1923) suggests that there are four marks which enable us to identify a mystical experience:

- Ineffability: It cannot be described in words; it can only be felt. It must be experienced to be understood.
- Noetic (concerning the intellect) quality: Although it is like a state of feeling, it is also a state of knowledge. It communicates a truth or truths which cannot be communicated in any other way.
- Transiency: It does not last more than an hour or two.
- Passivity: It sometimes causes a feeling of being controlled by a higher power.

James considers a number of examples of mystical experience, including those of Hindus who have undergone training in yoga – the 'experimental union of the individual with the divine' (2014: 46 [1923]). Diet, posture, breathing, concentration and moral discipline lead disciples to a state known as *samadhi*, in which they learn that the mind has a higher state, beyond reason and above consciousness and in which there is no sense of self. In this state, they see the Truth and know themselves for what they really are: 'free, immortal, omnipotent, loosed from the finite, and its contrasts of good and evil altogether, and identical with the *Atman* or Universal Soul' (46).

Alston argues that, since God is spiritual, mystical experiences which are nonsensory are more likely to present God as Xe is. He questions why we should think that only the five senses of humankind are capable of mediating experiences, and suggests that other creatures may have sensitivities to other physical stimuli which are analogous to the five senses of humankind. Furthermore, he suggests, we can imagine that there might be 'presentations that do not stem from the activity of any physical sense organs, as is apparently the case with mystical perception' (2014: 53 [1996]).

Alston claims that perception of X simply consists of X's appearing to one, and that that is all there is to be said about it; no conceptualising or judgment is required. For X to appear to one, however, three requirements must be satisfied:

- X must exist.
- X must make a causal contribution to one's experience.
- The experience must give rise to beliefs about X.

Alston argues that, if God exists and causes experiences of Godself which give rise to beliefs about God, it is reasonable to say that mystical experience is mystical perception. He cites the numerous examples of cases in which people have taken themselves to be directly aware of God and says that he can see no reason to doubt their accounts of their experience, even if there may be reasons for doubting that God appeared to them. He suggests that, in describing sensory appearances, we generally use comparative concepts when these appearances involve something more complex than basic sensory qualities (e.g. round, red, acrid). So we say, for example, 'She looks like Susie', 'It tastes like pineapple' or 'It sounds like Bach' (56). And the same applies to mystical perceptions; people say that 'God presented himself to their experience as a good, powerful, compassionate, forgiving being could be expected to appear' (56).

Although, generally speaking, those who perceive God already possess beliefs about God, their perception usually gives rise to further beliefs about God – and so Alston's third requirement is satisfied. The second requirement is also satisfied, since, if God exists, Xe causally contributes to everything which happens, and it is reasonable to assume that Xe does make a specific causal contribution to at least some direct experiences of God.

Alston notes that, if he is right, it is possible for us to have a personal relationship with God in a literal sense. He acknowledges that there are still difficulties in ascertaining whether perceptions of God are genuine, but argues that these are no more significant than the similar difficulties associated with sense perception.

• AN ARGUMENT FROM RELIGIOUS EXPERIENCE

Alston is primarily concerned with demonstrating the coherence of believers' claims regarding mystical experiences of God. Swinburne is, however, concerned with the question of whether these, and other types of apparently religious experience, are genuine perceptions of God. He argues that we should apply the Principle of Credulity and the Principle of Testimony.

The Principle of Credulity

The Principle of Credulity states that, unless there is some special reason for doubt, we should accept that 'How things seem to be . . . are good grounds for a belief about how things are' (2004 [1979]: 303).

There are four things which might make us doubt that the way things seem to be indicates how things are:

1 The conditions or the person have been found in the past to be unreliable. For example, past experience may suggest that it is unwise to trust perceptions made under the influence of LSD, or by a particular person.

Swinburne responds that claims to have had a religious experience are not usually doubted on these grounds. Most religious experiences are had by those who have not taken drugs and are generally regarded as reliable.

2 Similar perceptual claims have proved false. For example, if a person claims that he has read ordinary-size print at a great distance but cannot do this on other occasions, it is likely that his original claim was false.

This challenge would be effective it if could be shown that alleged religious experiences are generally unreliable. This could be done if there were a good proof of God's non-existence – but, Swinburne claims, there is not.

Swinburne notes the suggestion that religious experiences are unreliable because they support conflicting beliefs, but responds that God may be known by different names to people of different cultures. In cases where there is a genuine conflict – a Jewish person would not accept a report of an experience of Christ, for example – if the opponent can give good reasons for regarding the experience as false, the person who had the experience must either withdraw the claim or 'describe it in a less committed way' (316) – for example, claim to have been aware of some supernatural, but unidentified, being.

Reflection

Do you think that the suggestion that God may be known by different names to people of different cultures constitutes a reasonable response to the objection that religious experiences are unreliable because they support conflicting beliefs?

Another way to suggest that alleged religious experiences are generally unreliable is to say that those who have such experiences have not had the kind of experiences which are needed to make such claims probably true. For example, it might be argued that a claim to have recognised a person is only likely to be correct if you have previously perceived that person in some way and been told who he is, or if you have been given a detailed description of him. But Swinburne suggests that a description of God as an omnipotent, omniscient and perfectly free person may enable us to recognise God, and, even if we find it difficult to recognise power, knowledge or freedom in human persons, we might be able to recognise extreme degrees of them.

3 Background evidence suggests that it is very probable that the thing perceived was not present. For example, a claim to have seen John in the corridor might be doubted if there were others in the corridor looking for John who did not see him.

Swinburne argues that this challenge would be effective if it could be shown that, very probably, God was not there to be perceived, but, as Swinburne has already suggested, this cannot be done.

4 Although the perception is genuine, it was not caused by the thing thought to have been perceived. For example, a person may genuinely have seen someone in the

corridor who looked like John, but their perception may have been of an actor dressed like John.

Swinburne admits that this challenge would be effective if it could be shown that alleged experiences of God were caused by something other than God. But, if God is omnipresent and the sustainer of all causal processes, *whatever* brings about an experience of God will, ultimately, be caused by God. It could only be shown that these alleged experiences were not caused by God if it could be shown that God does not exist.

Thus, Swinburne concludes, we should accept alleged experiences of God as genuine unless it is much more probable that God does not exist. And, he claims, the balance of probability may be tipped in favour of the genuineness of religious experiences if there is evidence that others have such experiences.

The Principle of Testimony

According to the Principle of Testimony, unless there is some special reason for doubt, we should accept that the experiences of others are as they report them. Most of our beliefs about the world are based on the perceptions of others. We might doubt someone's perception if we had evidence that, either generally or in that particular case, they were misremembering, exaggerating or lying. But, in most cases, none of these apply. In the case of religious experience, we can test whether they do by examining the person's life-style after the experience. If they act as if there is a God, it is likely that the experience was genuine. Although believing on the basis of others' experiences is not as good a reason for belief as believing on the basis of one's own experience, many of our beliefs about the world *are* based on the reports of others and, particularly when many people claim to have had the same experience, it is reasonable for us to accept their testimony.

So, if we accept the testimony of others (the Principle of Testimony) this may make it probable that God exists and show that there is no overriding reason to reject our own experience as genuine (the Principle of Credulity). Someone who has not had an experience of God will have less evidence for God's existence, but he or she will still have the testimony of others on which to base such a belief.

• OBJECTIONS TO AN ARGUMENT FROM RELIGIOUS EXPERIENCE

Responses to the Principle of Credulity

In support of the fourth challenge to the Principle of Credulity, that alleged experiences of God are caused by something other than God, Wayne Proudfoot (b. 1939) (1985) argues that such experiences can be explained in historical or cultural terms. He suggests that religious experiences are shaped by the religious traditions within which they occur, and within the particular forms of the tradition which shaped the person and his or her experience.

Michael Martin (1932–2015) (1990) suggests that religious experiences are caused not by external realities but by the workings of people's minds. This is known as the psychological hypothesis. Martin argues that the use of drugs and alcohol, mental illness and sleep deprivation provide experiences which are not trusted because they do not give us a coherent account of an external reality. He claims that religious experiences are like those caused by drugs and alcohol, mental illness and sleep deprivation because they do not tell a coherent story, and there is no plausible explanation for the discrepancies which occur.

Reflection

Do you agree with Martin that there is no plausible way to explain why some religious experiences seem to be incompatible with others? Look again at Swinburne's arguments in response to the second challenge to the Principle of Credulity.

Evan Fales (b. 1943) (2004) argues that mystical experience requires cross-checking. Although some (e.g. Alston) argue that mystical experience is similar to the apparently direct way in which we acquire perceptual knowledge, in both cases inference to the best explanation is still required. In order to know what we are perceiving, we need to know what is causing our experience, and we can do this by eliminating possible explanations until, ideally, a single cause explains our experience. Even when we think that we just 'see' something – e.g. that the refrigerator in the kitchen is white – there is 'subliminal information processing' in which cross-checking plays an important part. Thus, we see that the refrigerator is white because we already understand what refrigerators are and what they look like, expect to find them in kitchens and know how white things look in a certain light. Even though we are not aware of it, we use this knowledge to reason to the best explanation for the relevant sensory inputs.

Fales argues that mystical experiences are unlikely to be genuine, firstly because the research of the anthropologist I. M. Lewis (1930–2014) suggests that mysticism is either a means for mystics to achieve social justice for themselves and their group, or a way to support their claim on social leadership positions. Secondly, he argues that mystical experiences may be caused by micro-seizures of the temporal lobes of the brain; when these are severe, they result in epilepsy, but when they are mild, they lead to mystical experiences. We cannot argue that God uses this as a way to appear to believers, firstly because this would not explain why Xe apparently appears in different forms to the believers of different religions, and secondly because this would be a 'God-of-the-gaps strategy' (2008: 197 [2004]) – that is, an appeal to God to explain something for which there is no scientific explanation. As scientific knowledge progresses, the number of 'gaps' to be filled by a divine explanation gradually decreases. Such gaps are often filled by natural causes but, in addition, there are no constraints on the time, method and location of divine action, no agreed procedures for cross-checking alleged religious experiences and no recommended ways in which we might investigate and verify divine interactions with the world, and such experiences usually have few, if any, implications for the future (198).

Martin suggests that, if experiences of God are grounds for belief in the existence of God, experiences of the absence of God are good grounds for belief that God does not exist. So if we accept the Principle of Credulity we also have to accept the Negative Principle of Credulity, according to which 'If it seems . . . to a subject S that x is absent, then probably x is absent' (2014: 76 [1990]).

Swinburne argues that we cannot experience the absence of God because we do not know under what conditions God would appear if Xe existed, but Martin suggests that, if we do not know this, this would also mean that we cannot experience the presence of God.

Responses to the Principle of Testimony

As we saw earlier, Swinburne argues that we can test whether a person's experience is likely to be genuine by examining their lifestyle after the experience – whether, in the case of a religious experience, the person acts as if there is a God. Martin suggests that it is equally possible that someone might degenerate morally after such an experience as a consequence of a weak will or the dreadful nature of the vision. Furthermore, it is possible that someone could show moral improvement after an illusory religious experience.

Fales argues that mystical experiences are difficult to cross-check because they are not public. He notes Teresa of Avila's suggestion that they may be tested by examining:

1 The fruits of an experience (actions, personality, peace of mind).
2 The vividness of the memory.
3 Conformity to Scripture.
4 Validation by the mystic's confessor.

But Fales suggests that the authority of Scripture rests on the authority of the revelations on which it is based, and 1, 2 and 4 presuppose that there could be no other cause of experiences which have good fruits, are memorable and are convincing to confessors.

Fales thinks that the best hope for cross-checking would be successful prophecy, but this can only support mystical experiences if it is:

1 Of an intrinsically unlikely event.
2 Not self-fulfilling.
3 Not made after the events to which it refers.
4 Specific and unambiguous.
5 Verified independently of the prophet and his/her followers.

Fales argues that there is no recorded prophecy which clearly satisfies 1–5. Thus, mystical experiences may be checked, but are always found wanting.

• CONCLUSION

It would appear that none of the arguments in favour of the possibility that we can experience God are decisive. Nevertheless, if we already think that God's existence is probable, we may be more inclined to accept as genuine experiences which tend to confirm our beliefs.

Alternatively, we could, in the manner of T. R. Miles (1923–2008) (1972) argue that religious experience is not experience of an objectively-existing, personal deity but an experience of love or sense of holiness which may occur when someone attempts to come to terms with cosmic issues. As such, they do not show us a non-material world, but they do help us to understand better the world in which we live.

• REFERENCES

Alston, William (2014) 'Religious Experience' [no original place of publication given]; reprinted in Michael Peterson, William Hasker, Bruce Reichenbach and David Basinger (eds) *Philosophy of Religion: Selected Readings* (Oxford: Oxford University Press, 2014 [1996]), 52–58.

Fales, Evan (2004) 'Do Mystics See God?' in Michael Peterson and Raymond J. Van Arragaon (eds) *Contemporary Debates in Philosophy of Religion* (Malden, MA: Blackwell Publishers), 145–158; reprinted in Andrew Eshleman (ed.) *Readings in Philosophy of Religion: East Meets West* (Oxford: Blackwell Publishing, 2008), 191–199.

James, William (1923) *The Varieties of Religious Experience* (New York, NY: Longmans, Green and Co.); reprinted in Michael Peterson, William Hasker, Bruce Reichenbach and David Basinger (eds) *Philosophy of Religion: Selected Readings* (Oxford: Oxford University Press, 2014 [1996]), 44–51.

Martin, Michael (1990) *Atheism: A Philosophical Justification* (Philadelphia, PA: Temple University Press); reprinted in Michael Peterson, William Hasker, Bruce Reichenbach and David Basinger (eds) *Philosophy of Religion: Selected Readings* (Oxford: Oxford University Press, 2014 [1996]), 68–78.

Miles, T. R. (1972) *Religious Experience* (London: Macmillan).

Proudfoot, Wayne (1985) *Religious Experience* (Berkeley, CA: University of California Press), 169–184, 187–189, 216–225; reprinted in Michael Peterson, William Hasker, Bruce Reichenbach and David Basinger (eds) *Philosophy of Religion: Selected Readings* (Oxford: Oxford University Press, 2014 [1996]), 59–67.

Swinburne, Richard (2004 [1979]) *The Existence of God* (Oxford: Clarendon Press), Chapter 13.

• FURTHER READING

Encyclopedia articles

Webb, Mark (2011) 'Religious Experience', *Stanford Encyclopedia of Philosophy*, https://plato.stanford.edu/entries/religious-experience/.

Original articles in edited collections

Alston, William P. (2004) 'Religious Experience Justifies Religious Belief' in Michael Peterson and Raymond J. Van Arragon (eds) *Contemporary Debates in Philosophy of Religion* (Malden, MA: Blackwell Publishers), 135–144.

Gellman, Jerome I. (2005) 'Mysticism and Religious Experience' in William J. Wainwright (ed.) *The Oxford Handbook of Philosophy of Religion* (Oxford: Oxford University Press), 138–167.

Smart, J. J. C. (1996) 'The Argument from Religious Experience' in J. J. C. Smart and J. J. Haldane *Atheism and Theism* (Oxford: Blackwell), 48–52.

Wiebe, Phillip H. (2006) 'Religious Experience, Cognitive Science, and the Future of Religion' in Philip Clayton and Zachary Simpson (eds) *The Oxford Handbook of Religion and Science* (Oxford: Oxford University Press), 503–522.

Extracts from articles or books in edited collections

Al-Ghazali, Abu Hamid (1998 [original date unknown]) 'Divine Intoxication' from *The Niche of Lights*, trans. David Buchman (Provo, UT: Brigham Young University Press), 17–18; reprinted in Andrew Eshleman (ed.) *Readings in Philosophy of Religion* (Malden, MA: Blackwell Publishing, 2008), 221–222.

Black Elk (1984) *The Sixth Grandfather: Black Elk's Teachings Given to John G. Neihardt*, ed. Raymond J. DeMallie (Lincoln, NE: University of Nebraska Press); reprinted in Gary E. Kessler (ed.) *Philosophy of Religion: Toward a Global Perspective* (Boston, MA: Wadsworth, Cengage Learning, 1999), 164–171.

Dogen, Ehei (2002 [thirteenth century]) 'Manifesting Suchness' from *The Heart of Dogen's Shobogenzo*, trans. Norman Waddell and Masao Abe (Albany, NY: SUNY Press); reprinted in Andrew Eshleman (ed.) *Readings in Philosophy of Religion: East Meets West* (Malden, MA: Blackwell Publishing, 2008), 223–224.

Suzuki, D. T. (1956) 'Satori, or Enlightenment' in William Barrett (ed.) *Zen Buddhism: Selected Writings of D. T. Sukuki* (Garden City, NY: Doubleday Anchor Books), 83–108; reprinted in Chad Meister (ed.) *The Philosophy of Religion Reader* (New York, NY: Routledge), 491–501.

Saint Teresa of Avila (1976 [1562–1565]) 'The Difference Between Union and Rapture' from *The Collected Works of Teresa of Avila* Vol. 1, trans. Kieran Kavanaug and Otilio Rodriguez (Washington, DC: ICS Publications), 161–162, 172–175, 179–180; reprinted in Andrew Eshleman (ed.) *Readings in Philosophy of Religion: East Meets West* (Malden, MA: Blackwell Publishing, 2008), 218–220.

Yandell, Keith E. (2010 [1997]) 'Religious Experience' in Charles Taliaferro, Paul Draper and Philip L. Quinn (eds) *A Companion to Philosophy of Religion* (Malden, MA: Blackwell Publishing), 405–413.

Books

Davis, Caroline Franks (1989) *The Evidential Force of Religious Experience* (Oxford: Clarendon Press).

Davis, Stephen T. (1997) *God, Reason and Theistic Proofs* (Edinburgh: Edinburgh University Press), Chapter 7.

Gowans, Christopher W. (2003) *Philosophy of the Buddha* (London: Routledge), 195–196.

Griffin, David Ray (2014) *Panentheism and Scientific Naturalism: Rethinking Evil, Morality, Religious Experience, Religious Pluralism, and the Academic Study of Religion* (Claremont, CA: Process Century Press), Chapter 5.

Mackie, J. L. (1992) *The Miracle of Theism: Arguments For and Against the Existence of God* (Oxford: Clarendon Press), Chapter 10.

Otto, Rudolph (1936) *The Idea of the Holy*, trans. J. W. Harvey (New York, NY: Oxford University Press); selection reprinted in Charles Taliaferro and Paul J. Griffiths (eds) *Philosophy of Religion: An Anthology* (Malden, MA: Blackwell Publishing, 2003), 146–161.

Sharma, Arvind (1990) *A Hindu Perspective on the Philosophy of Religion* (Basingstoke: Macmillan Press), 14–16, 18–19.

Smart, J. J. C. and Haldane, J. J. (2002 [1996]) *Atheism and Theism* (Oxford: Blackwell), 43–47.

Taliaferro, Charles (1998) *Contemporary Philosophy of Religion* (Oxford: Blackwell), 264–287.

Wettstein, Howard (2012) *The Significance of Religious Experience* (Oxford: Oxford University Press).

Yaran, Cafer S. (2003) *Islamic Thought on the Existence of God: Contributions and Contrasts with Contemporary Western Philosophy of Religion* (Washington: The Council for Research in Values and Philosophy), Chapter 1.

Web resources

The Alister Hardy Religious Experience Research Centre, www.uwtsd.ac.uk/library/alister-hardy-religious-experience-research-centre/.

Wildman, Wesley 'Religious Experience Resources' http://people.bu.edu/wwildman/relexp/.

13

arguments for the existence of the divine: ontological arguments

• INTRODUCTION

In Chapters 9–12, we examined four *a posteriori* arguments for the existence of the Divine – that is, those based on (posterior to) human experience. We now turn to an *a priori* argument – that is, one which precedes (is prior to) human experience and is therefore based on the analysis of concepts alone. Broadly speaking, the ontological argument is based on analysis of the concept of the Divine; it claims that existence is part of the definition of God and that Xe must, therefore, exist.

The ontological argument is commonly said to have originated with Anselm of Canterbury, although some have suggested that versions of the argument may be found in Plato (b. 429/423 BCE), Chrysippus (280–207 BCE), Cicero (106–43 BCE), Augustine, and the ninth-century Neo-Platonist John Scotus Eriugena (d. c877 CE). Majid Fakhry (b. 1923) notes that all of these converge on the Platonic tradition, which had a profound influence on the development of Arabic philosophy, and thus that we should not be surprised to find a well-developed parallel to Anselm's argument in the writings of Abu Nasr Muhammad ibn Muhammad al-Farabi (c. 870–951) (Fakhry, 1986: 7).

• ANSELM'S ONTOLOGICAL ARGUMENT(S)

Some scholars (Charles Hartshorne [1897–2000] and Norman Malcolm [1911–1990], for example) argue that Anselm (1033–1109) produced two different forms of the ontological argument (1077–1078).

The first form

The first form can be found in Chapter 2 of his *Proslogion*. The structure of this argument is as follows:

1 God is 'that than which nothing greater can be conceived'.
2 Even the fool of Psalm 13.1 who thinks 'There is no God' can have this concept in his mind.
3 But does it exist only in the mind – or does it also exist in reality?
4 To exist both in the mind and in reality is greater than existing only in the mind.
5 If it only exists in the mind it is not that than which nothing greater can be conceived because we can conceive of something greater than a greatest conceivable being which exists only in the mind – that is, that same thing existing in reality.
6 Therefore, that than which nothing greater can be conceived cannot exist only in the mind but must exist in reality as well.

The second form

The second form of the argument is presented in Chapter 3 of the *Proslogion*.

Anselm argues that, although a person can be thought not to exist, the same is not true of God; God exists necessarily. This is because, if God did not exist necessarily, Xe would not be that than which nothing greater can be conceived.

In Chapter 4 of the *Proslogion*, Anselm distinguishes between the word 'God', which may be conceived not to exist, and the reality of God which exists necessarily.

In Chapter 9, we encountered two definitions of 'necessary' in our examination of the cosmological argument:

1 Eternal and imperishable.
2 Eternal, imperishable, and not dependent for its existence on anything else. This only applies to God, according to Aquinas.

Anselm uses the concept of necessity in a third sense:

1 Non-existence would be self-contradictory – that is, logical necessity. For Anselm, God's necessity is logical necessity; God cannot be thought not to exist.

A single argument?

Although it is often suggested that Anselm has two forms of the ontological argument, Davies (2004: 99–100) presents the so-called second version as a continuation of the first. On his view, the complete argument runs as follows:

1 God is 'that than which nothing greater can be conceived'.
2 Therefore God must have the attribute of necessary existence – otherwise Xe would not be 'that than which . . .'
3 Therefore God must exist.

On this interpretation, then, it is not merely the so-called second version but the whole argument which aims to prove that God's existence is necessary – that God cannot not exist.

Descartes' version of the argument can be similarly interpreted, and Kant's first objection to Descartes' argument (outlined on page 126) suggests that Kant did not think of the ontological argument as having two distinct forms.

• GAUNILO'S OBJECTIONS

Gaunilo of Marmoutier (c. eleventh century) (1078) argues as follows:

1 According to Anselm, God is in my understanding because I can understand what is meant by 'God'. But the same could be said of unreal objects. Unless we can say that it is only God who must exist in reality because Xe exists in my understanding, this would seem to imply that unreal objects must exist in reality because they exist in my understanding.
2 We cannot say that if God exists in my understanding Xe also exists in reality, because this would imply that:
   a There is no difference between understanding something and understanding that it exists.
   b We cannot conceive of God's non-existence; but we *can* conceive of God's non-existence – if we could not, Anselm's argument would not be needed.
3 We cannot conceive of God because we cannot understand God. Even if I try to conceive of God, Xe may not exist – just as if I try to conceive of a man I do not know, he may not exist; my conception of him as existing may be mistaken. We can only conceive of the *word* 'God', of which we do not know the object; we cannot conceive of a God who exists in reality.
4 Just as we cannot prove the existence of an island which is greater than all other islands, so we cannot prove the existence of a being than which none greater can be conceived. Conceivability does not entail actuality.

Replies to Gaunilo

Plantinga (1977) notes Anselm's reply that what he was attempting to prove was not the existence of something which is in fact greater than any other but the existence of something than which it is not possible that there could exist something greater. Plantinga suggests that Gaunilo's argument could, however, be revised so that he refers not to an island which is more excellent than all other islands but to an island than which a greater island cannot be conceived. But Anselm could respond by suggesting that, no matter how great an island is, there could always be a greater one because the qualities which make islands great – number of palm trees, quantity of coconuts, and so on – do not have an intrinsic maximum – that is, there is no number of trees or coconuts which it would be impossible to exceed. The same is not true with regard to the concept of God. If God is both omniscient and omnipotent, these are, Plantinga suggests, unsurpassable.

Reflection

How might Gaunilo respond to this?

• DESCARTES' ONTOLOGICAL ARGUMENT

In his *Meditations* (1986 [1641]) Descartes argues that:

1 God is 'a supremely perfect being'.
2 Existence is a perfection – that is, a desirable attribute which it is better to have than to lack.
3 Therefore, existence cannot be separated from God, just as having three angles equal to two right angles cannot be separated from the essence of a triangle, and the idea of a mountain cannot be separated from the idea of a valley.

Kant's objections to Descartes' ontological argument

In his *Critique of Pure Reason* (1965 [1781/1787]) Kant raises the following objections:

1 'To posit a triangle [say that it exists], and yet to reject its three angles, is self-contradictory; but there is no contradiction in rejecting the triangle together with its three angles. The same holds true of the concept of an absolutely necessary being' (2008: 301 [1781/1787]) – that is, although it may be contradictory to say that God exists without some of the attributes which Xe must have in order to be God, it is not contradictory to say that God, with all God's attributes, does not exist.

One possible response to Kant is to argue that some things do have a logically necessary existence – a number greater than one million, for example. But if the existence of God is like the existence of a number, it could be argued that this is not what people usually mean when they say that God exists.

2 'Exists' is not a real predicate – an attribute which, when added to the description of something, tells us more about it. One hundred existing thalers (a thaler was a unit of German currency) do not contain any more thalers than 100 possible thalers.

We could, perhaps, argue that 'exists' is only different from other kinds of predicate in that it describes something which is not described by other predicates. And this must be true of every predicate. This 'something' differs from that which is described by other predicates in that anything which does not have this particular property also lacks all other properties. But 'exists' is not the only property the absence of which also rules out other properties. For example, something which does not possess the property of being frozen cannot possess the property of being ice-cream. So, I would suggest, the difference between 'exists' and other properties is simply one of degree. The absence of the property of existence simply rules out a larger number of other properties – all of them – than the absence of any other property. So perhaps we can, after all, say that existence is a real predicate – that it does tell us something about an object.

Even if existence is a real predicate, however, it could be argued that the first of Kant's arguments remains a difficulty for both Anselm and Descartes and therefore that, if it is not contradictory to reject the existence of a triangle with its three angles, perhaps it is also not contradictory to reject the existence of God with all God's attributes.

• MALCOLM'S ONTOLOGICAL ARGUMENT

Malcolm (1960) appeals to what he regards as the second version of Anselm's argument. In this, according to Malcolm, Anselm is not saying that God must exist because existence is a perfection but that God must exist because the concept of God is the concept of a being whose existence is necessary – God cannot not exist.

Malcolm's argument is as follows:

1 If God does not exist, God's existence is impossible (because God's existence cannot be caused by something else, and it cannot just happen).
2 If God does exist, God's existence is necessary (because God's existence cannot be caused by something else, and it cannot just happen).
3 Therefore God's existence is either impossible or necessary.
4 Since the concept of God is neither self-contradictory nor absurd, the existence of God is not impossible.
5 Therefore the existence of God must be necessary.

An objection to Malcolm

A key difficulty with Malcolm's argument is that he appears to switch between two senses of 'impossible'. He begins by saying that, if God does not exist, it is impossible for God to come into existence because God, understood as a being which cannot depend upon anything other than God, cannot be caused by anything other than God to come into existence. Malcolm also claims that God's existence cannot just happen. But while it might be reasonable to argue that a being whose attributes include those required to create the universe cannot come into existence at some point after the creation of the universe, it is less clear that God could not have caused Godself to come into existence at some point prior to the creation of the universe.

Even if we accept this initial step, however, the impossibility implied in step 1 of the argument is not obviously the same as the logical impossibility which appears in step 4 of the argument. Therefore we cannot argue that the impossibility that a non-existent God could come to exist is somehow equivalent to logical impossibility and that, since the concept of God is not logically impossible, God necessarily exists.

• PLANTINGA'S ONTOLOGICAL ARGUMENT

Plantinga (1977) restates Malcolm's argument with the help of the idea of possible worlds. A possible world is a way things could be. So our world is a possible world, as is one in which elephants have two trunks.

Plantinga argues as follows:

1 There is a possible world in which there is a being with maximal greatness – that is, one which has maximal excellence in every world.
2 A being has maximal excellence in every world if it has omniscience, omnipotence and moral perfection in every world.
3 If 1 is true, there is a possible world, W, in which, if it had been actual, there would have existed an omniscient, omnipotent, morally perfect being which had these qualities in every possible world.
4 If the non-existence of an omniscient, omnipotent, morally perfect being is impossible in at least one possible world, then it is impossible in every possible world, since what is possible does not vary from one world to another.
5 Therefore, the non-existence of an omniscient, omnipotent, morally perfect being is impossible in our actual world.

What Plantinga's argument amounts to is this: it is possible that there is a being with maximal greatness – that is, one which has maximal excellence in every possible world. Since our world is a possible world, there must be a being with maximal greatness in it.

Plantinga does, however, acknowledge that only someone who accepts his main premise – that it is possible that there is a being with maximal greatness – would accept his argument.

• MURDOCH'S ONTOLOGICAL ARGUMENT

Murdoch (1992) claims that the ontological argument fails to support belief in a personal God, but that a version of the argument can be used to support belief in the Good, a concept of perfect goodness which we should contemplate in order to understand the true nature of goodness and how we can apply it in every situation in which we find ourselves. Murdoch's ontological argument may be summarised as follows:

1 The first or logical argument: That which is perfect, the 'object' of our best thoughts, must, in some sense, exist (from Chapters 2 and 3 of Anselm's *Proslogion*).
2 The supplementary argument: 'Everything that is less good, in so far as it is good, is like the greater good . . . [B]y ascending from the lesser good to the greater we can form a . . . notion of a being than which a greater is inconceivable' (Chapter 8 of Anselm's 'Reply to Gaunilo', quoted in Murdoch, 1992: 394).

(This step of Murdoch's argument has much in common both with al-Farabi's earlier version of the argument and with the later Fourth Way of Aquinas [1265–1274]. Al-Farabi, developing an argument of Aristotle to the effect that immaterial entities have varying degrees of perfection, argues that these immaterial entities may be ranked in order of increasing perfection, culminating in 'a perfect being (kamil), nothing more perfect than which can exist' [quoted in Fakhry, 1986: 12]. This being existed before all other entities, and gives unity and reality to everything. A being with these attributes, al-Farabi concludes, 'is the being who ought to be believed to be God Almighty' [quoted in Fakhry, 12].)

3 We cannot believe in a personal God, partly as a consequence of scientific developments, and partly because belief in a personal God offers false consolation.

4 But the ontological argument can support belief in the necessary existence of the Good by means of an *a posteriori* argument from our experience of goodness. From the existence of imperfect examples of goodness we can see that there are degrees of goodness (derived from 2 above), and deduce from this the concept of perfect goodness.

Objections to Murdoch's ontological argument

Perhaps the most obvious objection to this argument which comes to mind is that it is not, in fact, an ontological argument because it is not entirely an *a priori* argument which argues to the existence of the Good by means of analysis of the concept of the Good, but an *a posteriori* argument from human experience of degrees of goodness. It does, however, begin by adapting Anselm's *a priori* argument from *Proslogion* Chapters 2 and 3; the part of the argument which is *a posteriori* is a supplementary argument, and, since this is also derived from Anselm, this shows that even Anselm thought that the *a priori* version of the argument could not stand alone. As Sarvepalli Radhakrishnan (1888–1975) argued some sixty years before Murdoch:

> The Ontological argument is a report of experience. We cannot have certain ideas without having had the experience of the objects of which they are the ideas. In such cases it is not illegitimate to pass from the ideas to the objects referred to by them. We should not have had an idea of absolute reality if we had never been in immediate cognitive relation with it, if we had not been intuitively conscious of it. The proof of the existence is founded on the experience.
>
> (2009 [1932]: 224)

A second objection is that this version of the argument, if it works, does not prove the existence of anything which might be recognised by others as 'religious'. For example, Peter Byrne (1998) suggests that Murdoch's Good might be just a name for human aspiration which does not refer to anything beyond the language in which we speak of it. He suggests that, if the Good existed independently of our perception of it, it would guarantee that we would make moral progress, and that we would be rewarded in proportion to our moral actions.

Although the Good does not guarantee that we make moral progress and reward us appropriately, however, this does not mean that it has no reality. The Good – or that for which it is a metaphor – is real because it is not something which we invent; moral values cannot be 'thought away' from human experience (Murdoch, 1992: 396). The Good is a real Idea, but it is also 'incarnate in knowledge and work and love . . . experience of the reality of good . . . is a discovery of something independent of us' (508). As we saw in Chapter 1, 'religion' is difficult to define, but Murdoch's view has some characteristics in common with other belief-systems which are described as religious. In particular, it aims to increase moral virtue and to help humankind to live well in the light of evil and suffering, and it is or may be associated with individual and communal practices which enable the individual to become more virtuous.

• CONCLUSION

The Buddha appears to have thought that questions such as those which we have considered in this chapter are of little value if they involve only metaphysical speculation, since they are not helpful in the search for salvation (Sharma, 1997: 27). If they do succeed in demonstrating the existence of the Divine, which supports moral behaviour and offers the believer a sense of purpose, however, these argument are not merely idle speculation.

In this chapter we have examined several of the most influential versions of the ontological argument, most of which ultimately encounter the difficulty of demonstrating the mind-independent existence of the Divine by means of analysis of the concept of the Divine. We also saw that Murdoch attempts to side-step this difficulty, partly by reconceiving the concept of the Divine, and partly by supplementing her version of the argument with an argument from moral experience.

• REFERENCES

Anselm (1077–1078) *Proslogium*, in *St Anselm: Basic Writings*, trans. S. N. Deane (La Salle, IL: Open Court Publishing Company, 1962), 47–80.

Aquinas, Thomas (2016 [1920] [1265–1274]) *The Summa Theologica of St Thomas Aquinas*, trans. Fathers of the English Dominican Province, www.newadvent.org/summa/ Part I, Question 2, Article 3.

Byrne, P. A. (1998) *The Moral Interpretation of Religion* (Edinburgh: Edinburgh University Press).

Davies, Brian (2004) *An Introduction to the Philosophy of Religion* (Oxford: Oxford University Press).

Descartes, René (1986 [1641]) *Meditations on First Philosophy With Sections from the Objections and Replies*, trans. John Cottingham (Cambridge: Cambridge University Press), Meditations 3 and 5.

Fakhry, Majid (1986) 'The Ontological Argument in the Arabic Tradition: The Case of al-Farabi', *Studia Islamica* 64: 5–17.

Gaunilo (1078) *On Behalf of the Fool*, in *St Anselm: Basic Writings*, trans. S. N. Deane (La Salle, IL: Open Court Publishing Company, 1962), 303–311.

Kant, Immanuel (1965 [1781/1787]) *Critique of Pure Reason*, trans. Norman Kemp Smith (New York, NY: St Martin's Press), 500–507; reprinted in Chad Meister (ed.) *The Philosophy of Religion Reader* (New York and Abingdon: Routledge, 2008), 300–305.

Malcolm, Norman (1960) 'Anselm's Ontological Arguments', *The Philosophical Review*, 69, 1: 41–62.

Murdoch, Iris (1992) *Metaphysics as a Guide to Morals* (London: Chatto and Windus).

Plantinga, Alvin (1977) *God, Freedom, and Evil* (Grand Rapids, MI: Wm. B. Eerdmans Publishing Co.).

Radhakrishnan, Sarvepalli (2009 [1932]) *An Idealist View of Life* (New Delhi: HarperCollins Publishers, India).

Sharma, Arvind (1997 [1995]) *The Philosophy of Religion: A Buddhist Perspective* (Delhi: Oxford University Press), 26–27.

• FURTHER READING

Encyclopedia articles

Himma, Kenneth Einar 'Anselm: Ontological Argument for God's Existence', *Internet Encyclopedia of Philosophy*, www.iep.utm.edu/ont-arg/.

Oppy, Graham (2016) 'Ontological Arguments' *Stanford Encylopedia*, http://plato.stanford.edu/entries/ontological-arguments/.

Original articles in edited collections

Inwagen, Peter van (2010) 'Ontological Arguments' in Charles Taliaferro, Paul Draper and Philip L. Quinn (eds) *A Companion to Philosophy of Religion* (Malden, MA: Blackwell Publishing), 359–367.

Leftow, Brian (2005) 'The Ontological Argument' in William J. Wainwright (ed.) *The Oxford Handbook of Philosophy of Religion* (Oxford: OUP), Chapter 4.

Mayer, Toby (2008) 'Theology and Sufism' in Tim Winter (ed.) *The Cambridge Companion to Classical Islamic Theology* (Cambridge: Cambridge University Press), 278–279.

Shihadeh, Ayman (2008) 'The Existence of God' in Tim Winter (ed.) *The Cambridge Companion to Classical Islamic Theology* (Cambridge: Cambridge University Press), 211–214.

Smart, J. J. C. (1996) 'The Ontological Argument' in J. J. C. Smart and J. J. Haldane (eds) *Atheism and Theism* (Oxford: Blackwell), 36–38.

Article

Johnson, J. Prescott (1963) 'The Ontological Argument in Plato', *The Personalist*, 44: 24–34.

Books

Brecher, R. (1985) *Anselm's Argument – The Logic of Divine Existence* (Aldershot: Gower).

Davis, Stephen T. (1997) *God, Reason and Theistic Proofs* (Edinburgh: Edinburgh University Press), Chapter 2.

Dombrowski, Daniel A. (2006) *Rethinking the Ontological Argument: A Neoclassical Theistic Response* (Cambridge: Cambridge University Press).

Harrison, Jonathan (1999) *God, Freedom and Immortality* (Aldershot: Ashgate), Chapters 4–5.

Mackie, J. L. (1992) *The Miracle of Theism: Arguments For and Against the Existence of God* (Oxford: Clarendon Press), Chapter 3.

Oppy, Graham (1995) *Ontological Arguments and Belief in God* (Cambridge: Cambridge University Press).

Taliaferro, Charles (1998) *Contemporary Philosophy of Religion* (Oxford: Blackwell), 378–381.

Yaran, Cafer S. (2003) *Islamic Thought on the Existence of God: Contributions and Contrasts with Contemporary Western Philosophy of Religion* (Washington: The Council for Research in Values and Philosophy), Chapter 7.

Audio

Bragg, Melvyn (2012) 'The Ontological Argument', *In Our Time*, BBC Radio 4, first broadcast 27 September 2012, www.bbc.co.uk/programmes/b01mwx64.

14

arguments against belief in the divine: the problem of evil

• INTRODUCTION

In this chapter we will consider the first of three significant challenges for religious belief – the problem of evil. The problem of evil represents a difficulty for any version of theism which holds that God is omnipotent (in the sense that God can do anything), omniscient (in the sense that God knows everything about the past, present and future) and good, since the presence of evil in our world would seem to suggest that it is irrational to suppose that our world is presided over by a divine being with these attributes. The problem of evil may therefore represent a reason for rejecting theism, or, for the theist, a problem to which he or she must find a satisfactory answer in order to maintain his or her faith.

Since the publication of William Rowe's (1931–2015) (1979) 'The Problem of Evil and Some Varieties of Atheism', analytic philosophers have distinguished between two forms of the problem of evil:

1 The 'logical problem of evil', according to which theists hold contradictory beliefs (belief in a God who is omnipotent, omniscient and good, and belief that there is evil in the world); and
2 The 'evidential argument from evil', in which the existence or quantity of evil is said to count against the existence of God.

• THE LOGICAL PROBLEM OF EVIL

The logical problem of evil runs as follows:

1 The world contains two kinds of evil:

    a Moral evil, which is brought about by the free choices of human beings – e.g. torture, murder, etc.

b   Natural evil, which is all that is evil in the physical universe – e.g. earthquakes, cancer, and so on.

2 If God exists, God would have the following characteristics:

a   Omnipotence (in the sense that God can do anything), including the power to prevent evil.

b   Omniscience (in the sense that God knows everything about the past, present and future), including knowledge of evil which is happening in the present or will happen in the future.

c   Goodness, which means that Xe would not wish sentient beings to suffer.

3 1. (There is evil) and 2. (God exists) are incompatible.

• FREE WILL AS A RESPONSE TO THE LOGICAL PROBLEM OF EVIL

A common response to the logical problem of evil is to argue that evil arises from the misuse of human free will, for which evil is a price worth paying. In this section we will examine a tenth-century account of a free will defence from Saadya, and, from the twentieth century, a much-discussed objection from Mackie. We will then turn to Plantinga's attempt to reformulate the free will theodicy in response to Mackie's criticism as a free will defence, and Hick's so-called Irenaean Theodicy, which incorporates some elements of a free will defence but attempts to explain not only moral evil but also natural evil.

Saadya's free will theodicy

Saadya (1960 [933]) argues that, because God is just and merciful towards human beings, God gives human beings the power and the ability to choose to do what God commands, and to refrain from what is forbidden.

Both an action and abstaining from an action are positive acts, because when someone abstains from an action he chooses the opposite. For example, a person who abstains from love chooses to hate, while a person who is not favourably disposed chooses to be angry. Unintentional wrong actions do not count as actions, however. So, if a man freely chooses to cut wood but kills a person in the process of doing so, his failure to prevent the accident does not count as an action because it was unintentional.

Saadya offers four proofs that God has given humankind free will based on the following:

1 Sense perception (we know from our own experience that we have the power to choose our actions).

2 Reason (if the Creator interfered with human actions, there would be no point in commandments and prohibitions; if Xe compelled a person to perform an action it would be unreasonable to punish him for it, and if human beings acted under

compulsion then it would be necessary to reward both believers and unbelievers on the grounds that they did only what they were ordered to do).

3 Scripture (examples include: 'Therefore choose life' [Deuteronomy 30:19] and 'Woe to the rebellious children, saith the Lord, that take counsel, but not of me' [Isaiah 30:1]).

4 Tradition (ancient Teachers have told us that everything except the fear of God lies in God's hands).

Saadya argues that God dreads human disobedience because of its harmful effects upon us, but gives four reasons why God gives commandments and prohibitions knowing that human beings will disobey:

1 The commandments tell human beings what God requires of them.

2 If a human being acted in accordance with God's will without being commanded he would have no right to be rewarded.

3 If it were acceptable to reward a human being for something not commanded, it would be equally acceptable to punish a human being for something not prohibited – which would be unjust.

4 The commandments reinforce those which may be established by Reason, so that human beings might be very careful to follow them.

Mackie on evil and omnipotence

Mackie (1955) examines several possible responses to the logical problem of evil, each of which, he argues, compromises divine omnipotence and thereby renders the resulting position no longer recognisably theistic.

He rejects the argument that God gave human beings free will because it is better that they should act freely than that they should be automata on the following grounds:

1 Why could God not have made human beings who always freely choose the good? If it is not logically impossible to choose the good freely on one or several occasions, it is logically possible to choose the good freely on every occasion.

2 If the wills of human beings really are free, even God cannot control them; therefore God is not omnipotent. Even if God merely refrains from controlling them, why should God refrain from controlling evil wills? This suggests that freedom outweighs wrongness. This leads to the 'Paradox of Omnipotence' which asks whether an omnipotent being is able to create things which God is unable to control, or to make rules by which even God is bound, thus rendering God no longer omnipotent. One solution is to say that God has unlimited power to determine what powers to act things will have, but does not, Godself, have unlimited power to act, but this, again, is to modify the divine attribute of omnipotence.

Plantinga's free will defence

Plantinga's free will defence (1974) is one of the best-known responses to Mackie's paper. Whereas a free will theodicy attempts to say what God's reason for permitting evil *is*, according to Plantinga, a free will defence suggests what God's reason for permitting evil might *possibly* be.

Plantinga admits that there is a contradiction between God's attributes of omnipotence, omniscience and goodness if it is held that:

1 A good thing always eliminates evil as far as it can.
2 There are no limits to what an omnipotent being can do.

He observes that few would argue that God can bring about logically impossible states of affairs, or cause necessarily false propositions to be true. And, in response to the first of these propositions, he argues that something may not eliminate evil because it does not know about the evil. But, even if it does know about the evil (and the theist who holds that God is omniscient would want to say this), it might choose not to eliminate an evil because there are two evils and it is not possible to eliminate both of them.

Reflection

If there are two evils and God cannot eliminate both of them, what might this imply about the concept of God?

Plantinga therefore considers the following modifications:

1 A being which is omnipotent, omniscient and good will eliminate every evil which it is possible for such a being to eliminate; and
2 An omnipotent being can perform only actions which are permitted by the laws of logic.

He argues that there are some evils which cannot be eliminated without eliminating goods which outweigh them. For example, suffering and adversity might lead to heroism which creates a good situation from a bad one and inspires others.

Reflection

How might someone object to this argument?

Plantinga concludes that there is no explicit or formal contradiction between statements asserting God's omnipotence, omniscience and goodness. So those who say that there is a contradiction between these statements must mean that there is an implicit contradiction.

He suggests that we can argue that this is not the case, on the grounds that an omnipotent, omniscient, good God does not eliminate evil because there is a good reason why Xe does not do this. He cites Augustine's response to the view that God should have created humankind without the ability to sin – that it is better to have a world containing human beings with free will who sin than a world containing human beings who do not sin only because they do not have free will.

Plantinga argues for a version of this view, although his view is a free will defence, rather than a free will theodicy. For him, a free will defence tries to show that there may be goodness which God cannot bring about without permitting evil.

Plantinga notes that the free will defence requires that a person is free with respect to an action; i.e. he is free to perform it, and free to refrain from performing it. The action might be predictable, but it must still be a free choice. He argues that a world containing free creatures who perform more good than evil actions is more valuable than a world which contains no free creatures. God can create free creatures, but Xe cannot cause or determine them to do only what is right. In exercising their freedom, some of these creatures go wrong, and this is the source of moral evil. However, Plantinga suggests, the fact that free creatures sometimes make wrong moral choices does not count against divine omnipotence or goodness because God could only have prevented such moral evil by creating a world which contained no possibility of moral goodness.

Plantinga considers the following objections to his view:

1 Freedom and determinism are compatible.

   This is the 'compatibilist' position, which, as we saw in Chapter 6, is argued for, among many others, by Flew. Flew suggests that God could have created creatures who were free, but also causally determined to do only what is right. He gives the example of Murdo, who decides to marry Mairi. Murdo does not choose his wife at random; his choice could have been predicted by anyone who knew him well. Similarly, God could have made human beings in such a way that their natures determined that they would always choose to do what is good. A human being would be free in that they would act in accordance with their nature, but, since their nature was made by God, it would always cause them to choose what is right. Since God has not made human beings in this way, Flew argues, God cannot be good.

   Plantinga thinks that this objection is implausible because it seems to imply that someone could equally well say that being in jail does not limit her freedom because if she were not in jail she would be free to go where she pleases. The force of this objection is unclear, however. It would appear that Plantinga is objecting to a view like Flew's by claiming that we cannot say that being constrained by our God-given nature allows us complete freedom on the grounds that not being constrained by our God-given nature would allow us unlimited freedom; the concept of freedom in the context of a situation without constraints cannot be applied in the context of a situation in which our actions are constrained.

2 An omnipotent God could create a world in which creatures are free to do wrong but never in fact do so.

   This is Mackie's view, summarised above. Plantinga considers:

   a Whether it would have been possible for God to create any possible world Xe wished to create.

He argues that this is not the case. For example, as a necessary being, Xe could not have created a world in which Xe did not exist. And there are many possible worlds in which it is partly up to free human beings whether God can create them.

b   Whether, of the worlds which God *could* have created, Xe could have created a world containing moral good but no moral evil.

He concludes that it would not have been in God's power to create a world in which Curley Smith, who, in Plantinga's story, is the corrupt mayor of Boston, produces moral order but no moral evil. He suggests that every possible world which God could create is of the kind that, if Curley is free in it, he will perform at least one wrong action. In other words, Curley Smith, like the rest of humankind of whom he is an example, suffers from 'transworld depravity': in every possible world in which human beings could be created, every one of them will perform at least one wrong action. If all human beings suffer from transworld depravity, not even God could create a world in which human beings are free but never choose to perform any wrong actions. Therefore, the price for creating a world in which free creatures produce moral good is the creation of a world in which free creatures also produce moral evil.

Hick's Irenaean Theodicy

Hick's Irenaean Theodicy (2010 [1966]) contains elements of a free will defence but, he claims, it also provides a better explanation for the existence of natural evil.

Following the thought of Irenaeus (d. c202 CE), Hick constructs his theodicy on the basis of a two-stage conception of the creation of humankind:

- At the first stage, human beings are created in the 'image' of God – that is, they are animals who are intelligent and ethical and have the potential to attain knowledge of and have a relationship with God.
- The second stage is a gradual process of further growth and development, in which these human animals are brought, through their own free responses, into what Irenaeus called the divine 'likeness'. During this stage, the human animal gradually becomes a child of God.

Hick says that humankind was created in this way for two reasons:

- To preserve the 'epistemic [concerned with knowledge] distance' between human beings and God. God has created the world and human beings in such a way that God's existence is not obvious to us; there is a distance between what we know and complete knowledge of God. The world is 'religiously ambiguous' so that we have the freedom to choose whether or not to be open to the gradual awareness of God which is a possibility for all humankind.
- Freely chosen goodness is more valuable than ready-made virtues. Hick thinks that Mackie and Flew were correct to argue that God could have created free beings who always choose the good – and suggests that Xe did so in the case of Jesus Christ.

But Hick argues that virtues which are developed as a consequence of our own decisions in the context of challenge and temptation are more valuable than virtues which are created without the need for any effort on our part. God therefore created imperfect creatures who would attain the more valuable kind of goodness through their own free choices.

Hick argues that what we know about human beings and the world is compatible with this hypothesis. The many examples of human sin support the view that human beings are self-regarding animals. But the many examples of human goodness support the view that God is gradually creating children of God. A dangerous world, containing natural disasters and illnesses, constitutes an appropriate environment for the second stage of creation; it is because our world is one in which we can be harmed that our actions are morally significant. An action which is morally wrong harms others, while one which is morally right prevents or alleviates harm, or maintains or increases the well-being of humankind. In a world without pain and suffering, there would be no distinction between right and wrong, and therefore no opportunity for moral growth and development. Conversely, in the world as it is, we can develop courage and determination, and in our relationships we can develop the values of love and care, self-sacrifice, and commitment to the common good.

An objection to Hick's theodicy

Nick Trakakis (2008) argues that natural evil is not necessary in order to maintain an 'epistemic distance' between human beings and God. He describes a 'Twin Earth' which is like Earth in most respects but in which the law of predation and the evolution of species by natural selection are not operative. He suggests that such a world could still contain moral evil, and that this would generate sufficient evil for the purposes of soul-making, but that the presence of benevolent natural laws – that is, the absence of natural evil – would not immediately indicate the interventions of a benevolent deity.

Reflection
How might Hick respond to this objection?

Determinism and the problem of evil

Clearly, a free will theodicy or defence is a possible solution to the problem of evil only if we think that human beings have free will. If, as al-Ghazali (1984) argues, human beings do not have free will, and God is ultimately responsible for our evil actions, it is necessary not only to provide an alternative explanation of why an omnipotent and good God permits evil but also to explain how determinism can be compatible with divine goodness.

Al-Ghazali argues that, even if God had created all creatures with the intelligence, knowledge and wisdom of the most learned, or if Xe had created all creatures with the intelligence, knowledge and wisdom of all of them, and this had included all morally-relevant knowledge and wisdom, and if God had commanded them to arrange this world and the next in accordance with the knowledge and wisdom which they had received, that arrangement would not require us to add to or subtract from the way in which God has, in fact, arranged creation in this world and the next; in other words, even perfect creatures could not create a world more perfect than the one in which we live. Therefore, everything which God gives to human beings, whether it be a source of pleasure or of pain, must be regarded as the product of divine justice. If God had the power to create something better but did not, God would be guilty of miserliness and injustice. If, on the other hand, Xe were unable to create something better, this would entail divine incapability, which is not compatible with the nature of divinity.

Al-Ghazali argues that, in the next world, everything which one individual lacks is a bonus for someone else. Without night we would not recognise the value of the day, without ill health, those who were healthy would not appreciate their good health, and the existence of hell enables those in paradise to appreciate the extent to which they have been blessed. He claims that it is just to give precedence to the perfect – to enable the faithful to live in paradise by increasing the punishment of those in hell, just as someone might preserve life by amputating a gangrenous hand. If God had not created the imperfect, the perfect would be unrecognisable, and if God had not created animals, we would not be able to appreciate the dignity of humankind: 'Divine generosity and wisdom require the simultaneous creation of the perfect and the imperfect' (1999: 191 [1984]).

Al-Ghazali claims that only 'the knowing' are able to understand this. It is like a deep and perilous sea in which large groups of people who do not possess this understanding drown. Behind this sea lies the mystery of predestination where 'the many wander in perplexity'. Those who have been permitted to understand it are forbidden to communicate their understanding to others. Nonetheless, al-Ghazali claims, it is possible for us to understand that, as a consequence of a divine judgement, good and evil are foreordained. Therefore, 'What strikes you was not there to miss you; what misses you was not there to strike you' (191).

Reflection

On what grounds does al-Ghazali argue for determinism? How might someone object to his view?

• THE EVIDENTIAL ARGUMENT FROM EVIL

Many scholars now agree that the logical problem of evil fails to show, without doubt, that there is an inconsistency between the relevant propositions. The evidential argument from evil claims only that the existence or quantity of evil counts against belief in the existence of God.

Rowe's evidential argument

Rowe (1979) argues that, if we can find one or more examples of intense suffering which do not lead to any greater good, this counts against belief in the existence of an omnipotent, omniscient, supremely good creator of the world.

Rowe put forward several versions of his argument but, in outline, it runs as follows:

1 There are instances of intense suffering which an omnipotent, omniscient being could have prevented without losing some greater good or permitting an equally bad or worse evil. (This is sometimes called the 'factual premise' because it appears to make a factual statement about the world.)
2 An omniscient, wholly good being would prevent intense suffering, unless it could not do so without losing some greater good or permitting an equally bad or worse evil. (This is sometimes called the 'theological premise'.)
3 Therefore, an omnipotent, omniscient, wholly good being does not exist.

Rowe argues that, since the second premise accords with our basic moral principles, any fault with the argument must lie with the first premise. He asks us to consider the case of a fawn which is burned in a forest fire and lies in agony for several days before it dies. In a later paper (1988) he adds a difficult example of moral evil, that of that of a five-year-old girl who was beaten, raped and strangled to death by her mother's boyfriend. These examples are referred to respectively by Alston (1991) as 'Bambi' and 'Sue'. Rowe argues that, since we do not know of any good state of affairs which would justify an omnipotent, omniscient being in allowing the suffering of Bambi and Sue, there probably is no good state of affairs which would justify an omnipotent, omniscient being in allowing such suffering.

He acknowledges that this does not prove the truth of the first premise, since the suffering in question may lead to some good which outweighs it which we cannot see. But, he claims, there are no rational grounds for disbelieving the first premise. Indeed, he suggests, even if it is possible in the case of the fawn that there is some otherwise unachievable outweighing good which cannot be perceived, it seems unlikely that this applies to all instances of intense suffering.

Marilyn McCord Adams on horrendous evils

One influential attempt to address the problem of intense suffering is offered by Marilyn McCord Adams (b. 1943) (1989), who defines 'horrendous evils' as evils which cause someone to doubt whether their life has any positive meaning.

Adams dismisses attempts to solve the problem of evil by postulating reasons why God permits evil which are both general – that is, which cover all kinds of evil – and global – that is, which focus on one feature of the world as a whole; in other words, she rejects arguments to the effect that God permits a world containing evil because this is the best of all possible worlds. She argues that such theodicies do not offer consolation to individuals who experience horrendous evils.

Some believers simply argue that God does not guarantee to all God's creatures a life which is, on balance, positive. But this requires us to admit that human life in our world is 'a bad bet'.

Adams suggests that we do not need to find logically possible reasons why God permits horrendous evils; we need only show that God is sufficiently good to God's creatures to give them lives which they regard as, on balance, positive, despite the experience of horrendous evils.

Adams suggests that, for the Christian, the good of beatific, face-to-face communion with God in the afterlife by far outweighs any other goods or ills, including horrendous evils, which someone might experience, and that this thereby renders their life worth living.

Adams suggests that, in addition to 'engulfing' horrendous evils, perhaps God also 'defeats' them by making them part of a person's relationship with God. She suggests three possible ways in which this could be done:

1 Human experience of horrendous evils could be a way of identifying with Christ's suffering – either by understanding his pain (sympathetic identification) or by sharing it (mystical identification).
2 Horrendous evils are defeated through divine gratitude for suffering, as suggested by Julian of Norwich. The experience of divine gratitude outweighs the experience of suffering.
3 Human suffering provides a vision into the inner life of God – that is, if God is not impassible (unable to suffer), our suffering enables us to understand God's suffering as a consequence of human sin and the sufferings of Christ. Even this would be good in that it is a vision of God. Any form of divine intimacy is an incommensurate good which would cancel out the experience of evil and the desire to understand why God permits it.

Reflection

Michael P. Levine describes the claim 'that God will make it up to people in heaven for the horrors unjustly suffered on earth' as a 'simplistic solution' (2000: 99). Do you agree?

Sceptical theism

A common response to the evidential argument from evil has recently come to be known as 'sceptical theism', although it is derived from the scriptures of the Abrahamic faiths. For example, in Romans 11:33–34, we find the apostle Paul proclaiming: 'Oh, the depth of the riches of the wisdom and knowledge of God! How unsearchable his judgements, and his paths beyond tracing out! Who has known the mind of the Lord!' (New International Version, quoted in Trakakis, 2016: 10).

Stephen J. Wykstra (1984) develops as a response to Rowe the idea that, as mere human beings, we cannot reasonably expect to be able to understand the mind of God. He does this by means of the epistemic principle known as CORNEA – 'Condition Of ReasoNable Epistemic Access'. According to this principle, a human, H, can reasonably claim of situation s 'It appears that p' only if it is likely that s would appear differently if p were not the case. Applied to Rowe, the principle entails that Rowe is reasonably entitled to claim 'It appears that there are no goods which justify divine permission of horrendous evils' only if it is likely that, if there were goods justifying divine permission of horrendous evils, we would be able to recognise them. Wykstra and his many followers argue that our cognitive faculties are so limited in comparison to those of the divine being that we cannot reasonably hope to be able to know whether there are goods which justify divine permission of horrendous evils.

Various analogies have been offered in an attempt to show that, for example, just as a baby cannot understand the intentions of its parent (Wykstra, 1984), and a beginning chess player cannot understand why Kasparov makes the move he does (Alston, 1996), we cannot hope to understand the intentions of God, and therefore cannot conclude that God has no legitimate reasons for allowing horrendous evils.

Rowe responds (2001), however, by suggesting that, while Kasparov has good reason not to reveal how his move supports his game-plan, God has good reason to reveal to us the goods for the sake of which we suffer horrendous evils, since this would help us more easily to bear our suffering – and yet God does not do so. This, for Rowe, strongly suggests that an omnipotent, omniscient, omnibenevolent being does not exist.

Evil after Auschwitz

Another possible response to the problem of intense suffering is offered by Hans Jonas (1903–1993) (1987), who considers what the suffering and death of Jewish people at Auschwitz, the paradigmatic example of a horrendous evil in the twentieth century, added to what was already known about the extent of the suffering which human beings can inflict on others. He considers whether Jewish people could, as the prophets did, say that they suffered because they had been unfaithful to their covenant with God. In the Maccabeean age, this was replaced by the idea of witness and the concept of the martyr; the innocent and the just suffer the most. But, Jonas argues, this idea is of no help to us in attempting to understand why Auschwitz occurred because the victims did not die for the sake of their faith. Christians might appeal to the idea of original sin but, for Jewish people, God is the 'Lord of History'. Such evil leads us to question the concept of God. Those who do not wish to give up the concept must therefore rethink it.

Jonas argues for:

1 A suffering God – but not, as in Christianity, a deity who sends part of itself into a particular situation; rather, God suffers from the time of creation onwards.
2 A becoming God – that is, a God who emerges in time. Jonas argues that, although the ancient Greek idea of a timeless, unchanging God has come to be regarded as the

orthodox view, the concept of a God who changes represents a much better fit with biblical texts. Jonas argues that creation changes God's own state because Xe is no longer alone, and that God's relation to the creation means that Xe has changing experiences as the world changes.

3 A caring God – but not a kind of 'sorcerer' who acts in accordance with God's own concerns; God has taken the risk of giving other agents the power and right to act on their own.

4 A God who is not omnipotent. Jonas argues that no viable theology can maintain the medieval doctrine of absolute, unlimited divine power and gives two reasons for this:

a The concept of omnipotence is self-contradictory. Something can be omnipotent only if nothing else exists, because the existence of something else would constitute a limitation. But power without an object is powerless. Power is only power in relation to something else which has the power to resist it.

b The divine attributes of intelligibility, absolute goodness, and omnipotence are not compatible. Judaism cannot sacrifice intelligibility or goodness. Therefore, the existence of evil is compatible with divine goodness only if God is not omnipotent. We could say that God simply chooses not to exercise God's omnipotence in order to preserve the autonomy of God's creatures, but this is inadequate because we would expect a good, omnipotent God to make a miraculous intervention when God's creatures inflict intense suffering on each other. But there were no miracles at Auschwitz – except those which were brought about by human beings. God did not intervene because God could not.

Thus, Jonas gives the opposite solution to the one which we find in the book of Job: Job suggested that God's power is too great for human beings to understand – the response of the sceptical theist – but Jonas suggests that God has chosen to relinquish God's omnipotence.

Reflection

Why might a theist wish to maintain divine omnipotence?

• HINDU AND BUDDHIST ACCOUNTS OF EVIL AND SUFFERING

Brahman, creation and evil

Shankara (1971) argues that *Brahman* (in Hinduism, the Ultimate Reality which underlies everything) cannot be the cause of the world because, if that were the case, *Brahman* would be guilty of creating inequality, and cruelty to creatures.

Gods are eminently happy, animals are eminently unhappy, and human beings occupy an intermediate position. If a God were responsible for bringing about such inequality, such a God would be malicious. Such a God would also be responsible for inflicting pain and destruction and would therefore be guilty of great cruelty. Both malice and cruelty are incompatible with divine goodness.

But *Brahman* is not responsible because the inequality in creation is caused by the merit given for good deeds and lack of merit brought about by bad deeds, both of which are freely chosen by creatures and for which *Brahman* is therefore not to blame. Just as Parjanya, the Giver of Rain, is the common cause of rice, barley and other plants, while the differences between them are caused by the differing potentialities in the seeds, so *Brahman* is the common cause of the creation of gods and human beings, and the differences are caused by the different merit of individual souls.

Shankara considers the objection that, before the creation, there was no distinction between beings and so no merit which would cause the creation to become unequal. He responds that the world had no beginning and therefore that merit and inequality are like the seed and its sprout in being both caused and causes. If this were not the case, he argues, souls would be rewarded or punished irrespective of previous good or bad actions.

Reflection

Shankara argues that suffering is a consequence of failing to perform good deeds or choosing to perform bad deeds, either in this life or in a previous life. To what extent does this constitute an adequate response to the problem of human and animal suffering?

A Buddhist account of suffering

David J. Kalupahana (1933–2014) (1987) notes that philosophers such as Arthur Schopenhauer (1788–1860), Friedrich Nietzsche (1844–1900) and Karl Jaspers (1883–1969) have given us the impression that Buddhism is a pessimistic religion because it teaches that 'all is suffering'. But, he claims, this interpretation was derived from a misunderstanding by the Sarvastivadins, a group of Buddhists which arose during the third century BCE, and was perpetuated by Brahmanical philosophers in India.

Kalupahana argues, instead, that the Buddha teaches that birth is a source of suffering only if the craving for survival which is a condition for the birth of a human being continues to dominate a person's life. The same is true of decay and old age; it is the unwillingness to accept these as part of life which leads to frustration and unhappiness. To overcome the suffering associated with death, we must realise the impermanence of life and cease to crave for life to continue beyond its possible limits. Excessive craving for life can lead to rebirth, which is regarded as undesirable, whereas a complete lack of this tendency might lead to suicide. The Buddha therefore recommends a middle way which will enable us to enjoy the pleasures of life without being enslaved by them or facing frustrations and anxiety. We should learn to recognise the 'life instinct', but it should not be an obsession. To avoid suffering we must avoid 'grasping' – excessive craving or obsession. For Kalupahana, then, the Buddha's view of life is therefore neither pessimistic nor optimistic. Life is not a tragedy but an opportunity.

> **Reflection**
>
> Can there be a 'problem of evil' for a religion without a deity?

• CONCLUSION

As we have seen, some scholars argue that the logical problem of evil fails because we cannot show, without doubt, that there is an inconsistency between the relevant propositions. The evidential argument from evil claims only that the existence or quantity of evil counts against belief in the existence of God. Responses to the evidential version of the argument may offer further attempts to show why a God who is omnipotent, omniscient and good permits even horrendous evils, or claim scepticism regarding our human ability to understand the mind of God. Others argue that the Divine cannot be conceived in terms of classical theism, perhaps suggesting that God is not omnipotent, that God is not the cause of the universe, or that there is no God and that suffering represents a challenge which we must overcome.

• REFERENCES

Adams, Marilyn McCord (1989) 'Horrendous Evils and the Goodness of God', *Proceedings of the Aristotelian Society*, supp. vol. 63: 297–310.

Al-Ghazali, Abu Hamid (1984) Extract reprinted in Eric Ormsby (ed.) *Theodicy in Islamic Thought: The Dispute over Al-Ghazali's 'Best of All Possible Worlds'* (Princeton, NJ: Princeton University Press, 1984) 38–41; reprinted in Eleanore Stump and Michael J. Murray (eds) *Philosophy of Religion: The Big Questions* (Oxford: Blackwell, 1999) 190–191.

Alston, William (1991) 'The Inductive Argument from Evil and the Human Cognitive Condition', *Philosophical Perspectives* 5: 29–67.

Alston, William (1996) 'Some (Temporarily) Final Thoughts on the Evidential Argument from Evil' in Daniel Howard-Snyder (ed.) *The Evidential Argument from Evil* (Bloomington, IN: Indiana University Press), 311–332.

Flew, Antony (1955) 'Divine Omnipotence and Human Freedom' in Antony Flew and Alasdair Macintyre (eds) *New Essays in Philosophical Theology* (London: SCM Press), 149–150.

Hick, John (2010 [1966]) *Evil and the God of Love* (Basingstoke: Palgrave Macmillan).

Jonas, Hans (1987) 'The Concept of God after Auschwitz: A Jewish Voice', *The Journal of Religion* 67, 1: 1–13.

Kalupahana, David (1987) *The Principles of Buddhist Psychology* (Albany, NY: State University of New York Press), 79–87; reprinted in Chad Meister (ed.) *The Philosophy of Religion Reader* (New York and Abingdon: Routledge, 2007), 576–584.

Levine, Michael P. (2000) 'Contemporary Christian Analytic Philosophy of Religion: Biblical Fundamentalism, Terrible Solutions to a Horrible Problem, and Hearing God', *International Journal for the Philosophy of Religion* 48, 2: 89–119.

Mackie, J. L. (1955) 'Evil and Omnipotence', *Mind* 64, 254: 200–212.

Plantinga, Alvin (1974) *The Nature of Necessity* (Oxford: Clarendon Press), Chapter 9, 'God, Evil and the Metaphysics of Evil', 164–193.

Rowe, William (1979) 'The Problem of Evil and Some Varieties of Atheism', *American Philosophical Quarterly* 16, 4: 335–341.

Rowe, William (1988) 'Evil and Theodicy', *Philosophical Topics* 16, 2: 119–132.

Rowe, William (2001) 'Reply to Howard-Snyder and Bergmann' in William Rowe (ed.) *God and the Problem of Evil* (Malden, MA: Blackwell), 155–158.

Saadya Gaon (1985 [1960, 933]) *Book of Doctrines and Beliefs*, in Alexander Altmann (ed.) *Three Jewish Philosophers* (New York, NY: Meridian Books), 118–123; reprinted in Eleanore Stump and Michael J. Murray (eds) *Philosophy of Religion: The Big Questions* (Oxford: Blackwell, 1999), 192–195.

Shankara, Adi (1971) 'Brahman, Creation, and Evil' from *Brahmasutrabhasya*, II.1. 34–6 in *A Sourcebook of Advaita Vedanta*, Eliot Deutsch and J. A. B. Buitenen (Honolulu: University of Hawaii Press), 191–192; reprinted in Andrew Eshleman (ed.) *Readings in Philosophy of Religion: East Meets West* (Oxford: Blackwell, 2008), 296–297.

Trakakis, Nick (2008) *The End of Philosophy of Religion* (London: Continuum).

Trakakis, N. (2016) 'The Evidential Problem of Evil', *Internet Encyclopedia of Philosophy*, www.iep.utm.edu/evil-evi, accessed 6 March 2016.

Wykstra, Stephen J. (1984) 'The Humean Obstacle to Evidential Arguments from Suffering: On Avoiding the Evils of "Appearance"', *International Journal for Philosophy of Religion* 16, 2: 73–93.

• FURTHER READING

Encyclopedia articles

Beebe, James R. 'Logical Problem of Evil', *Internet Encyclopedia of Philosophy*, www.iep.utm.edu/evil-log/.

Dougherty, Trent (2014) 'Skeptical Theism', *Stanford Encyclopedia of Philosophy*, https://plato.stanford.edu/entries/skeptical-theism/.

McBrayer, Justin P. (n.d.) 'Skeptical Theism', *Internet Encyclopedia of Philosophy*, www.iep.utm.edu/skept-th/.

Pessin, Sarah (2003) 'Saadya', https://plato.stanford.edu/entries/saadya/#2.

Tooley, Michael (2015) 'The Problem of Evil', https://plato.stanford.edu/entries/evil/.

Trakakis, Nick 'The Evidential Problem of Evil', *Internet Encyclopedia of Philosophy*, www.iep.utm.edu/evil-evi/.

Original articles in edited collections

Bergman, Michael (2009) 'Skeptical Theism' in Thomas P. Flint and Michael C. Rea (eds) *The Oxford Handbook of Philosophical Theology* (Oxford: Oxford University Press), 374–399.

Draper, Paul (2009) 'The Problem of Evil' in Thomas P. Flint and Michael C. Rea (eds) *The Oxford Handbook of Philosophical Theology* (Oxford: Oxford University Press), 332–351.

Gale, Richard M. (2013 [2007]) 'The Problem of Evil' in Chad Meister and Paul Copan (eds) *The Routledge Companion to Philosophy of Religion* (Abingdon: Routledge), 457–467.

Murray, Michael J. (2009) 'Theodicy' in Thomas P. Flint and Michael C. Rea (eds) *The Oxford Handbook of Philosophical Theology* (Oxford: Oxford University Press), 352–373.

Oppy, Graham (2010 [1997]) 'The Evidential Problem of Evil' in Charles Taliaferro, Paul Draper and Philip L. Quinn (eds) *A Companion to Philosophy of Religion* (Chichester: Wiley-Blackwell), 500–508.

Peterson, Michael L. (2010 [1997]) 'The Logical Problem of Evil' in Charles Taliaferro, Paul Draper and Philip L. Quinn (eds) *A Companion to Philosophy of Religion* (Chichester: Wiley-Blackwell), 491–499.

Extracts from articles or books in edited collections

Ghuly, Mohammed (2014) 'Evil and Suffering in Islam' in Michael Peterson, William Hasker, Bruce Reichenbach and David Basinger (eds) *Philosophy of Religion: Selected Readings* (Oxford: OUP), 383–391.

Herman, A. L. (1971) 'Indian Theodicy: Samkara and Ramanuja on Brahma Sutra II. 1. 32–36', *Philosophy: East and West* 21, 3: 265–281.

Levinas, E. (1988) 'Useless Suffering', trans. Richard Cohen, in M. Larrimore (ed.) *The Problem of Evil* (Oxford: Blackwell Publishing), 371–380.

Matilal, Bimal K. (1992) 'A Note on Śamkara's Theodicy', *Journal of Indian Philosophy* 20: 363–376; reprinted in Andrew Eshleman (ed.) *Readings in Philosophy of Religion* (Malden, MA: Blackwell Publishers), 273–278.

Plantinga, Alvin (1996) 'On Being Evidentially Challenged' from Daniel Howard-Snyder (ed.) (Bloomington, IN: Indiana University Press), 244–261; reprinted in Eleanore Stump and Michael J. Murray (eds) *Philosophy of Religion: The Big Questions* (Oxford: Blackwell), 176–198.

Southwold, Martin (1985) 'Buddhism and Evil' from David Parkin (ed.) *The Anthropology of Evil* (Oxford: Blackwell Publishers), 128–141; reprinted in Charles Taliaferro and Paul J. Griffiths (eds) *Philosophy of Religion: An Anthology* (Oxford: Blackwell), 424–431.

Articles

Barnhart, J. E. (1977) 'Theodicy and the free will defence: Response to Plantinga and Flew', *Religious Studies* 13, 4: 439–453.

Basinger, David (1999) 'Infant Suffering: A Response to Chignell', *Religious Studies* 35, 3: 363–369.

Chignell, Andrew (1998) 'The Problem of Infant Suffering', *Religious Studies* 34, 2: 205–217.

Chryssides, George D. (1987) 'Evil and the Problem of God', *Religious Studies* 23, 4: 467–475.

Dougherty, Trent (2011) 'Recent Work on the Problem of Evil', *Analysis* 71, 3: 560–573.

Kane, G. Stanley (1975) 'The Failure of Soul-Making Theodicy', *International Journal for Philosophy of Religion* 6, 1: 1–22.

Levine, Michael P. (1994) 'Pantheism and the Problem of Evil', *International Journal for Philosophy of Religion* 35, 3: 129–151.

Mawson, T. J. (2004) 'The Possibility of a Free-Will Defence for the Problem of Natural Evil', *Religious Studies* 40, 1: 23–42.

Mesle, C. Robert (1986) 'The Problem of Genuine Evil: A Critique of John Hick's Theodicy', *The Journal of Religion* 66, 4: 412–430.

Pruss, Alexander (2003) 'A New Free-Will Defence', *Religious Studies* 39, 2: 211–223.

Trakakis, Nick (2005) 'Is Theism Capable of Accounting for Any Natural Evil at All?', *International Journal for Philosophy of Religion* 57, 1: 35–66.

Books

Adams, Marilyn McCord (1999) *Horrendous Evils and the Goodness of God* (Ithaca, NY: Cornell University Press).

Bernstein, R. J. (2002) *Radical Evil: A Philosophical Interrogation* (Cambridge: Polity Press).

Crosby, Donald A. (2008) *Living With Ambiguity: Religious Naturalism and the Menace of Evil* (New York, NY: State University of New York Press).

Davies, Brian (2006) *The Reality of God and the Problem of Evil* (London: Continuum).

Inwagen, Peter van (2004) *Christian Faith and the Problem of Evil* (Grand Rapids, MI: Eerdmans).

Jonas, Hans (1996) *Mortality and Morality: A Search for the Good After Auschwitz*, ed. Lawrence Vogel (Evanston: IL: Northwestern University Press).

15

arguments against belief in the divine: the problem of divine hiddenness

---

• INTRODUCTION

The argument from divine hiddenness was first developed in J. L. Schellenberg's (b. 1959) book, *Divine Hiddenness and Human Reason* (2006 [1993]) and has been much discussed by philosophers of religion in recent years. Schellenberg argues that, since there are nonbelievers who are not resistant to a relationship with a personal God and yet are unable to have such a relationship, and it is reasonable to expect that a loving God would make it possible for them to do so, there cannot be a loving God.

• THE ARGUMENT FROM NONRESISTANT NONBELIEF

Schellenberg has produced a number of reformulations of his argument in response to criticism but, in outline, the argument runs as follows:

1 If God exists, God perfectly loves finite persons.
2 If 1. God is open to being in a meaningful and reciprocal relationship with every capable finite person.
3 If 2. no capable finite person who is nonresistant to belief in God's existence is a non-believer in God's existence.
4 There is at least one capable finite person who is nonresistant to belief in God's existence who is a nonbeliever in God's existence.
5 Therefore God does not exist.

Schellenberg argues for the first premise on the basis of ultimism, the claim that there is a reality which is ultimate in the following three ways:

a Metaphysical ultimacy: It is 'something whose existence is the ultimate or most fundamental fact about the nature of things, in terms of which any other fact about what things exist and how they exist would have to be explained in a comprehensive and correct account' (2015: 19).
b Axiological ultimacy: It is the greatest possible reality, like Anselm's account of the Divine as 'that than which nothing greater can be thought'.
c Soteriological ultimacy: It enables humankind to attain the deepest or ultimate human good, for themselves as individuals and for humankind in its entirety.

With regard to the second premise, Schellenberg explains that someone may be regarded as being open to a meaningful and reciprocal relationship if they never do anything which would make such a relationship unavailable to someone who is not resistant to that relationship.

Regarding the third premise, that no one who is nonresistant to belief in God can be a nonbeliever, Schellenberg says that, by failing to reveal God's existence, God is doing something which makes it impossible for someone who is nonresistant to belief in God to be a believer.

As a consequence of this, the nonbeliever loses both moral benefits and experiential benefits, as follows:

a Moral benefits: The ability to use the relationship as a way of overcoming character-flaws, enabling her to love others in the manner in which she is loved and increasing her chances of human flourishing.
b Experiential benefits: The experience of peace and joy as a consequence of her belief that she is correctly related to her Creator, the security of believing that all will ultimately be well even if she suffers, and the pleasure of the presence of God.

As consequence of both a and b, Schellenberg suggests, it is also likely that the believers' relationships with other finite beings would improve.

Finally, the claim that there is at least one person who is nonresistant to belief in God but is, nonetheless, a nonbeliever, is supported by an appeal to a multitude of historical examples of nonresistant nonbelievers (NNs) (e.g. 2015: 76–79).

• EXPLANATIONS FOR NONRESISTANT NONBELIEF

Many defences of theism against the argument from divine hiddenness suggest, in response to the second premise (that God is open to being in a meaningful and reciprocal relationship with every capable finite person), that there might be good reasons why a perfectly loving God would do something which would lead some creatures to have nonresistant nonbelief. Daniel Howard-Snyder and Adam Green (2016) provide a list derived from the extensive literature which includes the following:

1 The NN has not chosen her nonresistant attitude to God and needs to show that she has chosen her own positive attitude to God.
2 The NN has improper motives for her nonresistance – e.g. fear of punishment, desire for approval.
3 The moral autonomy of the NN would be reduced if God were to allow her to believe now.
4 The intensity of the NN's desire for God would be reduced if God were to allow her to believe now.
5 If God were to allow the NN to believe now, she would not have the opportunity to respond virtuously to various intellectual temptations.

Howard-Snyder and Green note four common responses to explanations such as these:

1 It is unlikely that any one reason can provide a complete explanation for non-resistant belief. Different types of NN might require different explanations, and, even for a group of NNs who are relevantly similar, a single reason might be unable to provide a total explanation for nonresistant nonbelief of that kind. Howard-Snyder and Green acknowledge, however, the possibility that a collection of explanations, taken together, might provide a complete explanation for nonresistant nonbelief.
2 It might be difficult to ascertain which of the possible explanations apply to any particular NNs. It is therefore possible that no one can say that there are NNs.
3 It is possible that none of the reasons suggested offer us an adequate explanation, either individually or collectively, of why God apparently allows nonresistant non-belief, either because it would be possible for God to bring about its desirable con-sequences in the context of a meaningful and reciprocal relationship or because the good of such a relationship exceeds the good of the consequences of nonresistant nonbelief.
4 If God exists, why did God not create a world without nonresistant nonbelief?

Reflection

How might a theist respond to objections 1–4 above?

• FURTHER OBJECTIONS TO THE ARGUMENT FROM NONRESISTANT NONBELIEF

Further objections cited by Howard-Snyder and Green include the following:

Objection to premise 1: If God exists, God perfectly loves finite persons

God does not, as far as we know, love human persons, either because God is transcendent and beyond human understanding and therefore non person-like or because, as some Deists would say, God is indifferent to human persons.

Objection to premise 2: If 1. God is open to being in a meaningful and reciprocal relationship with every capable finite person

There are different kinds of loving relationship. It is possible that God loves us by providing for our greatest good, which consists in being virtuous and caring for our environment and other creatures. The relationship between God and humankind need not be of the kind which Schellenberg regards as necessary.

Objections to premise 3: If 2. no capable finite person is a nonresistant nonbeliever

Here, the theist may appeal to a form of sceptical theism and suggest that, although we might expect that, if God is open to a relationship with humankind, no capable finite person would be an NN, there might be reasons why God does allow the existence of NNs which we, as mere human beings, cannot understand.

Howard-Snyder and Green also suggest that it is possible to have a personal relationship when we are less than completely certain of the existence of the other party. They question, however, whether a perfect God would make Godself available for a relationship in such less-than-ideal circumstances.

Objection to premise 4: There is at least one capable finite person who is a nonresistant nonbeliever

Some might argue that there are no persons who are open to belief in God who do not believe in God because everyone possesses basic knowledge of God, even if they do not call it 'God'.

Reflection

How might a supporter of the argument from divine hiddenness respond to these objections?

• CONCLUSION

In this chapter, we have outlined Schellenberg's argument from divine hiddenness, along with a selection of possible objections. At the time of writing, a lively debate about this relatively new topic in philosophy of religion is ongoing. It is, however, worth noting that Schellenberg's argument focuses very much on the God of classical theism, as Schellenberg himself points out. This by no means rules out all forms of religious belief, however.

• REFERENCES

Howard-Snyder, Daniel and Green, Adam (2016) 'Divine Hiddenness', *Stanford Encyclopedia of Philosophy*, https://plato.stanford.edu/entries/divine-hiddenness/.

Schellenberg, J. L. (2006 [1993]) *Divine Hiddenness and Human Reason* (Ithaca, NY: Cornell University Press).

Schellenberg, J. L. (2015) *The Hiddenness Argument: Philosophy's New Challenge to Belief in God* (Oxford: Oxford University Press).

• FURTHER READING

Original articles in edited collections

Moser, Paul K. (2004) 'Divine Hiddenness Does Not Justify Atheism' in Michael L. Peterson and Raymond J. Vanarragon (eds) *Contemporary Debates in Philosophy of Religion* (Malden, MA: Blackwell Publishing), 42–53.

Murray, Michael J. and Taylor, David E. (2013 [2007]) 'Hiddenness' in Chad Meister and Paul Copan (eds) *The Routledge Companion to Philosophy of Religion* (Abingdon: Routledge), 368–377.

Schellenberg, J. L. (2004) 'Divine Hiddenness Justifies Atheism' in Michael L. Peterson and Raymond J. Vanarragon (eds) *Contemporary Debates in Philosophy of Religion* (Malden, MA: Blackwell Publishing), 30–41.

Schellenberg, J. L. (2010 [1997]) 'Divine Hiddenness' in Charles Taliaferro, Paul Draper and Philip L. Quinn (eds) *A Companion to Philosophy of Religion* (Chichester: Wiley-Blackwell), 509–518.

Articles

Cullison, Andrew (2010) 'Two Solutions to the Problem of Divine Hiddenness', *American Philosophical Quarterly* 47, 2: 119–134.

Dougherty, Trent and Poston, Ted (2007) 'Divine Hiddenness and the Nature of Belief', *Religious Studies* 43, 2: 183–198.

McCreary, Mark L. (2010) 'Schellenberg on Divine Hiddenness and Religious Scepticism', *Religious Studies* 46, 2: 207–225.

Oakes, Robert (2010) 'Life, Death, and the Hiddenness of God', *International Journal for Philosophy of Religion* 64, 3: 155–160.

Books

Green, Adam and Stump, Eleanore (eds) (2016) *Hidden Divinity and Religious Belief: New Perspectives* (New York, NY: Cambridge University Press).

Howard-Snyder, Daniel and Moser, Paul K. (eds) (2002) *Divine Hiddenness: New Essays* (Cambridge: Cambridge University Press).

McKim, Robert (2001) *Religious Ambiguity and Religious Diversity* (Oxford: Oxford University Press).

Web resources

Schellenberg, J. L. and Jordan, Jeffrey (2008) 'Section 4: Faith and Uncertainty' in *God or Blind Nature? Philosophers Debate the Evidence*, Paul Draper (ed.), https://infidels.org/library/modern/debates/great-debate.html.

16

arguments against belief in the divine: the problem of religious diversity

• INTRODUCTION

Like the problems of evil and divine hiddenness, the problem of religious diversity is also both a challenge to belief and an issue to which the theist must find an answer in order to maintain faith. But this topic is, perhaps, even more important than the previous two because, as Hick notes in a lecture delivered to the Institute for Islamic Culture and Thought in Tehran (2005), the fact that, for many centuries, religions have commonly regarded themselves as the only true faith has meant that religion has been a 'validating and intensifying factor' in most wars. Although in the twentieth and twenty-first centuries it has become common for people of different faiths to live side by side in the same city, this has often led to an increase in merely superficial encounters with those of other faiths, and therefore not to an increase in understanding and tolerance but to an increase in the use of newer and more destructive ways to maim and kill those regarded as holding the 'wrong' beliefs.

• THREE APPROACHES TO RELIGIOUS DIVERSITY

Broadly speaking, there are three ways of approaching religious diversity:

1 Exclusivism: Only one religion offers religious truth and a pathway to salvation. Other religions should therefore be rejected and their adherents should be converted to the one true faith.
2 Inclusivism: Only one religion offers religious truth and a pathway to salvation, but those who follow another religion faithfully and live in accordance with its teachings may still achieve salvation.

3 Pluralism: There is a common Reality underlying each of the religious traditions, each of which is said to be a different manifestation of the common Reality. Therefore, more than one religion can offer religious truth and a pathway to salvation.

In the following sections we will consider each of these in turn.

• EXCLUSIVISM

Plantinga is one of the best-known Christian exclusivists. He notes (1995) that, although he personally agrees with the prophet Nathan's condemnation of David's actions regarding Bathsheba (he arranged for her husband, Uriah the Hittite, to be killed in battle so that he could marry her himself [II Samuel 12]), he recognises that others disagree. He suggests that he is justified in holding his own view, even though he cannot argue for it. Similarly, he asks whether he is wrong to think that racial bigotry is despicable, even though he knows that others disagree and hold their views just as strongly.

Plantinga suggests that, in each case, although both believers may acknowledge that each of them is equally convinced of his/her belief, neither really thinks that both beliefs are equally true; they both think that the other has made some kind of mistake.

Plantinga admits that he could be wrong about his beliefs, but argues that he does not avoid the risk of being wrong by treating all religious beliefs as equally acceptable; to do that, he thinks, could be just as wrong because that is still to hold one view and reject an alternative (e.g. exclusivism). He suggests that there is no alternative strategy since we cannot do better than to believe and reject beliefs in accordance with what, after we have thought carefully about the matter, seems to us to be right.

Hick's objections to religious exclusivism

Hick (2005) suggests that the view that only one religion is the right religion is problematic because, in most cases, a person's religion depends upon where they were born. So, someone born in a predominantly Christian family is likely to become a Christian, while someone born in a Muslim family will probably become a Muslim – and both will probably believe that theirs is the one true faith.

Hick questions whether we can reasonably ignore our global context and claims that other religions, particularly Islam, 'turn human beings away from selfish self-concern to serve God, just as much as Christianity does' (6). He suggests that Plantinga neither takes this into account nor considers salvation or the moral and spiritual consequences of faith outside of Christianity. Hick suggests that Plantinga would probably say that only God knows whether the non-Christian majority of the human race will be saved, but argues that, if it is only God who knows this, no exclusivist can claim that only their own faith is in possession of the final truth.

Hick says that the main objection to exclusivism, whether it be Christian, Muslim or of some other kind, is that 'it denies by implication that God, the sole creator of the world and of all humanity, is loving, gracious and merciful, and that His love and mercy extend to all humankind' (6). He questions whether, if God created all humankind, we can reasonably believe that God has 'set up a system by which hundreds of millions of men, women and children, the majority of the human race, are destined through no fault of their own to eternal torment in hell' (6–7).

He observes that Craig, also a Christian exclusivist, has tried to address this problem by appealing to the idea of 'middle knowledge'. If God has middle knowledge, God knows what every person would do in every possible set of circumstances. Craig argues that, for all those who have not encountered the Christian Gospel, God knows that, if they had encountered it, they would have rejected it and that their punishment is therefore not unjust. Hick responds that this is to condemn hundreds of millions of people without having any knowledge of them, and notes that even other conservative Christian philosophers think that this claim is objectionable.

> ### Reflection
>
> **What, in your view, is the most significant objection to the exclusivist position? How could an exclusivist respond?**

• INCLUSIVISM

The inclusivist position is particularly associated with the Roman Catholic theologian Karl Rahner (1904–1984). Rahner (1966) argues that the plurality of religions is a greater threat for Christianity than it is for other religions because no other religion maintains to the same extent that it is the only revelation of God. He therefore suggests the following interpretation of other religions.

First thesis

Christianity understands itself as the absolute religion, for all human beings, and no other religion is equal. But, since Christianity had a beginning in history, it has not in every time and place been the only way to achieve salvation. Therefore Christianity is only the absolute and only religion for all people with respect to their ultimate destination. It is recognised that the obligation of Christianity comes to different people at different times.

Second thesis

Until an individual encounters the Christian Gospel, a non-Christian religion can contain elements of a natural knowledge of God. It can also contain supernatural elements through the grace of Christ. This means that non-Christian religions can be recognised as lawful (in various degrees).

This thesis has two parts:

1 Although it is possible that non-Christian religions contain supernatural, grace-filled elements, this does not entail that every aspect of a non-Christian religion is harmless. But God wishes every human being to be saved, including those who lived before Christ. Therefore, we must conclude that every person is somehow exposed to the influence of divine grace. It is senseless and cruel to suggest that most people living beyond the reach of Christianity are so evil that they should not receive the offer of grace. Thus, it is not impossible that grace is at work in the spiritual life of the individual wherever the individual makes a moral decision.
2 Even if pre-Christian religions contain corruption, error and moral mistakes, they can also have positive significance. Religions other than Christianity contain elements of supernatural influence by grace. Human beings can live in relationship to God only in society and must therefore have the right and the duty to live in relationship to God in the religious and social realities available.

Third thesis

Members of religions other than Christianity are 'anonymous Christians'. Proclamation of the Gospel does not turn someone abandoned by God into a Christian, but turns an anonymous Christian into someone who knows about their Christian belief. Nevertheless, a Christian still has a better chance of salvation than someone who is an anonymous Christian.

Fourth thesis

Missionary activity is still required to bring anonymous Christians to explicit consciousness of Christianity. It may seem presumptuous to think of non-Christians as anonymous Christians, but God is greater than human beings and the Church.

Hick's objections to religious inclusivism

Hick notes that the idea of the 'anonymous Christian' has been regarded as offensive to many non-Christians, who question whether Christians would find it acceptable to be described as 'anonymous Muslims'. Nevertheless, Hick suggests, inclusivism, minus the offensive description, is the most common view among Christian theologians and church leaders. It allows them to say that Christianity is distinctive and central, but does not require them to say that non-Christians are destined for hell. In Islam, he suggests, the idea of the People of the Book might be thought of as a form of inclusivism, with the full truth being found in Islam, but Jews and Christians having at least some of it.

Hick argues that this view still has some unacceptable implications, however. He suggests that we think of the solar system as an analogy, with the sun as God in the centre and the planets as the religions. For inclusivism, the sun falls directly on the Earth (Christianity), whereas the other planets receive only the light which is reflected from the Earth. Alternatively, thinking in terms of economics, wealth (divine grace) 'trickles down in diluted forms' (8) to other faiths below.

Hick acknowledges that, historically, neither Christians nor Muslims have lived up to the divine will. But, he asks, can we say that the people of one faith are better behaved than those of the other? Or is it, rather, the case that saints and sinners seem to exist about equally in both? Furthermore, he suggests, as far as he can tell, the fruits of religious belief are not obviously concentrated within his own religion, Christianity, but are spread evenly across a range of cultures and religions. If this is so, then, he argues, we cannot be inclusivists.

Reflection

On what grounds does Hick object to inclusivism? How might an inclusivist respond to Hick's objections?

• PLURALISM

Radhakrishnan

Radhakrishnan observes (1967) that religious believers sometimes become 'missionaries of hatred' towards other religions, and that this is inconsistent with the spirit of true religion (1967: 117–118). He quotes Hugo Grotius' assertion that:

> there was no sense at all in Catholics and Protestants seeking to impose their special dogmas on each other and that, if only they would *think* quietly, instead of *feeling* wildly, humanity would be relieved of much meaningless wastage and much atrocious suffering.

(118)

Radhakrishnan suggests that, in all religions, we see the universal through the concrete; we see 'The One Luminous, the maker of all, the great self always dwelling in the hearts of people, revealed through love, intuition, intelligence. Whoever knows him becomes immortal' (Upanishads, quoted at 118). Reality is immutable, but our perception of it changes. All theologies are human attempts to try to explain experience of the Divine, which is so great that it cannot be described in human language.

Radhakrishnan claims that, when talking about Ultimate Reality, the concepts used are symbols which should be regarded more in the manner of poetry than logic. When we emphasise the ineffable character of Ultimate Reality we refer to it as the Absolute, but when we see it as the creative principle of everything which exists, we refer to it as God. So the Absolute and God are two aspects of the same Reality.

Radhakrishnan notes that there are many descriptions of God, and that these are opinions rather than objects of knowledge. For the Greeks, God is absolute reality, whereas for the Romans God is a lawgiver who intervenes in the world and is subject to human passions. In many religions, God is 'an aggressive despot, full of phobias and complexes' (123), while Paul Tillich (1886–1965) favours a God who is the 'ground of all being' and the source of our 'ultimate concern', and John Robinson (1919–1983) similarly rejects the idea of a God who exists 'out there'. Radhakrishnan suggests that, in the various representations of God we catch a glimpse of 'a substantial being superior to the world', but talk about God is merely symbolic. For Radhakrishnan, religion is 'the will of the creature to raise himself above himself through toil and effort. All people, religious or non-religious, have this urge' (125). God is not a being who interferes with the natural laws of the universe, neither is God responsible for disease and disaster. Rather, 'God is the deepest in us which we have to get at through prayer and meditation' (126). Radhakrishnan suggests that spiritual experience is described by many different writers in different times and languages, but that the world must be united by the realisation that we must find again the sense of community which we have lost, get rid of hatred and intolerance, and 'recognize the super-natural reality in which we are all one' (127). All religions require the practice of brotherly love; knowledge of divine things is not sufficient without love. The religious life is also marked by dedication; we must have a purpose to live and die for and it is this lack of purpose which makes our lives meaningless.

Radhakrishnan suggests that, fifty years earlier (than 1967), it would have been regarded as a betrayal of one's own faith to look for that which is valuable in other religions, but now we can see that the different religious traditions are governed by the same spirit and work for the salvation of humankind and the universe. The religions may call God by different names, but they all apply to the same Supreme being. All the religions, at their best, require that human beings attempt to understand each other 'in a spirit of humility and friendliness' (129) and whatever enables us to sense the Divine is permitted. Thus, for example, Gandhi said:

> I do not believe in the exclusive divinity of the Vedas. I believe the Bible, the Koran and the Zend-Avesta to be as divinely inspired as the Vedas . . . Hinduism is not a missionary religion. In it there is room for the worship of all the prophets in the world . . . Hinduism tells everyone to worship God according to his own faith or dharma, and so it lives in peace with all religions.
>
> (quoted in Radhakrishnan, 129–130)

Radhakrishnan suggests that we should adopt a tentative attitude towards our own faith because we are aware of the limitations of the human mind with regard to the nature of truth. Although we might be tempted to claim that only our own religion has an adequate grasp of the truth, we know that others make similar claims. Further, if God is Love and is the creator of all creatures, it is unlikely that God has favourites among humankind and must therefore be perceptible to all. Thus, all revelations of the Divine must be regarded as valid. This is not to say that we should ignore the differences between religions altogether, however; diversity contains 'precious spiritual insight' and thus we should aim for 'a joining together of differences so that the integrity of each is preserved' (134).

Hick

Hick was, perhaps, the best-known religious pluralist of recent times and wrote prolifically on the subject across several decades. For Hick (2005), religious pluralism is the belief that no single religion has the truth, or the only way to salvation, but that each religion is a different manifestation of the same divine reality which we cannot know about directly but which lies behind the religions of humankind.

By 'salvation', Hick means 'a process of human transformation in this life from natural self-centredness to a new orientation centred in the transcendent divine reality, God, and leading to its fulfilment beyond life' (11). He argues that, as far as it is possible to tell, this process is taking place, or failing to take place, to the same extent in all the world's great religions.

Hick suggests that there are two main approaches:

1 To begin from one's own faith and explore the ways in which it supports the belief that salvation may be found to the same extent in other religions. He gives an example from the Qur'an:

> If God had pleased He would surely have made you one people (professing one faith). But He wished to try and test you by that which He gave you. So try to excel in good deeds. To Him you will all return in the end, when He will tell you of what you were at variance.
>
> (5:48, quoted in Hick, 12)

Hick notes that this can only be done from within a faith by its believers. He therefore favours the following:

2 All the great religious traditions teach that Ultimate Reality cannot be completely understood or described by human beings. For example, Aquinas said that 'God surpasses every form that our intellect reaches' ([1261–1263]: I, 14:3, quoted in Hick, 13). So there is a difference between God in Godself, and God as known by humankind. This distinction is seen in, for example, the work of Christian mystics such as Meister Eckhart, who made a distinction between the unknowable Godhead, and the knowable God of the scriptures, and the doctrines and worship of the Church. Teaching about the unknowability of God in Godself is also found in the work of Islamic mystics such as Kwaja Abdullah Ansari (1006–1088), while the contrast between the unknowable God and God as known by humankind is found in the work of Ibn Arabi, who said that, generally speaking, most human beings have:

> an individual concept of their Lord, which they ascribe to Him and in which they seek Him. So long as the Reality is presented to them according to it they recognize Him and affirm Him, whereas if presented in another form, they deny Him, flee from Him and treat Him improperly, while at the same time imagining that they are acting toward Him fittingly.
>
> (quoted in Hick, 14)

So, Hick argues, the Ultimate as it is itself is experienced and described by humankind in different ways which depend upon their historical and cultural situations, and these different ways are the world's religions. This way of understanding the relationship between different religions seems to Hick to be the best way to make sense of the situation.

Brian Hebblethwaite's objection to Hick's religious pluralism

Brian Hebblethwaite (b. 1939) (1993) argues that Hick's pluralism leads him ultimately to a non-realist view of God – in other words, to the view that the idea of God is just a human creation; there is no God independently of our thoughts about God. Hebblethwaite notes that Hick has, for decades, argued against the view that talk about God is not concerned with truth-claims about the transcendent (as, indeed, he continues to do in his 2005 paper). But, Hebblethwaite suggests, his understanding of the nature of the truth which underlies the experiences and claims of the different religions has changed significantly over time. In his early work, he spoke of faith in a personal God revealed in Jesus Christ, whereas in his later works, he talks of an 'Ultimate' or a 'Real' which is manifested in both the personal deities of the monotheistic faiths and the impersonal representations of the Divine found in Theravada Buddhism or Vedantic Hinduism.

For Hick, all experience is 'experiencing-as' – i.e. everything we experience is interpreted by us in some way. When we experience the natural world, we apply concepts to our experience so that we see ourselves as living in a world of interacting material objects. Similarly, moral experience sees inter-personal life as imposing demands and obligations on us. So, Christian religious experience is experience of the world as created by God and as the sphere in which God's providence operates. In each case, Hick follows Kant in arguing that the mind contributes to the interpretation of the experience. Thus, there is a Kantian distinction between the noumenon, the thing as it is in itself, and the phenomenon, the thing as it appears to us – between the Real as it is in itself and its various divine manifestations.

Just as Willard Van Orman Quine (1908–2000) sees the possibility of many different ways of interpreting our experience of the world, so Hick now sees a plurality of religious interpretations of the world. In his early writings he spoke of religion in solely Christian terms, but now this is only one of a range of phenomenal interpretations of a noumenal reality. Much of what was originally ascribed to the object of religious experience is now seen as just one way in which a noumenal object appears to those in a particular religious tradition. Hick now uses the term 'the Real' for the noumenal religious object, and the God of Judaeo-Christian theism is one of the 'personae' of the Real – i.e. the ways in which the Real is represented as a being worthy of worship, which sustains and transforms the lives of human beings. In these traditions, the resources of the transcendent are experienced as grace and love. In other traditions the Real is represented through 'impersonae' – a non-personal Absolute – e.g. *Brahman* in

Vedantic Hinduism, or *Nirvana* or *Sunyata* in Buddhism. In these, union with the Absolute leads to peace, bliss and compassion.

Hebblethwaite claims that Hick moves from the view that experience of the Christian God as a source of grace and love is an experience of the noumenal reality, to the view that experience of the Christian God as a source of grace and love is experience only of a phenomenal reality and not of Ultimate Reality as it is in itself. Thus, Christianity is just one of a number of personalist manifestations of the Real, and descriptions of God are understood as myths which express religious attitudes conducive to ethical and spiritual transformation.

Hebblethwaite argues that Hick seems to move from a half-way stage regarding the truth content of religious beliefs, in which he thinks that the religions are ultimately complementary rather than rival truths, to a later view in which religious doctrines refer at the phenomenal level to personae or impersonae of the Real, but function mythologically at the noumenal level. The former seems to suggest that religious beliefs are mythological only at the phenomenal level; the latter argues that they are mythological at both the phenomenal and the noumenal levels and that there is therefore little or no underlying truth.

This means that the ultimate referent of religious language, the noumenal Real, becomes more unknown as Hick's view develops. Almost nothing can be said of the noumenon. But it is necessary to retain a vague transcendent Real? Cupitt suggests that the 'personae' and 'impersonae' can be understood as human social constructs without a transcendent Real. They may be spiritually effective in the lives of faith communities with no object of faith at all. So the noumenal Real has become redundant, and this threatens Hick's critical realism.

But Hick does still seem committed to belief in something which is transcendent. Hebblethwaite suggests that this belief takes three forms:

1 There is an ultimate transcendent Reality;
2 Human transformation requires non-human spiritual resources; and
3 Human life will be extended after death and there will be some kind of perfected consummation.

According to Hebblethwaite, Hick's pluralism requires that all other religious assertions are mythological. But, Hebblethwaite asks, might these three claims not, themselves, collapse into redundancy? And can religious believers accept that these three truth-claims represent their tradition's central doctrines?

Reflection

What is Hebblethwaite's objection to Hick's religious pluralism? To what extent do you think his objection is justified?

• AN ALTERNATIVE INTERPRETATION OF RELIGIOUS PLURALISM

Masao Abe (1915–2006) (1985) acknowledges Cobb's objection to religious pluralism that, although we can identify a number of respects in which the world's religions are similar, there are also fundamental differences between them. For example, what Christians mean by 'God the Father' is not the same as what Buddhists mean by 'Emptiness'. But Cobb argues that, although the ultimacy of the Buddhist's 'Emptiness' and the Christian's 'God the Father' are not the same, they are complementary in that they do not exclude each other; the concept of Emptiness does not necessarily conflict with the claim that I should trust God.

Abe claims that the reason for this complementarity is not clear, however. Even if we accept that the doctrine of Emptiness answers questions about what things are, and the Christian God answers questions about how and why things are, the relationship between the what/how/why questions is unclear.

Abe therefore develops a version of religious pluralism which features the Buddha's teaching of the doctrine of *madhyama pratipad* (the Middle Way), a 'positionless position' concerning the nature of Ultimate Reality. *Pratitya-samutpada* (dependent co-origination) is another term for this Middle Way and was described by Nagarjuna (c. 150–250) in terms of 'Emptiness' which can be realised only existentially, not conceptually. On this view, there is no theory about the nature of 'Ultimate Reality' and no notion of a common denominator in all religious traditions. From the positionless position there is no Absolute, because of the Emptiness or nonsubstantiality of everything, but the relative ultimacy of different traditions is recognised without denying their distinctiveness.

Abe's proposal also features the Mahayana Buddhist three-body (*tri-kaya*) doctrine. According to this doctrine, there are three kinds of body in which the Buddha is manifested:

1 The *nirmana-kaya*, or assumed-body/apparitional-body/transformation-body – i.e. the historical Buddha which was the means by which the suprahistorical Buddha revealed himself to his earthly disciples.
2 The *sambhoga-kaya*, or bliss-body/reward-body/enjoyment-body – i.e. the suprahistorical Buddha who has fulfilled the requirements of Dharma (teaching about the moral laws of the universe) and is enjoying virtues as a consequence of the merit obtained.
3 The *dharma-kaya*, or truth-body – i.e. an impersonal 'body' beyond time and space, without form or colour and identified with *sunyata* or Emptiness. This can take the form of the other two bodies (and has done so on many occasions), and is the ground of everything.

Abe suggests a threefold understanding of reality in terms of:

1 'Lord' (equivalent to 1. above – that is, a historical religious figure who is the centre of faith – e.g. Jesus Christ or Gautama Buddha – or, applying the term 'Lord' in the sense of 'Master', Moses or Muhammad);

2 'God' (2. – that is, a supra-historical personal and virtuous God – e.g. Yahweh, Allah, *Ishvara*, etc);

3 'Boundless Openness' or 'Formless Emptiness' (3. – that is, Truth, the ultimate ground for both historical religious figures and personal Gods).

On Abe's view, the Gods of the world's religions are understood as deities which have attained the fulfilment of Ultimate Reality but have a particular name and form which enable them to be distinguished from each other. Behind these there is an Ultimate Reality which is revealed both in personal Gods and in historical religious figures. He concludes that each religion should realise that 'Boundless Openness' is its basis, in order to develop understanding between religions and to encourage them to learn from each other in interfaith dialogue.

Reflection

How does Abe address the problems with religious pluralism? To what extent do you think that he is successful?

• THEOLOGIES OF DIALOGUE

Many Christian theologians now argue that none of the three ways of approaching religious diversity which we have considered in this chapter are adequate for the task of religious dialogue. Rowan Williams (b. 1950) (2000) suggests that exclusivism rules out dialogue, while inclusivism 'makes a bid for ownership of all that is tolerable and recognizable in other traditions', and pluralism 'allows no more than unquestioning co-existence' (95).

Gavin D'Costa (b. 1958) (2011) aims to expound the teaching of the Roman Catholic Church, drawing in particular on the documents 'The Dogmatic Constitution on the Church' (*Lumen Gentium*, 1964), section 16, and 'The Declaration on the Relation of the Church to Non-Christian Religions' (*Nostra Aetate*, 1965) of the Second Vatican Council (1962–1965). He notes that the basic teaching of the Catholic Church is that salvation is possible for non-Christians, although the work of developing and defending this teaching is still ongoing. With regard to the major world religions he identifies in these documents the following points:

Judaism:

1 Catholics are encouraged to learn from Judaism and appreciate it.
2 Neither all Jewish people at the time of Jesus nor all Jewish people in the present day can be regarded as responsible for the death of Jesus.
3 Anti-Semitism at any time, whether past or present, is strongly condemned.

Islam:

1 Both Christians and Muslims worship the same God.
2 Christians and Muslims have in common the patriarch Abraham, and the high esteem given to Jesus and Mary the mother of Jesus.
3 It is necessary to move on from times of troubled relations with Muslims for the sake of the 'common good'.

Hinduism and Buddhism:

1 The New Testament includes an account of Paul's speech on the Areopagus in which he refers to those who believe in an 'Unknown God', and in I Timothy 2:4, God is said to desire the salvation of all people. This shows that a genuine search for God might be found even in non-theistic religions.
2 In Hinduism, the Divine is sought in myth, philosophy and, in the non-theistic traditions, practices such as asceticism and, in the bhakti traditions, in the love of God.
3 In some forms of Buddhism the practitioners seek divine assistance.
4 Buddhist teaching concerning the unsatisfactoriness of a constantly changing world and the need to seek liberation or enlightenment is also affirmed.

D'Costa notes that, although the Second Vatican Council referred only briefly to a limited number of religions, it began an engagement with other religions which is both positive and critical. It is positive in that Catholic theologians are encouraged to:

1 Acknowledge that the Spirit of God may be at work within other religions.
2 Engage in dialogue with the members of other faiths in order to focus on that which they have in common, and to work together to help humankind in their struggle with evil and to encourage selfless service.

It is not uncritical, however, in that the Church is not regarded as just one of a number of equivalent ways to salvation. While the Holy Spirit (one of the three Persons of the Trinity, the other two of which are God the Father and God the Son [i.e. Jesus]) may be seen at work in other religious traditions, each of which may contain truth and goodness, for D'Costa, the Catholic Church is the only true way to salvation.[1]

Reflection

To what extent, in your view, does D'Costa's approach to religious diversity address the problems associated with religious diversity which were outlined in the introductory paragraph of this chapter?

• CONCLUSION

In this chapter we have examined one of the most challenging problems for the philosopher of religion and considered three common approaches to religious diversity – exclusivism, inclusivism and pluralism. Exclusivism appears to rule out dialogue between the members of different faiths, while inclusivism might be offensive to those who do not wish to be regarded as anonymous members of a faith tradition which is not their own. Pluralism, on the other hand, seems to gloss over the distinctive aspects of each faith in the hope of finding a single divine common denominator. D'Costa attempts to side-step the difficulties associated with each of these approaches but, since he claims that Christianity somehow includes or may be found in other faiths, it is difficult to avoid the conclusion that he has simply offered us a variant of religious inclusivism.

Therefore, perhaps we might return to Abe's interpretation of religious pluralism which acknowledges the distinctive aspects of the world's religions and enables us to say that *Ishvara*, Yahweh, God and Allah are not merely different manifestations of the same Ultimate Reality but that there might, nonetheless, be an underlying 'Boundless Openness' which is the ultimate ground of all divine and human existence.

• NOTE

1 I am grateful to Dr Elizabeth Phillips of Westcott House and the University of Cambridge for drawing my attention to theologies of dialogue.

• REFERENCES

Abe, Masao (1985) 'A Dynamic Unity in Religious Pluralism: A Proposal from the Buddhist Point of View' in John Hick and Hasan Askari (eds) *The Experience of Religious Diversity* (Brookfield, VT: Gower Publishing Co); reprinted in Andrew Eshleman (ed.) *Readings in Philosophy of Religion: East Meets West* (Malden, MA: Blackwell Publishing, 2008), 395–404.

Aquinas, Thomas (1955–1957 [1261–1263]) *Summa contra Gentiles* ed. Joseph Kenny Book I, trans. Anton C. Pegis (New York: Hanover House). http://dhspriory.org/thomas/ContraGentiles.htm Book I, Chapter 14:3.

D'Costa, Gavin (2011) 'Christianity and the World Religions: A Theological Appraisal' in Gavin D'Costa, Paul Knitter and Daniel Strange (eds) *Only One Way? Three Christian Responses to the Uniqueness of Christ in a Religiously Pluralist World* (London: SCM Press), 3–46.

Hebblethwaite, Brian (1993) 'John Hick and the Question of Truth in Religion' in Arvind Sharma (ed.) *God, Truth and Reality: Essays in Honour of John Hick* (New York, NY: St Martin's Press); reprinted in Andrew Eshleman (ed.) *Readings in Philosophy of Religion: East Meets West* (Malden, MA: Blackwell Publishing, 2008), 383–389.

Hick, John (2005) 'Religious Pluralism and Islam', www.johnhick.org.uk/article11.pdf.

Plantinga, Alvin (1995) 'Pluralism: A Defence of Religious Exclusivism' in Thomas D. Senor (ed.) *The Rationality of Belief and the Plurality of Faith* (Cornell, NY: Cornell

University Press); reprinted in Chad Meister (ed.) *The Philosophy of Religion Reader* (New York and Abingdon: Routledge, 2008) 40–59.

Radhakrishnan, Sarvepalli (1967) *Religion in a Changing World* (London: George, Allen and Unwin), Chapter 6.

Rahner, Karl (1966) *Theological Investigations*, Vol. V, 'Christianity and Non-Christian Religions' (Baltimore, MD: Helicon Press), 115–134; reprinted in Michael Peterson, William Hasker, Bruce Reichenbach and David Basinger (eds) *Philosophy of Religion: Selected Readings* (Oxford: Oxford University Press, 2014 [1996]), 606–613.

Williams, Rowan (2000) *On Christian Theology* (Oxford: Blackwell).

• FURTHER READING

Encyclopedia articles

Basinger, David (2015) 'Religious Diversity (Pluralism)', *Stanford Encyclopedia of Philosophy*, https://plato.stanford.edu/entries/religious-pluralism/.

Original articles in edited collections

Byrne, Peter (2004) 'It is Not Reasonable to Believe that Only One Religion is True' in Michael L. Peterson and Raymond J. Vanarragon (eds) *Contemporary Debates in Philosophy of Religion* (Malden, MA: Blackwell Publishing), 201–210.

Cobb, John B. (1996) 'Metaphysical Pluralism' in Joseph Prabhu (ed.) *The Intercultural Challenge of Raimon Panikkar* (Maryknoll, NY: Orbis Books), 49–54; extracts reprinted in Andrew Eshleman (ed.) *Readings in Philosophy of Religion: East Meets West* (Malden, MA: Blackwell Publishing, 2008), 390–394.

Quinn, Philip L. (2005) 'Religious Diversity: Familiar Problems, Novel Opportunities' in William J. Wainwright (ed.) *The Oxford Handbook of Philosophy of Religion* (Oxford: OUP), Chapter 16.

Yandell, Keith (2004) 'How to Sink in Cognitive Quicksand: Nuancing Religious Pluralism' in Michael L. Peterson and Raymond J. Vanarragon (eds) *Contemporary Debates in Philosophy of Religion* (Malden, MA: Blackwell Publishing), 191–200.

Extracts from articles or books in edited collections

Gellman, Jerome (2000) 'In Defence of a Contented Religious Exclusivism', *Religious Studies* 36, 4: 401–417; extract reprinted in Andrew Eshleman (ed.) *Readings in Philosophy of Religion: East Meets West* (Malden, MA: Blackwell Publishing, 2008), 374–382.

Gyatso, Tenzin (the fourteenth Dalai Lama of Tibet) (1999) *Ancient Wisdom, Modern World: Ethics for the New Millennium* (London: Abacus Books, 2001), 219–231; reprinted in Chad Meister (ed.) *The Philosophy of Religion Reader* (New York and Abingdon: Routledge, 2008), 79–85.

Halevi, Judah (1960 [c1140]) *Kuzari: A Book of Proof and Argument: An Apology for a Despised Religion*, ed. Isaaak Heinemann (New York, NY: Meridian Books), Book I, 27–37; extract reprinted in Eleonore Stump and Michael J. Murray (eds) *Philosophy of Religion: The Big Questions* (Oxford: Blackwell, 1999), 435–440.

Rahner, Karl (1966) *Theological Investigations*, Vol. V (London: Darton, Longman and Todd Ltd); extract reprinted in 'Christianity and the Non-Christian Religions' in John Hick and Brian Hebblethwaite (eds) *Christianity and Other Religions: Selected Readings* (Oxford: Oneworld Publications, 2001), 19–38.

Articles

Hick, John (2001) 'Is Christianity the Only True Religion, or One Among Others?' www.johnhick.org.uk/jsite/index.php/articles-by-john-hick/16-is-christianity-the-only-true-religion-or-one-among-others.

Books

Coward, Harold (ed.) (1987) *Modern Indian Responses to Religious Pluralism* (Albany, NY: State University of New York Press).

Dupres, Jacques (2001) *Toward a Christian Theology of Religious Pluralism* (Maryknoll, NY: Orbis Books).

Hick, John (1985) *Problems of Religious Pluralism* (New York, NY: St Martin's Press, LLC).

Quinn, Philip L. and Meeker, Kevin (eds) (2000) *The Philosophical Challenge of Religious Diversity* (New York, NY: Oxford University Press).

Schmidt-Leukel, Perry (ed.) (2008) *Buddhist Attitudes to Other Religions* (St Ottilien, Germany: EOS-Verlag).

Web resources

The Cambridge Interfaith Programme, www.interfaith.cam.ac.uk/.
Scriptural Reasoning, www.scripturalreasoning.org/.

17

voluntarist theories of religious belief

• INTRODUCTION

In Chapters 4–13 we considered various ways in which reason can be used to tell us about God's nature and existence. In each case, we saw that there are limits to what reason can accomplish. It may be able to show that belief in the Divine is not unreasonable, or it may be used to *support* belief in Divinity – but, at least in the case of classical theism, it cannot tell us conclusively what God is like, or prove that God exists. In this chapter and the next we will consider historical and contemporary versions of the claim that, even in the absence of conclusive arguments for the existence of the Divine, it is still rational to believe in the existence of the Divine.

• PASCAL'S WAGER

In his *Pensées*, Blaise Pascal (1623–1662) (1669) argues that, if there is a God, Xe is beyond our comprehension, and we are therefore unable to give rational arguments for belief. But God either exists or does not exist. Since we cannot use reason to determine which of these is or is not the case, we must wager (gamble) in favour of one or the other. In response to the objection that the right course of action is not to wager at all, Pascal replies that we have no choice but to wager.

Pascal argues that neither of the two choices represents a threat to our rationality. But the balance tips in favour of a wager that God exists when we consider the amount of happiness which we are likely to attain from each of the choices. If a wager that God exists turns out to be the correct choice, an infinity of infinitely happy life will result. Should it turn out to be the wrong choice, no happiness will have been lost. Since the 'prize' for correctly wagering that God exists is so great, Pascal argues, even if the chance of the wager being the correct one is much smaller than the chance of the wager turning out to be mistaken, it is rational to wager that God exists.

In response to someone who objects that he is made in such a way that he is unable to believe, Pascal suggests that, since inability to believe is caused by the passions, he should focus not on finding more proofs of God's existence but upon reducing his passions. In particular, Pascal recommends that, like others before him, he should behave as if he believed by taking holy water, attending masses, and so on, as this will bring about a natural religious belief.

Pascal claims that no harm will come to anyone who follows this course of action. Indeed, he says, such a person will be of good character and a true friend. Admittedly, he will be denied the pleasures associated with corrupt living, but this will be outweighed by the pleasures which will be available to him.

> ## Reflection
>
> To what extent does reason feature in Pascal's account of faith?

Objections to Pascal's wager

George Schlesinger (1925–2013) (1994) considers three objections:

Objection 1

Pascal's wager appeals to the scheming, calculating aspect of the human personality.

Schlesinger replies:

The wager was only a first step. Once the wager has been made, the wagerer is instructed to behave as if he believed in the hope of attaining genuine belief in God.

Schlesinger admits that we could still object to this on the grounds that, no matter how desirable the end result, it is still achieved by appealing to selfish motives; the person who eventually believes may live a good life in the process of attaining that belief, but he does so only because he wants to attain some good for himself.

But Schlesinger responds that almost every act fulfils some wish; even a philanthropist could be satisfying the need to reach the pinnacle of 'other-directedness'. He suggests that an action is deplorable only when it harms others or oneself by preventing us from striving after higher order pleasures. And the pleasure which Pascal recommends is of the highest order; so, if craving for this pleasure is counted as greed, then it is a form of greed which may be recommended.

The way of life which leads to genuine belief is not just a way of attaining a selfish end, however. Just as we may come to a genuine love of our fellow human beings by acting as if we genuinely loved them, so we may come to a genuine love for God by acting as if we loved God. So the wagerer who acts as if he believes is not simply doing something which is calculating or even commendable but is doing something which is essential for reaching his noble goal.

Objection 2 – The 'many gods' objection

Pascal seems to present us with only two options. But there are many others. Why could we not, for example, wager in favour of Osiris, Baal, Dagon, Zeus or Blodenwedd?

Might there not be, as Richard Gale (1932–2015) has suggested, an infinite number of logically possible deities, including the sidewalk crack deity who rewards only those who step on only one sidewalk crack during their lifetime? And might it not be the case, as Mackie has suggested, that there is a god who regards more favourably doubters or atheists who, in the manner of Hume, proportion their beliefs to the available evidence?

Schlesinger has three responses to the 'many gods' objection:

1 The existence of the greatest conceivable being is more probable than the existence of any other deity. Belief in this God is associated with theologies which have been developed across many centuries and have an internal coherence. They consist of propositions which appeal both to the intellect and to our nobler sentiments. Nothing equivalent exists for, for example, the sidewalk deity.
2 Statisticians such as Harold Jeffreys (1891–1989) have suggested that, although there may be many hypotheses which explain one set of experimental results, we should choose the simplest one – that is, the one with the smallest number of terms. With respect to deities, the concept of an absolutely perfect being is the simplest hypothesis.
3 The Principle of Sufficient Reason (PSR) shows that only some hypotheses are reasonable. For example, since there is no reason to believe that the melting point of gold will change from 1,604 degrees Celsius, there is sufficient reason to believe that it will remain the same. The PSR can be used to justify the rule that we should prefer the simplest explanation. The reason why we should prefer the simplest hypothesis is that it is unique – it is the only one in connection with which we cannot ask for a simpler hypothesis. For example, in mathematics, the PSR shows that the rectangle of greatest area which can be drawn in a circle is a square.

Schlesinger argues that the PSR can also be used to restrict the number of possible deities on which we might wager. He suggests that we could not give a sufficient reason why a deity was 95, 96 or 94% benevolent. But we can give a reason why there should be a deity who is 100% benevolent – and this is that it is impossible for a deity to be more than 100% benevolent. We could not, however, argue in a similar way that there must be a deity who is 0% benevolent on the grounds that it is impossible for there to be a deity who is less than 0% benevolent. This is because such a being would not be worthy of worship.

Objection 3

Schlesinger cites the objection of Antony Duff that the wager works regardless of how small the probability is (as long as its value is not zero), and that it promises infinite salvation. Therefore there is no point in acting religiously because, even if I do not do this, there must still be some probability that I will come to belief.

Schlesinger replies:

It is unreasonable to claim that the size of the reward means that the degree of probability of gaining it makes no difference. So, we should still try to increase the chances of our gaining faith. A rational wagerer will always bet on the outcome which has the best reward, but it is possible that the quality of the reward in this case, eternal life, might vary in accordance with the amount of effort used to attain it. Therefore, someone who follows their wager by acting as if they believed will have much longer to purify their soul than someone who merely wagers and waits for genuine faith to come at some future time.

> ## Reflection
>
> To what extent, in your view, does Schlesinger mount a successful defence of Pascal's argument?

• WILLIAM JAMES ON 'THE WILL TO BELIEVE'

James (1896) defends the rationality of 'voluntarily adopted faith' in his famous essay 'The Will to Believe'. He argues that a genuine choice between two sets of possible beliefs must be:

1 Live (in other words, both alternatives must be real possibilities, things which we have no reason not to believe);
2 Forced (it cannot be avoided – some choice has to be made); and
3 Momentous (it must make a real difference to our life).

But, James asks, can we change our opinions simply by choosing to do so? Can we, for example, choose to believe that Abraham Lincoln's existence was a myth? He cites Pascal's view of faith and admits that believing by our own volition does, at first sight, seem to be 'simply silly'. And, he asks, does this understanding of the nature of belief imply that we can choose which scientific beliefs to accept? Here, he refers to William Clifford's (1845–1879) essay 'The Ethics of Belief' (1877), in which Clifford argues that it is always wrong to accept a belief on the basis of insufficient evidence.

James responds, however, that what makes some hypotheses live for us and others dead often does not have much to do with reason. We might like to think that our opinions are the product of insight and logic, but we often believe as a consequence of 'fear and hope, prejudice and passion, imitation and partisanship, the circumpressure of our caste and set' (1990: 200 [1896]). James suggests that his listeners believe in such things as 'molecules and the conservation of energy, in democracy and necessary progress, [and] in Protestant Christianity . . . all for no reasons worthy of the name' (200). In such cases, he claims, our reason is satisfied, in most cases, if it is able to find 'a few arguments that will do to recite in case our credulity is criticized by someone else' (200). Therefore, Pascal's argument is, after all, 'a regular clincher' (201).

James therefore defends the view that, when a question is a genuine option and we cannot find the answer by means of intellectual arguments, we not only may but must use 'our passional nature' to find an answer. We cannot simply refuse to find an answer because this, too, is 'a passional decision' and risks losing the truth to the same extent as answering yes or no.

James observes that almost everything, except that there is consciousness, can be doubted because no concrete test of truth has ever been agreed upon. He remarks that there is nothing which at least someone has thought to be undeniably true while another has thought it to be uncontrovertibly false. We nevertheless have to believe something. James says that Clifford recommends that we should believe nothing rather than risk being mistaken. But, James says, Clifford is merely expressing a horror of being deceived. James shares that horror, but claims that there are worse things which can happen to a person: Clifford 'is like a general informing his soldiers that it is better to keep out of battle forever than to risk a single wound' (205), but we do not gain victory over our enemies or Nature in this way.

James admits that there may be some things about which our beliefs do not matter. For example, he suggests, it may make no practical difference to most of us whether we have a theory about Röntgen rays (X-rays, discovered in 1895 by Wilhelm Röntgen, who called this type of radiation X-radiation to indicate that it was of an unknown type) or the causality of conscious states, but some decisions – about morality, for example – are forced upon us because they cannot wait for proof.

In some cases, James suggests, the desire for truth can bring about that truth. For example, a man who believes that a woman loves him may find that she does, and a man in whose life a promotion or appointment is a live hypothesis will make sacrifices for them in advance and may find that his faith 'creates its own verification' (208). Therefore, he concludes, there are some situations which are only brought about as a consequence of prior faith in their realisation.

According to James, religion makes two claims upon us. Firstly, it says that 'the best things are the more eternal things' (209), and, secondly, it maintains that we are better off if we believe this.

Assuming that religious belief is a live option (since anyone who thinks that it is not would be unable to continue the discussion), James argues that it is momentous because our choice may lead us to gain or lose something of great benefit, and that it is forced because we cannot avoid the issue by remaining sceptical while waiting for further evidence; if we do that, we may avoid making a mistake if religious belief is untrue, but we risk losing the benefits of religion if it is true. James says that he prefers to choose belief and take the risk that he may be mistaken since, he says:

> I do not wish . . . to forfeit my sole chance in life of getting upon the winning side – that chance depending, of course, on my willingness to run the risk of acting as if my passional need of taking the world religiously might be prophetic and right.
>
> (210)

Reflection

To what extent does reason remain useful, for James? What are its limitations?

Objections to James on the nature of religious belief

Although Mackie (1982) is, in some respects, sympathetic towards James's arguments, he identifies three possible causes of concern:

1 James gives us little guidance regarding how we are to make our choice. He says only that the best things are the more eternal things, but it is not clear how this might help us decide what to believe.
2 James exaggerates the extent to which we decide what to believe on the basis of passion. Some of the beliefs which James lists in this category are, in fact, beliefs which we hold on the basis of authority, where we have good reason to believe that the authority has knowledge, or at least a rational opinion, and has no reason to deceive us. We may even have evidence from our own experience that the authority is usually reliable in the area under discussion. Mackie suggests that, in the case of religion, it is by no means clear that decisions about faith must be made on the basis of our passions because rational discussion has reached an impasse.
3 Mackie argues that belief in a personal God should no longer be a live hypothesis. But, if it is, and we choose to believe it, we must, at the same time, allow our belief to remain constantly open to testing and the possibility that it may be falsified. If faith is a kind of experiment, it must allow itself to be tested in accordance with the principles of experimental inquiry. Mackie suggests that any favourable result of such an experiment would have to consist in a series of religious experiences which could not be explained by other means.

Reflection

Which, if any, of these objections do you think are fatal to James's position?

• CONCLUSION

Both Pascal and James argue that it is in our best interests to believe in eternal things, more specifically, in the case of Pascal, eternal happiness. Both scholars acknowledge that we do not know whether or not there are eternal things or eternal happiness – which is why we must wager or choose on the basis of our passions – but if the concept of eternal things or eternal happiness could be shown to be incoherent, the argument would be substantially weakened.

In Chapter 19, we will consider an argument for the view that the concept of eternal happiness is incoherent. For James, however, the eternal aspect of the universe is represented in the world's religions in personal form, which means that the universe is not an *It* but a *Thou*, and that any relationship which is possible between human persons might also be possible in this context. He argues that, although we do not know its origin, the feeling that, in believing that there are gods, we are doing the universe the deepest possible service, appears to be 'part of the living essence of the religious hypothesis' (210). Freedom to believe does not, however, apply to the kind of faith defined by the schoolboy who said that 'Faith is when you believe something that you know ain't true' (211). Faith of this kind is a dead religious hypothesis; we are free to believe only live options – those which cannot be shown by reason to be absurd – which cannot be decided by the intellect alone.

• REFERENCES

Clifford, William Kingdon (1901 [1877]) 'The Ethics of Belief' in *Lectures and Essays* (New York, NY: Macmillan), 163–176; reprinted in Brian Davies (ed.) *Philosophy of Religion: A Guide and Anthology* (Oxford: Oxford University Press, 2000), 31–35.

James, William (1896) 'The Will to Believe' in *The Will to Believe and Other Essays in Popular Philosophy* (New York, NY: Longmans, Green and Co.); extract reprinted in John Hick (ed.) *Classical and Contemporary Readings in the Philosophy of Religion* (Englewood Cliffs, NJ: Prentice Hall, 1990), 196–212.

Mackie, J. L. (1982) *The Miracle of Theism: Arguments for and Against the Existence of God* (Oxford: Oxford University Press), 207–210.

Pascal, Blaise (1966 [1669]) *Pensées*, trans. with an introduction by A. J. Krailsheimer (Harmondsworth: Penguin Books), 150–153; reprinted in Michael Palmer *The Question of God: An Introduction and Sourcebook* (London: Routledge, 2001), 326–328.

Schlesinger, George N. (1994) 'A Central Theistic Argument' in Jeff Jordan (ed.) *Gambling on God: Essays on Pascal's Wager* (Lanham, MD: Rowman and Littlefield), 83–99; reprinted in Eleonore Stump and Michael J. Murray (eds) *Philosophy of Religion: The Big Questions* (Oxford: Blackwell, 1999), 302–312.

• FURTHER READING

Encyclopedia articles

Goodman, Russell (2013) 'William James', *Stanford Encyclopedia of Philosophy*, http:// plato.stanford.edu/archives/win2013/entries/james.

Hajek, Alan (2012) 'Pascal's Wager', *Stanford Encyclopedia of Philosophy*, http://plato. stanford.edu/archives/win2012/entries/pascal-wager.

Jordan, Jeff (2013) 'Pragmatic Arguments and Belief in God', *Stanford Encyclopedia of Philosophy*, https://plato.stanford.edu/entries/pragmatic-belief-god/.

Simpson, David (2017) 'Blaise Pascal', *Internet Encyclopedia of Philosophy*, www.iep. utm.edu/pascal-b/.

Original articles in edited collections

Golding, Joshua (2013 [2007]) 'The Wager Argument' in Chad Meister and Paul Copan (eds) *The Routledge Companion to Philosophy of Religion* (Abingdon: Routledge), 445–453.

Jordan, Jeff (2005) 'Pascal's Wagers and James's Will to Believe' in William J. Wainwright (ed.) *The Oxford Handbook of Philosophy of Religion* (Oxford: OUP), Chapter 7.

Jordan, Jeffrey (2010 [1997]) 'Pragmatic Arguments' in Charles Taliaferro, Paul Draper and Philip L. Quinn (eds) *A Companion to Philosophy of Religion* (Chichester: Wiley-Blackwell) 425–433.

Articles

Christian, Rose Ann (2005) 'Truth and Consequences in James' "The Will to Believe"', *International Journal for Philosophy of Religion* 58, 1: 1–26.

Saka, Paul (2001) 'Pascal's Wager and the Many Gods Objection', *Religious Studies* 37, 3: 321–341.

Schlecht, Ludwig F. (1997) 'Re-reading "The Will to Believe"', *Religious Studies* 33, 2: 217–225.

Wetzel, James (1993) 'Two Ways of Wagering with Pascal', *Religious Studies* 29, 2: 139–149.

Books

Davis, Stephen T. (1997) *God, Reason and Theistic Proofs* (Edinburgh: Edinburgh University Press), Chapter 9.

Evans, C. Stephen (1998) *Faith Beyond Reason* (Edinburgh: Edinburgh University Press), 47–52.

Jordan, Jeff (ed.) (1994) *Gambling on God: Essays on Pascal's Wager* (Lanham, MD: Rowman and Littlefield).

Mackie, J. L. (1982) *The Miracle of Theism: Arguments For and Against the Existence of God* (Oxford: Clarendon Press), 199–210.

Sharma, Arvind (1997) *The Philosophy of Religion: A Buddhist Perspective* (Oxford: Oxford University Press), Chapter 5.

Taliaferro, Charles (1998) *Contemporary Philosophy of Religion* (Oxford: Blackwell), 381–384.

Web resources

James, William (n.d.) A collection of resources may be found at: www.uky.edu/~eushe2/Pajares/james.html.

Audio

Bragg, Melvyn (2005) 'Pragmatism', *In Our Time*, BBC Radio 4, first broadcast 17 November 2005, www.bbc.co.uk/programmes/p003k9f5.

Bragg, Melvyn (2013) 'Pascal', *In Our Time*, BBC Radio 4, first broadcast 19 September 2013, www.bbc.co.uk/programmes/b03b2v6m.

18
reformed epistemology

• INTRODUCTION

In the previous chapter, we examined the views of Pascal and James on the relationship between reason and faith. In both cases, we saw that there are some religious beliefs which can be accepted only on the basis of faith – and that both argued that it is rational to accept these beliefs on the basis of faith.

Reformed Epistemologists have argued that there are some religious beliefs which must be accepted on the basis of our experience of God, and that all other religious beliefs are dependent on these beliefs. Such beliefs are known as 'properly basic' – they are beliefs on which other beliefs depend, and which can be accepted without proof.

• PLANTINGA'S REFORMED EPISTEMOLOGY

Plantinga is, perhaps, the best-known exponent of Reformed Epistemology, developed in a number of books and papers over several decades, culminating in *Warranted Christian Belief* (2000). More recently, Plantinga has produced a shorter and more accessible account of the arguments of this book in his *Knowledge and Christian Belief* (2015). Anthologies of readings (e.g. Peterson et al., 2014) tend to reproduce his earlier essays, however, which provide a short introduction to the key arguments which are developed in more detail in his later work. We therefore begin this chapter by considering the arguments put forward by Plantinga in a very early account of Reformed Epistemology, noting some more recent developments in Plantinga's thought later in the chapter.

Plantinga argues (1982) that theologians in the Reformed tradition reject natural theology, and gives five reasons derived from the work of Herman Bavinck (1854–1921):

1 People do not, as a matter of fact, believe in God on the basis of arguments for God's existence.
2 Belief in God can be rational without arguments for God's existence.
3 It is not *possible* to come to belief on the basis of arguments because the arguments of natural theology [arguments about the nature and existence of God based on observation of nature] do not work.
4 Scripture begins with God as the starting point, and the believer should do the same.

5 We believe in the existence of the self and the external world without arguments, so it
   is acceptable to believe in God without arguments.

Plantinga cites the view of John Calvin (1509–1564) that all human beings have a *sensus
divinitatis*, a sense of divinity, and that it is human sinfulness which prevents us from being
aware of this. Furthermore, God not only put the seeds of religion into human minds but
reveals Godself daily in the divine workmanship which can be seen throughout the
universe, and in particular in the heavens. Therefore, human beings, even those with the
least education, cannot open their eyes without being compelled to see God. Plantinga
suggests that no argument is implied; in such circumstances, Calvin claimed, a person
simply *knows* that God exists. Thirdly, Plantinga, again following Calvin, claims that it is
not simply the case that the Christian does not need arguments; a person ought not to
believe on the basis of argument because faith based on argument is unstable.

According to Plantinga, the Reformers thought that belief in God can be taken as basic; a
person is rational to believe in God without arguments, and without basing this belief on
any other beliefs. They rejected classical foundationalism, however. Foundationalism is
the view that some of our beliefs must be based on other, foundational, beliefs. Plantinga
suggests that there are different forms of foundationalism, as follows:

Strong (classical) foundationalism	Weak foundationalism
Ancient/medieval foundationalism (e.g. Aquinas) A proposition is properly basic only if it is: i self-evident, or ii evident to the senses (e.g. 'There is a tree before me').	A proposition is properly basic if it is: i self-evident, ii evident to the senses, or iii incorrigible for the subject.
Modern foundationalism (e.g. Descartes) A proposition is properly basic if it is: i self-evident, ii incorrigible for the subject (something which a person cannot doubt) (e.g. '*It seems to me that* I see a tree'; there may or may not be a tree there, but I cannot doubt that it seems to me that there is one).	But other kinds of propositions may also be properly basic, including belief in the existence of God.

So, according to Plantinga, foundationalism is the view that some beliefs are properly
basic, but different types of foundationalism imply different views about which beliefs
may be regarded as properly basic. The Reformers rejected classical foundationalism
because it excluded beliefs about God, but leaned towards weak foundationalism
because it included beliefs about God.

The Great Pumpkin objection

Plantinga defends Reformed Epistemology against the objection that, if belief in God is
properly basic, why can we not say that any belief is properly basic – such as the belief

that the Great Pumpkin returns every Halloween? Or that if I flap my arms hard enough, I will be able to fly around the room?

Plantinga says that Reformed Epistemology does not allow us to hold that beliefs such as these are properly basic. Although some propositions seem self-evident when they are not, it would not be rational to accept as a basic belief the denial of a statement the truth of which seems to you to be self-evident. For example, if it seems to you that you see a tree, it would be irrational to take as basic the proposition that you do not see a tree.

Plantinga thinks that there are no arguments which show us what is and is not properly basic. But we can tell the difference between propositions which are and are not properly basic by collecting *examples* of statements which are properly basic and those which are not. We can then construct hypotheses regarding the necessary and sufficient conditions (a necessary condition is a set of circumstances which must exist for an event to occur; a sufficient condition is one which may enable an event to occur, although there may be other possible causes of the event) of proper basicality and use our examples to test these hypotheses. So, under the right conditions it is rational to believe that you see a human person before you, but this belief is not based on others you hold – it is properly basic for you, even though it is neither self-evident nor incorrigible for you.

For Plantinga, then, the Reformed Epistemologist can say that belief in the Great Pumpkin is not properly basic, even though they hold that belief in God *is* properly basic. But they must say that there is a relevant difference between the two beliefs, and there are plenty of these. For example, they can say, like Calvin, that God has implanted in us a natural tendency to see God's work in the world, and that the same cannot be said of the Great Pumpkin – because there is no Great Pumpkin, and there is no natural tendency to accept beliefs about the Great Pumpkin.

Reflection

Do you think that this is a good response to the Great Pumpkin objection?

• PLANTINGA ON WARRANTED CHRISTIAN BELIEF

Warranted Christian Belief (2000) is the third of Plantinga's trilogy of books on warrant. 'Warrant' is defined as 'that property . . . enough of which is what makes the difference between knowledge and mere true belief' (2000: xi). In this book, Plantinga argues that there are two kinds of possible objection to Christian belief – *de jure* objections, those which claim that religious belief is rationally unacceptable in some way, and *de facto* objections, objections to the truth of Christian belief. Plantinga argues that there are no good *de jure* objections which do not depend on *de facto* objections. He considers key defeaters (things which would count against it, to the extent that one must reject it) for religious belief – the findings of biblical scholarship, religious pluralism and the problem of evil – and argues that, in each case, the Christian has a source of warrant for his/her beliefs which others do not – i.e. the Bible and the testimony of the Holy Spirit.

• POSSIBLE DEFEATERS FOR BELIEF IN GOD

Robert Pargetter (1990) notes that some alleged experiences of God are problematic because they occur in circumstances which might be expected to produce such experiences; Pargetter suggests that this includes the experiences of St John of the Cross and other mystics. But, where there are no such circumstances, is the belief that many people do not believe in God's existence a defeater for belief in God? If, in similar circumstances, person A experiences God and person B does not, does this mean that A is mistaken?

Pargetter says that we could respond that:

1 Many others share A's experience.
2 A and those who share A's experience usually agree about experiences with most other people most of the time.

> ### Reflection
> To what extent do these make A's experience more likely to be genuine?

Pargetter says that we need not doubt the reliability of A's experience for two reasons:

1 There are physiological and neurological similarities between A and B which make it unlikely that A has a special mechanism for having experiences of God.
2 Difference in beliefs does not require a difference in sensory mechanisms; just as there is not a special mechanism for acquiring mathematical beliefs, so there is no special mechanism for acquiring beliefs about God.

So, how do we account for the different experiences? Pargetter suggests that perhaps A has acquired some kind of relevant skill or developed an improved awareness, and that musicians have such skills.

So the fact that some experience God and others do not does not constitute a defeater for the proper basicality of belief in God. This means that, provided B has no other reasons for accepting defeaters for A's belief, B should accept A's belief on the basis of A's testimony.

Even if there *is* a potential defeater (in addition to others' belief that God does not exist), however, how do we decide whether it outweighs an apparent religious experience? Plantinga considers the problem of evil as a possible defeater, but Pargetter argues that we cannot be sure which belief is defeated by which, since many theists do not consider that the existence of evil cancels out their experience of God.

Pargetter suggests that A's claim that her belief in God is properly basic ultimately depends on a holistic evaluation of the system of beliefs which accompany this belief. We must therefore consider such things as the cohesiveness, meaningfulness, explanatory potential, usefulness, contribution to well-being and survival potential of competing systems of beliefs.

Pargetter concludes that, for many people, theism may, indeed, be a basic belief which is grounded in experience, and which may be shown to be properly basic by means of a holistic examination of the belief-system of which it is a part.

> **Reflection**
>
> **Does Pargetter's requirement for 'holistic evaluation' undermine the claim that belief in God is properly basic?**

We have seen that Pargetter rejects two possible defeaters for the proper basicality of belief in God. William Hasker (b. 1935) (1998) does, however, think that:

1 The existence of evil counts against belief in God.
2 Psychological projection theories of the origin of religious beliefs suggest that religious experience can be explained without reference to the activity of God and therefore cannot be used to justify beliefs about God.
3 The existence of a plurality of religions weakens support for religious experience of any one system of beliefs about God or Ultimate Reality.

Hasker suggests that, even if the theist can overcome the three defeaters he has considered, they are still likely to trouble her and it would be to her advantage to have further answers available. This further support could simply consist of responses to the defeaters ('defeater-defeaters'), but, he asks, why does it need to be so limited? Why should the theist not use plausible theistic arguments as part of a cumulative case?

Plantinga is, of course, well known for his arguments for theism, in particular for a version of the ontological argument and, in response to the problem of evil, a form of the free will defence. He has also given a series of lectures (n.d.) on 'Two dozen (or so) theistic arguments' in which he suggests that, although theistic belief does not need to be supported by arguments, such arguments can, nonetheless, 'serve to bolster and confirm ("helps" a la John Calvin); perhaps to convince' (1).

> **Reflection**
>
> **Are there non-religious basic beliefs which may conflict with religious beliefs?**

• CONCLUSION

In this chapter, we have examined Plantinga's argument that the theist has no need to seek arguments in support of her belief; rather, religious belief can be regarded as properly basic – as based on direct experiences of God. However, we also saw that arguments may still have a role to play in explaining how to counter arguments and experiences which seem to 'defeat' the view that belief in God is a properly basic belief, and how to choose between apparently conflicting basic beliefs.

• REFERENCES

Hasker, William (1998) 'The Foundations of Theism: Scoring the Quinn-Plantinga Debate', *Faith and Philosophy* 15, 1: 60–67.

Pargetter, Robert (1990) 'Experience, Proper Basicality, and Belief in God', *International Journal for Philosophy of Religion* 27, 3: 141–163; reprinted in Michael Peterson, William Hasker, Bruce Reichenbach and David Basinger (eds) *Philosophy of Religion: Selected Readings* (Oxford: Oxford University Press, 2014), 217–228.

Peterson, Michael, Hasker, William, Reichenbach, Bruce and Basinger, David (eds) (2014 [1996]) *Philosophy of Religion: Selected Readings* (Oxford: Oxford University Press).

Plantinga, Alvin (n.d.) 'Two Dozen (or so) Theistic Arguments' www.calvin.edu/academic/philosophy/virtual_library/articles/plantinga_alvin/two_dozen_or_so_theistic_arguments.pdf.

Plantinga, Alvin (1982) 'The Reformed Objection to Natural Theology', *Christian Scholar's Review* 11, 3: 187–198; reprinted in Michael Peterson, William Hasker, Bruce Reichenbach and David Basinger (eds) *Philosophy of Religion: Selected Readings* (Oxford: Oxford University Press, 2014), 207–216.

Plantinga, Alvin (2000) *Warranted Christian Belief* (Oxford and New York, NY: Oxford University Press).

Plantinga, Alvin (2015) *Knowledge and Christian Belief* (Grand Rapids, MI: Wm. B. Eerdmans Publishing Company). (This is a shorter and more accessible account of the proposals of *Warranted Christian Belief*.)

• FURTHER READING

Encyclopedia articles

Bolos, Anthony and Scott, Kyle (n.d.) 'Reformed Epistemology', *Internet Encyclopedia of Philosophy*, www.iep.utm.edu/ref-epis/.

Clark, Kelly James (n.d.) 'Religious Epistemology', *Internet Encyclopedia of Philosophy*, www.iep.utm.edu/relig-ep/.

Forrest, Peter (2013) 'The Epistemology of Religion', *Stanford Encyclopedia of Philosophy*, https://plato.stanford.edu/entries/religion-epistemology/#RefEpi.

Original articles in edited collections

Greco, John (2013 [2007]) 'Reformed Epistemology' in Chad Meister and Paul Copan (eds) *The Routledge Companion to Philosophy of Religion* (Abingdon: Routledge), 689–699.

Plantinga, Alvin (2010 [1997]) 'Reformed Epistemology' in Charles Taliaferro, Paul Draper, and Philip Quinn (eds) *Companion to Philosophy of Religion* (Chichester: Wiley-Blackwell), 674–680.
Wolterstorff, Nicholas (2005) 'Religious Epistemology' in William J. Wainwright (ed.) *The Oxford Handbook of Philosophy of Religion* (Oxford: Oxford University Press).

Reprinted article in edited collection

Martin, Michael (1991) *The Case Against Christianity* (Philadelphia, PA: Temple University Press), 22–34; reprinted in Andrew Eshleman (ed.) *Readings in Philosophy of Religion: East Meets West* (Malden, MA: Blackwell Publishing, 2008), 179–182.

Articles

Baker, Deane-Peter (2005) 'Plantinga's Reformed Epistemology: What's the Question?', *International Journal for Philosophy of Religion* 57, 2: 77–103.
De Ridder, Jeroen (2011) 'Religious Exclusivism Unlimited', *Religious Studies* 47, 4: 449–463.
Dillier, Kevin S. (2011) 'Can Arguments Boost Warrant for Christian Belief? Warrant Boosting and the Primacy of Divine Revelation', *Religious Studies* 47, 2: 185–200.
Koons, Jeremy Randel (2011) 'Plantinga on Properly Basic Belief in God: Lessons from the Epistemology of Perception', *The Philosophical Quarterly* 61, 245: 839–850.
Long, Todd R. (2010) 'A Proper de Jure Objection to the Epistemic Rationality of Religious Belief', *Religious Studies* 46, 3: 375–394.
Plantinga, Alvin, Links to online papers may be found at www.andrewmbailey.com/ap/.

Books

Davis, Stephen T. (1997) *God, Reason and Theistic Proofs* (Edinburgh: Edinburgh University Press), Chapter 5.
Evans, C. Stephen (1998) *Faith Beyond Reason* (Edinburgh: Edinburgh University Press), 40–47.
Taliaferro, Charles (1998) *Contemporary Philosophy of Religion* (Oxford: Blackwell), 260–262.
Trigg, Roger (1998) *Rationality and Religion* (Oxford: Blackwell), Chapter 6.

19

life, death and hope

• INTRODUCTION

Beliefs about what happens to human beings at the end of their lives on Earth take many forms. Generally speaking, for those who accept a realist view of God at least, such beliefs are concerned with a continued existence of some kind. This may be in some kind of heaven (for Jews and Christians) or paradise (for Muslims). Alternatively, it may take the form of a time-limited rebirth which will eventually culminate (for Hindus) in *moksha*, liberation from life in this world which is achieved when the individual soul merges into *Brahman*, the reality which underlies everything, or (for Buddhists) *nirvana* (Sanskrit) or *nibbana* (Pali), which means 'extinction'.

• THE SURVIVAL OF THE DISEMBODIED SELF

Descartes on body–mind dualism

Belief in the survival of the disembodied self presupposes the belief that the self can be separated from the body. One of the most well-known arguments for this may be found in the sixth of Descartes' *Meditations* (1641). Descartes argues as follows:

1 I can doubt that I have a body. There are three arguments for this:

   a Although my senses tell me that I have a body, my senses have often proved to be unreliable. For example, sometimes towers which appear round when viewed from a distance look square when we are closer to them, and sometimes those who have had limbs amputated feel pain in the missing limb.

   b I have sensory experiences while asleep. Since these have no external cause, the same may be true of sensory experiences which occur when I am awake.

   c Although my sensory perceptions seem to come from outside myself, it is possible that they were produced by some as yet unknown faculty.

2 Nevertheless, everything which I am able to understand clearly and distinctly is created by God to correspond with my understanding of it. If this were not the case, God would be a deceiver.

3 So the fact that I can understand clearly and distinctly that one thing is separate from another is good grounds for believing that the two things really are separate from each other.

4 Therefore, since I can have a clear and distinct idea of myself as a thinking thing and of my body as a non-thinking thing, this shows that I am distinct from my body and can live without it.

5 Although the body is divisible, the mind is not. A foot or arm can be cut off the body, but nothing can be taken away from the mind. This also shows that the mind is different from the body.

The implications of body–mind dualism for life after death

Swinburne (1986) considers the following arguments which suggest that the soul can function without the brain:

1 Arguments from parapsychology based on:

  a The alleged evidence of reincarnation. But even if there appear to be at least some genuine cases of children who can remember past lives, there is no evidence of continuity between the claimed memories of past lives and the brains of those who lived the past lives.

  b The alleged evidence of spiritualism. But there are no accounts of more than one medium offering the same account of the current afterlife experiences of the same deceased person. Secondly, mediums' accounts of afterlife experiences are very banal when one might expect that life in a very different, non-material world, would be very different from life in our world.

  c The alleged evidence of near-death-experiences. But even if accounts of experiences such as seeing a tunnel and hearing beautiful music or being able to see one's own body from a distance are genuine, they do not show that, at the time of such experiences, the brain had ceased to function.

2 Arguments for natural survival. There is no evidence that anyone has survived death, but, Swinburne argues, there is no reason why it should not be possible for someone to survive death. Our failure to find souls who have survived death shows only that they are not in the small number of places in which we have looked for them.

3 A God who is omnipotent would have the power to enable souls to survive and function after death. Furthermore, a good God might have an obligation to do so, or God might have announced God's intention of doing so.

Thus, Swinburne concludes, the only effective kind of argument for the survival and functioning of the soul after death requires a God who, in an afterlife which is not constrained by the natural laws which function in our world, can revive the soul and enable it to function again.

This does not, however, address the problems of personal identity which are associated with this view. Since, in this world, persons are usually identified by means of their bodies, it is difficult to understand how we might be able to recognise and differentiate between one disembodied soul and another. H. H. Price (1899–1984) (1953) suggests that an account of disembodied survival of death which resembles the kind of existence which we experience in our dreams is at least conceivable. But, although our dreams feature people and activities which exist only within our sleeping minds, they are still generated by a physical brain. Therefore, if an afterlife is a dream-like state, we might still question whether something physical is required to generate our dream-like experiences.

• SURVIVAL AS RESURRECTION

On this view, full human existence depends on the union of soul and body. Any afterlife existence would therefore require the resurrection of the body.

Clearly, the idea of an embodied afterlife avoids the problems associated with the idea that the mind can survive without the body. But it is not without problems of its own. In particular, the problem of personal identity appears again, but here in the form of the difficulty of being sure that a person who has died is the same person as one who is resurrected.

Hick (1976) gives us a series of three cases which, he argues, are logically possible:

1 A person disappears in London and an exact 'replica' of him appears in New York. Everything suggests that the person and the 'replica' are the same.
2 If the person in London dies and a 'replica' appears in New York, we still have to say that the 'replica' is the same person as the person who died in London.
3 If a person dies and his 'replica' appears in a different world – with the ability to remember having died, along with some experiences both before and after death – we must still say that the 'replica' is the same person as the person who died.

Note that Hick makes a distinction between a replica and a 'replica' in quotation marks. A replica is a copy which could exist at the same time as the original and may be one of several copies. A 'replica' in quotation marks cannot exist at the same time as the original, and cannot be one of many copies. It is God who ensures that we become 'replicas' of this kind.

It might be objected, however, that Hick's scenario is overly reliant on the role of memory in securing personal identity. For example, we would normally wish to say that a person with dementia is the same person as the child they were some decades ago, even when they are no longer able to remember anything which would associate them with that child. In such cases, it is the physical continuity and the record of that in, for example, photographs, which enables us to say that the person with memory loss and the child are one and the same. It is difficult to imagine what form such physical continuity might take in a life beyond life on Earth.

Both Price and Hick do only claim to show that their scenarios are logically possible, however; they give no reasons for believing that they describe actual states of affairs. If the scenarios were not logically possible, they would be less likely to represent actual states of affairs and this would be a helpful contribution to the debate. But, if the best we can hope for is to show that an afterlife is not logically impossible, this remains some way short of an argument in support of belief in life after death.

Reflection

To what extent are the difficulties associated with belief in life after death understood as either disembodied survival of the soul or resurrection concerned with personal identity? Can they be overcome?

• REBIRTH

The Abrahamic religions – Judaism, Christianity and Islam – generally claim that we begin to exist at a specific point in time, that we die once and that we continue to exist in some form after death.

By contrast, the Indian tradition – Hinduism and Buddhism – teaches that we exist without beginning, and that we live, die and are reborn many times – either as another human being or, in some traditions, as an animal, plant or inanimate object (Edwards, 2002 [1996]). This is often called 'reincarnation', but this implies belief in an immortal soul which transmigrates or reincarnates, and seems to conflict with the Buddhist doctrine of *anatta* ('not-self'), the belief that there is no enduring 'self', and thus no eternal soul which can be made incarnate again. Noble Ross Reat (1977) notes that, in the Buddhist *Milindapanha* (c. 100 BCE), the idea of rebirth without transmigration is illustrated by saying that the individual is like a fire which ignites another fire, whereas the Upanishads 'normally do incorporate a transmigrating entity in their theory of rebirth . . . [and] attribute the energy of the fire in their similes to the person (*purusa*) in the fire' (172). Roy W. Perrett (b. 1951) (1987) therefore suggests that the term 'rebirth' should be used in preference to 'reincarnation'.

Both the Upanishads and Buddhism teach that the will, expressed through *karma* (the sum of a person's actions), determines whether the next rebirth will be happy or otherwise, although neither system seems to value a 'good' rebirth, except insofar as it is more likely to enable the individual to lead the kind of life which will enable release from *samsara*, the cycle of birth, death and rebirth. The aim, in both cases, is not so much a happy rebirth as to stop rebirth (Reat: 175). There is no 'god' who is responsible for rebirth, so 'good' and 'bad' rebirths cannot be thought of as rewards or punishments; they are simply the impersonal product of the effects of *karma*.

Perrett on Karl H. Potter's arguments for the doctrine of pre-existence

Perrett examines Karl H. Potter's (b. 1927) argument (1968) for the pre-existence of the morally responsible agent. The argument seems to amount to the claim that, in order to perform an action, prior to performing that action an agent must possess the ability to perform that action. But if someone possesses the ability to perform an action, this means that they must previously possess the ability to try to perform that action, thus setting up a beginningless regress. If there were a first action in an agent's history, there could not have been any prior conditions – which means that the action could not have been performed. So, if an agent does perform actions, there must have been a beginningless series of prior causes.

Perrett points out that this argument depends on accepting that having the ability to perform an action precedes the action, and suggests that a cause need not necessarily precede its effect, but he argues that an infinite series of simultaneous events is no more plausible than a beginningless series of events (1987: 49).

Perrett considers three objections to the idea of a beginningless agent:

1 '[I]f there is no sense of strong personal identity across lives, then surely the theory is entirely void of any genuine personal significance?' (52)

Perrett suggests the following responses:

a Since we can remember how to tie shoelaces without remembering when and where we learnt this, it is possible that memories as abilities to perform certain actions might link successive lives in a way which is of personal relevance even if an individual has no memories of previous lives. He admits that continuity of this kind may be too weak to count as rebirth, and that some kind of memory is needed for the doctrine to have any significance for individuals, but seems to accept that latent memories may suffice (54).
b Some people do claim that they can remember previous lives. Perrett suggests that these do not provide conclusive evidence of rebirth but that they are 'strongly suggestive of rebirth' (53).

2 '[I]f my rebirth is not the same person as me, then why should I concern myself with his fate?' (52)

Perrett suggests that we have a moral obligation towards our karmic heirs (55). If we have a particularly strong obligation towards those closest to us, then our karmic heirs are our closest relations.

3 '[I]f he is not the same person as me, then how can he justly incur the karmic consequences of *my* actions?' (52)

Perrett suggests:

a If we accept deterrence or reformative theories of punishment as opposed to a retributive theory, it might be acceptable to punish someone for something they did not do.
b We can feel responsible for actions performed by others – e.g. the guilt of some white people about their ancestors' treatment of black slaves.
c We can still be responsible for the consequences of actions we cannot remember.

Whitley R. P. Kaufman on rebirth and the problem of evil

Whitley R. P. Kaufman (2005) objects to the notion of *karma* and rebirth on the grounds that it fails to offer a satisfactory account of evil and suffering. Although it might be thought that the problem of evil is applicable only to belief in the God of monotheism, the problem can be stated in non-theist terms, too. So, he suggests:

> The problem of evil in its broadest question simply asks such universal human questions as 'Why do the innocent suffer and the wicked flourish?' 'Why is the world not better ordered and more just?' 'Why is there suffering and death at all in the universe?'
>
> (2005: 17)

Kaufman suggests that this might be called the 'existential' problem of evil, as opposed to the 'theological' problem, and that it is shared by all people and religions.

Kaufman considers five moral objections to the doctrine of *karma*, as follows:

The Memory Problem

Kaufman suggests that someone who is suffering for a past crime should be aware of his crime and understand why he is being punished.

If the doctrine of *karma* promotes moral education, why is it that most suffering is the result of wrong choices in previous lives and most wrongs will be punished in a later life? There is no obvious connection between sin and suffering.

Since we cannot remember the sins of past lives, the doctrine is more like a revenge theory than a retributive one and is, for this reason, morally unacceptable.

The Proportionality Problem

Kaufman argues that some people suffer such horrendous evils that it is difficult to imagine what they might have done to justify such a punishment. Our practices suggest that we do not consider capital punishment an appropriate punishment even for serious crimes, and yet the doctrine of *karma* apparently determines that we will all die and that many of us will suffer terribly during the course of our lives. If the *karma* theory determines that someone who is raped in this life suffers because they were a rapist in a previous life, does the fact that we must all die mean that we were all murderers in a previous life?

The Infinite Regress Problem

If the doctrine of *karma* explains the suffering in our present life, what explains the suffering in the first life of the series? How did the process begin? If the process is said to be beginningless, this merely ignores the problem. In the debate between Russell and a woman who claimed that the world rests on the back of a giant turtle, which rests on the back of a giant turtle, and so on, the fact that each turtle supports the one above does not mean that she can avoid the question of what the whole series of turtles rests on.

The Problem of Explaining Death

Even if someone behaves well in their current life and will therefore have a better existence in their next life, they must still experience death – which, Kaufman suggests, is the greatest of evils.

Kaufman notes Max Weber's (1864–1920) suggestion that our life span is finite because our good deeds are finite, but argues that this would support a different law of *karma*, according to which we are punished not for our bad deeds but for failing to perform a sufficient number of good actions. It also implies that we must be infinitely good in order to avoid death, which seems implausible and undermines the claim that the law of *karma* is a fair system of rewards and punishments. Kaufman also points out that the argument is circular as in order to do an infinite number of good deeds someone would need an infinite amount of time.

An alternative response would be to deny that death is evil, on the grounds that it enables us to have another life in which we might be rewarded, but Kaufman suggests that there is no reason why death should be the means by which we attain our reward; we could be rewarded in our current life, or be transformed to a higher state. This also ignores the fact that death usually involves physical pain and separation from loved ones.

Again, we could argue that the ultimate reward is release from the cycle of rebirth. But this ignores the fact that life often contains much that is good – which we would then lose. So, why would it not be possible to reward perfect goodness with a perfectly happy earthly life? If life can be very good some of the time, why could it not be good all of the time?

The Free Will Problem

Finally, Kaufman objects that the doctrine of *karma* can often lead to fatalistic pessimism. In Christianity, a person has only one life in which to earn salvation but someone who believes in the doctrine of *karma* has many lives in which to achieve this and so there is less of an incentive to act well in the current life.

The doctrine also raises the question of whether we have free will at all. If the law of *karma* functions in a deterministic way, a terrorist would be merely the doctrine's agent, delivering punishment to those who deserve it. If he has a genuinely free choice of whether or not to kill his victims, this would suggest that his victims are, in fact, innocent. Even if they are compensated in a future life, this is a different theory from the doctrine of *karma*.

Some scholars have suggested that the law of *karma* explains only 'natural' evil and not 'moral' evil, but Kaufman points out that it is not always easy to distinguish clearly between the two – an earthquake might be regarded as a natural evil, for example, but people sometimes die as a consequence of failure to make buildings earthquake-proof – and that, on this view, we would no longer have any idea whether our sufferings were the consequence of past misdeeds or not.

Kaufman concludes his article by noting that the doctrine of *karma* is both unverifiable and unfalsifiable. Since any state of affairs is compatible with the doctrine, it is effectively meaningless. It also has no predictive value. Even if someone knows that they have done wrong, they do not know what the punishment will be or when it will occur. Kaufman suggests that the question of verifiability or falsifiability is important because these provide a check against dogmatism, ethnocentrism, and so on; it is, he says, 'widely acknowledged that the repressive caste system in India lasted so long in large part because the doctrine of *karma* encouraged Indians to accept social oppression as the mechanical workings of *karma*' (27).

Sri Aurobindo's revised understanding of rebirth

Sri Aurobindo (1872–1950) (1912) argues that the theory of rebirth can be neither proved nor disproved by science or philosophical argument.

He considers the objection that, since we cannot remember our past lives, there were no past lives. He responds that we cannot remember all of our present lives – e.g. infancy – so we cannot expect to be able to remember a time prior to infancy. If we could remember our past lives, it could only be by means of a 'psychical memory awakening' which could overcome physical limitations and enable us to remember things which have not left physical marks on our physical existence. But, he suggests, instances of psychical memory awakening can be challenged by the sceptic as merely fiction or the product of imagination. Even if there seems to be strong evidence, they do not constitute proof of rebirth because there are many possible explanations for one set of facts. For example, the phenomena of automatic writing or communication from the dead may come from the 'subliminal consciousness' (2014: 525 [1912]). Similarly, apparent memories of past lives may support the view that the consciousness can have knowledge of past events, but these events may have been experienced by persons other than ourselves.

Those who believe in rebirth argue that the theory accounts for the facts better than any alternative theory, but this does not guarantee its truth. For example, rebirth accounts for genius, but science argues that heredity provides an explanation for this.

The true foundation of the theory is 'the evolution of the soul' – that is, 'the continual growth of a divine knowledge, strength, love and purity' (526). The soul does not need proof of its rebirth because it will eventually become aware of its own immortality and the past which led to this state.

There is still room to question the means by which this is achieved. Sri Aurobindo rejects the view that the personality occupies a series of new bodies, on the grounds that memories, in which our personal identity is often said to lie, do not survive this process. The Buddhist holds that there is no self, no person; there is merely a continuous stream of energy which creates a false sense of identity. Therefore, there is no soul which is reincarnated. Karma 'creates the form of a constantly changing mentality and physical bodies that are . . . the result of that changing composite of ideas and sensations which I call myself' (526–527). But Sri Aurobindo adopts the Vedantist view, which holds that there is a self, but that this is not the same as my personality. Rather, there is a real Self which lies behind each series of rebirths and becomes immortal. The immutable Self adopts changing bodies and, by means of the 'mental being' or 'mental person', watches and enjoys the mutations, but is always unaffected by them. It is this which enables us to maintain the notion of a continuous identity throughout Time, as opposed to a Self with a timeless identity. The mental person forms a new personality for its terrestrial existence, and past experience, although not present in physical memory in order to avoid troubling the consciousness with the burden of the past, provides a 'fund on which we can always draw' (528).

Reflection

Is it rational to believe in rebirth?

• IS BELIEF IN ETERNAL LIFE DESIRABLE?

So far in this chapter we have considered various arguments for continued existence after death. However, in a famous article 'The Makropulos Case: Reflections on the Tedium of Immortality' (1973), Bernard Williams (1929–2003) argues that a life after death is not something to be desired.

The Makropulos Case

Williams cites the case of Elina Makropulos, a fictional character who appears in Karel Capek's play *The Makropulos Case*, and the opera by Leo Janacek of the same name. An expanded account is given by Lisa Bortolotti and Yujin Nagasawa (2009). Elina has lived for 300 years at the age of 42 but, to keep the secret of her longevity, she has had to change her name and country several times and leave those she loved or see them die. She therefore becomes detached from other people, claiming that she is not concerned about the well-being of her children and treating her suitors disdainfully. Finally, she concludes that it is the shortness of life which makes it valuable and meaningful. She decides not to take the elixir which would give her an additional 300 years of life and dies.

Williams suggests that Elina wishes to die because she has done all of the things that a woman of her character at her age would want to do. Although, in the play, Elina is one of only two or three people to drink the elixir and must keep it a secret, Bortolotti and Nagasawa suggest that Williams can still argue that there are other aspects of her story which might apply in a world of immortals – that is, that they would all eventually have fulfilled all of their categorical desires, those which give them a sufficient reason to wish for continued existence. Williams argues that the only way to be immortal without becoming bored with our existence would be to have a succession of unconnected lives, but this would destroy our personal identity.

J. Jeremy Wisnewski's response

J. Jeremy Wisnewski (b. 1975) (2005) offers one of many responses to Williams' paper. He argues that, while it is possible to tire of certain activities (boredom in the broader sense), it is not possible to reach a state in which we have satisfied all possible categorical desires (boredom in the narrower sense), since there is always the possibility of new ways of fulfilling old categorical desires.

Wisnewski illustrates his argument by means of an example in which, having lived for a million years, he has now satisfied his categorical desire to be the best musician ever by becoming a brilliant player of every possible instrument. He is bored for several hundred years, but then a new instrument is invented and he recognises that his categorical desire to master every possible instrument has not, in fact, been satisfied. This shows, Wisnewski suggests, that 'even if one enters a state where no categorical desires are present, it does not follow from this that the state is permanent' (34). Furthermore, we can imagine the invention of hundreds of new instruments, perhaps invented in order to satisfy Wisnewski's categorical desires.

In a second example, Wisnewski imagines being born in ancient Greece and having the categorical desire to experience all possible bodily pleasures. During the Middle Ages he thinks that he has satisfied this desire and is 'bored to death', only to discover, with the rise of technology which gives him access to film, video and virtual reality, that he has been mistaken. As in the previous scenario, a time of 'fatal boredom' is followed by the renewal of a previous categorical desire. Thus, Wisnewski claims:

> I no longer have a reason to find an immortal life necessarily unappealing. I recognize that, although there might be times in which I have no categorical desires, these periods are not permanent, nor will these periods necessarily be longer than those periods in which I maintain categorical desires.
>
> (35)

Finally, he suggests that, if the times in which he has categorical desires occur frequently enough, such that they outweigh periods in which he experiences fatal boredom, he is 'forced to want the immortal life' (35).

Mikel Burley's reply

Mikel Burley (b. 1972) (2009) notes that, while some philosophers have rejected Williams' suggestion that our categorical desires would eventually be satisfied during an immortal life, Wisnewski argues that, even if such desires are eventually satisfied, it is possible that at least some of them could be rekindled. As we saw above, Wisnewski offers two examples to illustrate his claim that categorical desires can be revived, but Burley objects that neither of them are able to support his case.

First he objects that Wisnewski's examples successfully respond to Williams' argument only if certain auxiliary conditions are met. So:

> claiming that the desire to be the most accomplished musician on every instrument could be perpetually renewed, and that this perpetually renewable desire can make immortal life desirable, makes no sense unless one assumes it to be conceivable, and desirable, that a world could exist forever in which a culture of

musical appreciation and musicianship flourishes. In the absence of such a culture, the desire in question would be senseless.

(81)

Although Burley is doubtful whether it is possible to imagine such a world, he pursues a different objection – that it is questionable whether Wisnewski's scenarios support the view that immortality is desirable. In the case of the first one, Burley suggests that the desire in question is a desire for a social status which is superior to that of mortal human beings – that is, to play any instrument more brilliantly than anyone with a finite life. Burley suggests that an immortal would not, or should not, find this satisfying.

Burley argues that fulfilment of the desire for superiority over others is usually thought to be satisfying only when we do not have a significant advantage over others. If we desire to achieve something which requires time, and we have a considerable temporal advantage over others, then that advantage seems so great that we are entitled to little, if any, satisfaction on fulfilment of the desire.

Burley gives two examples to illustrate his point. First, Alex, the basketball player who is an inch taller than any other player, desires to be the highest scorer in the league. He fulfils this desire and can feel justifiably satisfied since his height does not give him a big enough advantage to guarantee that he is the highest scorer. In the second scenario, Gulliver, without training, wins a race against some Lilliputians who have trained for many years, but is not entitled to feel satisfied because his advantage was so great.

Burley suggests that Wisnewski's musician example has something in common with both examples. Like Alex the basketball player, the musician must practice. The advantage in question does not guarantee success without practice in either case. But, like Gulliver, the musician's advantage is huge. Burley suggests that the Gulliver example is a better analogy than the basketball player example because someone with an infinite amount of time, or even just a considerable amount of time, has such an advantage over those who do not have the same amount of time that, in whatever task he attempted to become the best, we would say that his considerable advantage reduces the extent to which he is entitled to feel satisfied that he has achieved his goal.

Burley concludes that, if he is right, Wisnewski's musician example fails as an example of a categorical desire which might be rekindled during an immortal life because it is not a desire which would, or should, lead to satisfaction.

Burley suggests that Wisnewski's second example, the desire to experience every bodily pleasure, is even less satisfactory. It does have the advantage that it does not require a comparison with mortal humans. But it does assume that the number of possible bodily pleasures is inexhaustible, and slides between 'every possible bodily pleasure' and 'every possible means of acquiring some bodily pleasure' (83) in order to appeal to technological inventions in the hope of supporting the initial claim. But, Burley suggests, either way, pleasurable bodily sensations are likely to be just the kind of thing with which immortal beings will eventually become bored. He acknowledges that this might be simply a matter of personal intuition, but suggests that even if the desire to experience all bodily pleasures could continue for eternity, it is questionable whether such a life would be a desirable form of life. He notes the suggestion of other philosophers that immortality might be tolerable for animals, who are less intelligent than we are, or those who have infinite patience and tranquillity – in other words, who are more godlike than we are. For example, Christine Overall suggests of an immortal dog that 'if he could awake every day with the prospect of breakfast and a walk, he could probably be happy to go on awakening every day for eternity' (Overall, 2003: 147).

Finally, Burley suggests that Wisnewski has failed to think carefully enough about what a desirable human life consists of. Simply stating that the satisfaction of a particular kind of desire could constitute a worthwhile life does not establish that a life devoted to the satisfaction of that desire would be desirable. In fact, he suggests, the two desires which Wisnewski recommends 'appear closer to forms of pathological compulsion than to manifestations of a well-adjusted constitution' (84).

Burley therefore concludes that his discussion has shown the difficulty of finding an objective answer to the question of whether immortal life is something which we might desire. Williams' negative answer is based on his inability to imagine human projects and commitments which could interest us for an eternity, and this prompts respondents to consider what such projects might be like. But Burley is simply unable to see the point of the lives which Wisnewski describes.

• ETERNAL LIFE AS A BETTER QUALITY OF LIFE

Afterlife beliefs are sometimes described as beliefs about eternal life. For some, this can refer to our lives on Earth. Thus, Buddhists believe that rebirth takes place not only after death but also during life. Each of us is

> constantly changing during life, 'reborn' as a relatively 'different' person according to one's mood, the task one is involved in, or the people one is relating to. Depending on how one acts, one may experience 'heavenly' or 'hellish' states of mind.
>
> (Harvey, 2013: 47)

So the doctrines of *karma* and rebirth are ethical doctrines; they are concerned with the effects of our actions on both our own future well-being and that of the communities in which we live.

Nevertheless, a Buddhist might also say that 'it is reasonable to suppose that this process of change, determined especially by the nature of one's actions, does not abruptly stop at death, but carries on' (Harvey: 47), whereas Phillips would say that belief in eternal life has nothing to do with our destiny after bodily death. Phillips suggests that, '[t]o try to show that one should worship God because he will win in the end, is not to talk of worshipping God at all' (1970: 38). The 'soul' is not some kind of substance which may, or may not, survive death; rather, talk about the soul is simply a way of talking about human beings. Phrases such as 'the destiny of the soul', 'losing one's soul', 'selling one's soul', 'damning one's soul', and so on must all be understood 'in terms of the kind of life a person is living. To ask a question about the state of one's soul is to ask a question about the state of one's life' (45).

So, for Phillips to say that a person's soul is immortal is to say that she is living in accordance with eternal values, values which will not die, even when she does. Eternal life is not something which happens when life on Earth is over; 'Eternal life is the reality of goodness, that in terms of which human life is to be assessed' (48). In living in accordance with eternal values, we lose our concern for ourselves – we 'die to the self'. The believer ceases to see himself as the centre of his world, and realises that 'he has no claim on the way things go. Most of all, he is forced to realize that his own life is not a necessity' (52–53).

Perhaps some kind of middle way between the expectation of personal survival of death in some form and the belief that it is only our best moral values which will survive us may be found in the Chinese concept of *shen*. According to Cheng, *shen* is the power possessed by all living things which are able to exert a beneficial influence over other living things. So, a person of great virtue who performs great deeds and is respected and influential during his or her life leaves behind at his or her death his or her *shen* which continues to influence others, even when the person is no longer physically present. The life-generating and life-preserving aspects of the universe may also be thought of as its *shen*. Birth and death are both part of these aspects of the universe, which means that 'death is absorbed into the larger process and circulation of life and must be faced by a person with equanimity and peace of mind' (2008: 65 [1997]). To speak of the *shen* of the universe is to speak of the Divine, in which 'the spiritual is no longer confined to any projected or formerly existing person or thing, but pertains to the ever-present and ever-active life and vitality of the whole of nature' (65).

> ## Reflection
>
> To what extent does the concept of *shen* help to address difficulties with more personal conceptions of survival of death?

• CONCLUSION

It would appear that, at best, arguments about what happens to us at death can show only that an afterlife is not logically impossible. As we have seen, it is also questionable whether a continuation of our existence after death is something which might be desired. We also saw that talk of eternal life can refer not to our continued existence either in a future incarnation or in a world which is beyond our present world but to a commitment to eternal values, primarily that of goodness, which existed before our birth and will exist beyond the duration of our own, individual, lives. We might also draw on the Chinese concept of *shen*, our beneficial power which can continue to influence the world, even when we are no longer physically present, and the continuing beneficial power of the universe, in the context of which the lives and deaths of individuals are but a natural part of an eternally continuing process.

• REFERENCES

Bortolotti, Lisa and Nagasawa, Yujin (2009) 'Immortality Without Boredom', *Ratio* XXII, 3: 261–277.

Burley, Mikel (2009) 'Immortality and Boredom: A Response to Wisnewski', *International Journal for Philosophy of Religion* 65, 2: 77–85.

Cheng, Chung-Ying (1997) 'Reality and Divinity in Chinese Philosophy' in Eliot Deutsch and Ron Bontekoe (eds) *A Companion to World Philosophies* (Malden, MA: Blackwell), 185–197; reprinted in Andrew Eshleman (ed.) *Readings in Philosophy of Religion: East Meets West* (Malden, MA: Blackwell, 2008), 59–66.

Descartes, René (1641) *Meditations on First Philosophy*, Sixth Meditation; translations include John Cottingham *Meditations on First Philosophy with Selections from the Objections and Replies* (Cambridge: Cambridge University Press, 1986) and John Veitch *Meditations on First Philosophy* (1901), www.wright.edu/~charles.taylor/descartes/meditation6.html.

Edwards, Paul (2002 [1996]) *Reincarnation: A Critical Examination* (New York, NY: Prometheus Books).

Harvey, Peter (2013 [1990]) *An Introduction to Buddhism: Teachings, History and Practices* (Cambridge: Cambridge University Press).

Hick, John (1976) *Death and Eternal Life* (London: Collins).

Kaufman, Whitley R. P. (2005) 'Rebirth and the Problem of Evil', *Philosophy East and West* 55, 1: 15–32.

Overall, Christine (2003) *Aging, Death, and Human Longevity: A Philosophical Inquiry* (Berkeley, CA: University of California Press).

Perrett, Roy W. (1987) 'Rebirth', *Religious Studies* 23, 1: 41–57.

Phillips, D. Z. (1970) *Death and Immortality* (London: Macmillan).

Potter, Karl H. (1968) 'Pre-existence' in P. T. Raju and Alburey Castell (eds) *East-West Studies on the Problem of the Self* (The Hague: Martinus Nijhoff).

Price, H. H. (1953) 'Survival and the Idea of "Another World"', *Proceedings of the Society for Psychical Research* Vol. L, Part 182: 1–25.

Reat, Noble Ross (1977) 'Karma and Rebirth in the Upanisads and Buddhism', *Numen* 24, Fasc. 3: 163–185.

Sri Aurobindo (1912) 'On Rebirth', Sri Aurobindo Ashram Trust; reprinted in Michael Peterson, William Hasker, Bruce Reichenbach and David Basinger (eds) *Philosophy of Religion: Selected Readings* (Oxford: Oxford University Press, 2014), 524–528.

Swinburne, Richard (1986) *The Evolution of the Soul* (Oxford: OUP).

Williams, Bernard (1973) 'The Makropulos Case: Reflections on the Tedium of Immortality' in *Problems of the Self: Philosophical Papers 1956–1972* (Cambridge: CUP), 82–100; reprinted in J. M. Fischer (ed.) *The Metaphysics of Death* (Stanford, CA: Stanford University Press, 1993), 73–92.

Wisnewski, J. Jeremy (2005) 'Is the Immortal Life Worth Living?', *International Journal for Philosophy of Religion* 58, 1: 27–36.

• FURTHER READING

Encyclopedia articles

Luper, Stephan (2014) 'Death', *Stanford Encyclopedia of Philosophy*, https://plato.stanford.edu/entries/death/.

Original articles in edited collections

Baker, Lynne Rudder (2005) 'Death and the Afterlife' in William J. Wainwright (ed.) *The Oxford Handbook of Philosophy of Religion* (Oxford: Oxford University Press), 366–391.

Evans, Craig A. (2013 [2007]) 'Resurrection' in Chad Meister and Paul Copan (eds) *The Routledge Companion to Philosophy of Religion* (Abingdon: Routledge), 626–635.

Kvanig, Jonathan L. (2010 [1997]) 'Resurrection, Heaven, and Hell' in Charles Taliaferro, Paul Draper and Philip L. Quinn (eds) *A Companion to Philosophy of Religion* (Chichester: Wiley-Blackwell), 630–638.

Merricks, Trenton (2009) 'The Resurrection of the Body' in Thomas P. Flint and Michael C. Rea (eds) *The Oxford Handbook of Philosophical Theology* (Oxford: Oxford University Press), 476–490.

Reasoner, Paul (2010 [1997]) 'Reincarnation and Karma' in Charles Taliaferro, Paul Draper, and Philip L. Quinn (eds) *A Companion to Philosophy of Religion* (Chichester: Wiley-Blackwell), 639–647.

Walls, Jerry L. (2009) 'Heaven and Hell' in Thomas P. Flint and Michael C. Rea (eds) *The Oxford Handbook of Philosophical Theology* (Oxford: Oxford University Press), 491–511.

Extracts from articles or books in edited collections

Anonymous (1992 [1890]) *Questions of King Milinda*, trans. T. W. Rhys Davids (Delhi: Motilal Banarsidass Publishers), 63–64, 71–74; reprinted in Andrew Eshleman (ed.) *Readings in Philosophy of Religion: East Meets West* (Malden, MA: Blackwell Publishing, 2008), 355–356.

Averroes (Ibn Rushd) (1961) 'The Future Life', *Averroes on the Harmony of Religion and Philosophy*, trans. George F. Hourani (London: Luzac), 76–78; reprinted in Linda Zagzebski and Timothy D. Miller (eds) *Readings in Philosophy of Religion: Ancient to Contemporary* (Chichester: Wiley-Blackwell, 2009), 417–419.

Chakrabarti, A. (1983) 'Is Liberation (*moksa*) Pleasant?', *Philosophy East and West* 33, 2: 167–182; reprinted in Charles Taliaferro and Paul J. Griffiths (eds) *Philosophy of Religion: An Anthology* (Oxford: Blackwell, 2003), 589–599.

Cohen, Hermann (1972) *Religion of Reason out of the Sources of Judaism*, trans. S. Kaplan (Atlanta: Scholars Press); extract reprinted in Daniel H. Frank, Oliver Leaman and Charles H. Manekin (eds) *The Jewish Philosophy Reader* (London: Routledge, 2000), 433–440.

Le Poidevin, Robin (1996) *Arguing for Atheism: An Introduction to the Philosophy of Religion* (Abingdon: Routledge), 135–146; reprinted in Chad Meister (ed.) *The Philosophy of Religion Reader* (New York and Abingdon: Routledge, 2008), 642–651.

MacKay, Donald (1987) 'Brain Science and the Soul' in Richard L. Gregory (ed.) *The Oxford Companion to the Mind* (New York, NY: Oxford University Press), 723–725; reprinted in Andrew Eshleman (ed.) *Readings in Philosophy of Religion: East Meets West* (Malden, MA: Blackwell Publishing, 2008), 311–312.

Moser, Paul K. (2008) 'Death, Dying and the Hiddenness of God' [source not recorded]; reprinted in Chad Meister (ed.) *The Philosophy of Religion Reader* (New York and Abingdon: Routledge, 2008), 613–624.

Rubenstein, Richard (1966) *After Auschwitz* (New York, NY: Bobbs-Merrill); extract reprinted in Daniel H. Frank, Oliver Leaman and Charles H. Manekin (eds) *The Jewish Philosophy Reader* (London: Routledge, 2000), 440–441.

Russell, Bertrand (1957) 'Do we Survive Death?' in *Why I Am Not a Christian*. (London: George Allen & Unwin), 70–74; reprinted in Brian Davies (ed.) *Philosophy of Religion: A Guide and Anthology* (Oxford: Oxford University Press, 2000), Chapter 64.

Articles

Dunlap, Jeanetta W. (2007) 'Reincarnation and Survival of Life After Death: Is There Evidence That Past Life Memories Suggest Reincarnation?', Proceedings of the Academy of Spirituality and Paranormal Studies, Inc., Annual Conference 2007.

Kaufman, Whitley R. P. (2007) 'Rebirth and the Problem of Evil: A Reply to Critics', *Philosophy East and West* 57, 4: 556–560.

Phillips, D. Z. (1995) 'Dislocating the Soul', *Religious Studies* 31, 4: 447–462.

Preston, Ted M. and Dixon, Scott (2007) 'Who Wants to Live Forever? Immortality, Authenticity, and Living Forever in the Present', *International Journal for Philosophy of Religion* 61, 2: 99–117.

Rivas, Titus (2005) 'Rebirth and Personal Identity: Is Reincarnation an Intrinsically Impersonal Concept? (Literature Review and Philosophical Discussion)', *The Journal of Religion and Psychical Research* 28, 4: 226–233.

Stoeber, Michael (1990) 'Personal Identity and Rebirth', *Religious Studies* 26, 4: 493–500.

Books

Donnelly, John (ed.) (1978) *Language Metaphysics and Death* (New York, NY: Fordham University Press).

Edwards, Paul (ed.) (1997) *Immortality* (New York, NY: Prometheus Books).

Gowans, Christopher (2003) *Philosophy of the Buddha* (London: Routledge), Chapters 9, 12–13.

Harrison, Jonathan (1999) *God, Freedom and Immortality* (Aldershot: Ashgate), Chapter 23.

Irwin, H. and Watt, C. (2007) *An Introduction to Parapsychology* (London: McFarland & Co. Inc), Chapter 14.

Moreman, Christopher M. (2008) *Beyond the Threshold: Afterlife Beliefs and Experiences in World Religions* (Lanham, MD: Rowman and Littlefield), Chapter 11.

appendix 1: defining the divine

Type of theism	Key features	Key figures
Classical theism	God created time, the world, and everything in it from nothing, and everything depends for its continued existence upon God. The God of classical theism has a range attributes, but most commonly is said to be timeless (time does not pass for God; God sees everything which, for us, is past, present or future, simultaneously), omnipotent (all-powerful), omniscient (all-knowing) and good.	Thomas Aquinas (1225–1274) Brian Davies (b. 1951)
Deism	Deists have held such a variety of beliefs that it is difficult to provide a short definition of Deism which is also accurate. The website of the World Union of Deists defines Deism as recognition of a universal creative force which is greater than anything produced by humankind. This is supported by observation of the laws of nature and the use of human reason. Deists reject the claims of individuals and organisations who say that the Divine has revealed itself to them.	Matthew Tindal (d. 1733)
Integrative theism	Although God is not embodied in the world, the world functions like God's body because God loves the world. So, for example, the harm which human beings inflict on themselves, others and the world harms the life and love of God.	Charles Taliaferro (b. 1952)
Monotheism	Belief in one God.	Most adherents of the Abrahamic faiths – i.e. Judaism, Christianity and Islam.

(*Continued*)

Appendix 1 Continued

Type of theism	Key features	Key figures
Open theism	Although God knows everything up to and including the present, the future is open, for both God and human beings. One advantage of this view is that there is no apparent conflict between God's knowledge of the future and human freedom to choose our actions. It also enables us to say that God cannot be responsible for our bad moral choices if God does not know that we will make them.	David Basinger (b. 1947) William Hasker (b. 1935)
Panentheism	The view that the universe is contained within God, but that the universe and the world are not identical; God is something 'more than' the universe. Sometimes combined with process theism.	Pharaoh Ikhnaton (1375–1358 BCE) Karl Krause (1781–1832)
Pantheism	The view that God and the universe are identical.	Baruch Spinoza (1632–1677) John Toland (1670–1722) Grace Jantzen (1948–2006)
Panpsychism	Mind is a fundamental feature of the world which exists throughout the universe.	Alfred North Whitehead (1861–1947)
Polytheism	Either belief in many gods or belief that the one God is manifested in many different gods.	Most adherents of Hinduism.
Process theism	God created the world, but creation is an ongoing process; the universe grows and develops, and creatures contribute to this process. There is no contrast between a supernatural realm and a natural realm; there is only the creative activity of the things which exist. The beliefs of process theists are derived entirely from philosophical reasoning; the Divine does not reveal itself to humankind.	Alfred North Whitehead (1861–1947) Charles Hartshorne (1897–2000)
Religious fictionalism	The claim that religion is a useful fiction – it gives us a sense of meaning and purpose and helps us to behave ethically – but its claims about God, etc. are not to be understood as literally true. A form of religious non-realism (see below).	Andrew Eshleman

Appendix 1 Continued

Type of theism	Key features	Key figures
Religious naturalism	Broadly speaking, there are two types of religious naturalism: those which dispense with the concept of God altogether, and those which claim that God is a metaphor for the highest human ideals. In both cases it is claimed that there is nothing beyond Nature and that religious meaning may be found in Nature.	John Dewey (1859–1952) Loyal Rue (b. 1944) Donald A. Crosby (b. 1932)
Religious non-realism	Religious claims are, in some sense, true (they may be useful fictions [see religious fictionalism, above], and have some practical application in human life [see religious pragmatism, below]), but we cannot know whether there is any reality beyond religious language and the practices with which it is associated. This term is sometimes used interchangeably with religious anti-realism, which may also be understood as making the stronger claim that there is no objectively-existing religious reality beyond religious language and practices.	Don Cupitt (b. 1934)
Religious Platonism	This view claims either that God has much in common with the Form of the Good in the work of Plato (c. 428–c. 347 BCE), or that we should substitute the Form of the Good for the God of classical theism. The former has a long history in the development of Christian thought, while the latter was developed in the twentieth century most notably in the philosophical writings of Iris Murdoch.	St Augustine of Hippo (354–430) St Anselm of Canterbury (1033–1109) Iris Murdoch (1919–1999)
Religious pragmatism	The view that religion is so important to humankind that, since arguments for religious belief cannot prove its truth conclusively, we should choose the belief-system which has the best practical outcome. This may be associated with some forms of religious non-realism, although one can also be both a religious realist and a religious pragmatist – as, indeed, both Charles Sanders Peirce and William James, the originators of religious pragmatism, probably were.	Charles Sanders Peirce (1839–1914) William James (1842–1910)
Theistic personalism	God is a person without a body who created and sustains the universe and is omnipotent, omniscient and good.	Richard Swinburne (b. 1934)

appendix 2: list of further reading on the varieties of religious belief

• DEISM

Byrne, Peter (1989) *Natural Religion and the Nature of Religion: The Legacy of Deism* (London: Routledge).

Kadane, Matthew (2005) 'Deism', *New Dictionary of the History of Ideas*, www.encyclopedia.com/doc/1G2-3424300190.html.

• INTEGRATIVE THEISM

Taliaferro, Charles (1994) *Consciousness and the Mind of God* (Cambridge: Cambridge University Press), Chapter 6.

• OPEN THEISM

Rissler, James 'Open Theism', *The Internet Encyclopedia of Philosophy*, www.iep.utm.edu/o-theism/.

Robinson, Jeff 'Is Open Theism Still a Factor 10 Years After the ETS Vote?', www.thegospelcoalition.org/article/is-open-theism-still-a-factor-10-years-after-ets-vote.

Sanders, John *The Open Theism Information Site*: http://opentheism.info/ (John Sanders died in 2010, but much useful material remains on his website.)

• PANENTHEISM

Biernacki, Loriliai and Clayton, Philip (eds) (2013) *Panentheism Across the World's Traditions* (Oxford: Oxford University Press).

Cooper, John W. (2007) *Panentheism: The Other God of the Philosophers: From Plato to the Present* (Westmont, IL: IVP).

Culp, John 'Panentheism', *Stanford Encyclopedia of Philosophy*, http://plato.stanford.edu/archives/sum2015/entries/panentheism/.

Griffin, David Ray (2014) *Panentheism and Scientific Naturalism: Rethinking Evil, Morality, Religious Experience, Religious Pluralism and the Academic Study of Religion* (Claremont, CA: Process Century Press).

Johnston, Mark (2009) *Saving God: Religion After Idolatry* (Princeton, NJ: Princeton University Press).

• PANTHEISM

Jantzen, Grace (1984) *God's World, God's Body* (London: Darton, Longman and Todd).

Levine, Michael P. (1994) *Pantheism: A Non-Theistic Concept of Deity* (London: Routledge).

Mander, William (2013) 'Pantheism', *Stanford Encyclopedia of Philosophy*, http://plato.stanford.edu/archives/sum2013/entries/pantheism/.

• PANPSYCHISM

Seager, William and Allen-Hermanson, Sean (2015) 'Panpsychism', *Stanford Encyclopedia of Philosophy*, http://plato.stanford.edu/archives/fall2015/entries/panpsychism/.

• POLYTHEISM

Internet Sacred Text Archive (2010) 'Hinduism', www.sacred-texts.com/hin/.

Schneider, Laurel C. (2008) *Beyond Monotheism: A Theology of Multiplicity* (Abingdon: Routledge).

Sen, Sushana (2008) 'The Vedic-Upanisadic Concept of *Brahman* (The Highest God)' in Andrew Eshleman (ed.) *Readings in Philosophy of Religion: East Meets West* (Malden, MA: Blackwell Publishing), 43–51.

• PROCESS THEISM

Viney, Donald (2014) 'Process Theism', *Stanford Encyclopedia of Philosophy*, http://plato.stanford.edu/archives/spr2014/entries/process-theism/.

• RELIGIOUS FICTIONALISM

Eshleman, Andrew (2005) 'Can an Atheist Believe in God?' *Religious Studies* 41, 2: 183–199.

• RELIGIOUS NATURALISM

Crosby, Donald A. (2002) *A Religion of Nature* (New York, NY: SUNY Press).
Rue, Loyal (2011) *Nature is Enough* (New York, NY: SUNY Press).
Stenmark, Mikael (2013) 'Religious Naturalism and its Rivals', *Religious Studies* 49, 4: 529–550.

• RELIGIOUS NON-REALISM

Cupitt, Don, www.doncupitt.com/don-cupitt.

• RELIGIOUS PLATONISM

Murdoch, Iris (1985 [1970]) *The Sovereignty of Good* (London: ARK Paperbacks).

• RELIGIOUS PRAGMATISM

Peirce, Charles Sanders, James, William and Dewey, John, www.pragmatism.org/.

• THEISTIC PERSONALISM

Feser, Edward (2012) 'Craig on Theistic Personality', http://edwardfeser.blogspot.co.uk/2013/04/craig-on-theistic-personalism.html.

• TRANSCENDENTAL IDEALISM

Emerson, Ralph Waldo (2006 [1903]) *Nature Addresses and Lectures* (Elibron Classics [www.elibron.com], Adamant Media Corporation).

appendix 3: list of anthologies and their contents by topic

• ANTHOLOGIES

Adams, Marilyn McCord and Adams, Robert Merrihew (eds) (1988) *The Problem of Evil* (Oxford: Oxford University Press).

Davies, Brian (ed.) (2000) *Philosophy of Religion: A Guide and Anthology* (Oxford: Oxford University Press).

Eshleman, Andrew (ed.) (2008) *Readings in Philosophy of Religion: East Meets West* (Malden, MA: Blackwell Publishing).

Frank, Daniel H., Leaman, Oliver and Manekin, Charles H. (eds) (2000) *The Jewish Philosophy Reader* (London: Routledge).

Helm, Paul (ed.) (1999) *Faith and Reason* (Oxford: Oxford University Press).

Hick, John (ed.) (1990) *Classical and Contemporary Readings in the Philosophy of Religion* (Englewood Cliffs, NJ: Prentice Hall).

Kessler, Gary E. (ed.) (1999) *Philosophy of Religion: Toward a Global Perspective* (Boston, MA: Wadsworth, Cengage Learning).

Klemke, E. D. (ed.) (1992) *To Believe or Not to Believe: Readings in the Philosophy of Religion* (Orlando, FL: Harcourt Brace Jovanovich College Publishers).

McGinnis, Jon and Reisman, David C. (eds and trans.) (2007) *Classical Arabic Philosophy: An Anthology of Sources* (Indianapolis, IN: Hackett Publishing Company).

Meister, Chad (ed.) (2008) *The Philosophy of Religion Reader* (New York and Abingdon: Routledge).

Morris, Thomas V. (ed.) (1987) *The Concept of God* (Oxford: Oxford University Press).

Peterson, Michael, Hasker, William, Reichenbach, Bruce and Basinger, David (eds) (2014 [1996]) *Philosophy of Religion: Selected Readings* (Oxford: Oxford University Press).

Stump, Eleonore and Murray, Michael J. (eds) (1999) *Philosophy of Religion: The Big Questions* (Oxford: Blackwell).

Taliaferro, Charles and Griffiths, Paul J. (eds) (2003) *Philosophy of Religion: An Anthology* (Oxford: Blackwell).

Zagzebski, Linda and Miller, Timothy D. (eds) (2009) *Readings in Philosophy of Religion: Ancient to Contemporary* (Chichester: Wiley-Blackwell).

• CHAPTER 2 – WAYS WITH WORDS: THE MEANING OF RELIGIOUS LANGUAGE (SECTION A: THE NEGATIVE WAY)

Original source

Maimonides, Moses (1963 [1190]) *The Guide of the Perplexed*, trans. Schlomo Pines (Chicago, IL: University of Chicago Press).

Extracts are reprinted in the following anthologies:

Meister, Chad (ed.) (2008), 101–107; Peterson, Michael, Hasker, William, Reichenbach, Bruce and Basinger, David (eds) (2014 [1996]), 239–243; Ramsey, Ian T. (ed.) (1971) *Words About God: The Philosophy of Religion* (London: SCM Press), 23–35.

• CHAPTER 2 – WAYS WITH WORDS: THE MEANING OF RELIGIOUS LANGUAGE (SECTION B: RELIGIOUS LANGUAGE AS ANALOGICAL)

Original source

Aquinas, Thomas (1955–1957 [1261–1263]) *Summa contra Gentiles*, ed. Joseph Kenny Book I, trans. Anton C. Pegis (New York, NY: Hanover House), http://dhspriory.org/thomas/ContraGentiles.htm Book I, Chapters 28–34.

Reprinted in the following anthology:

Hick, John (ed.) (1990), 43–51. Hick gives a summary of these chapters in his introductory notes at the end of the volume (524–525).

Original source

Aquinas, Thomas (2008 [1920, 1265–1274]) *The Summa Theologica of St Thomas Aquinas*, trans. Fathers of the English Dominican Province, www.newadvent.org/summa/ Part I, Question 13, Article 5.

Reprinted in the following anthology:

Davies, Brian (ed.) (2000), 162–164.

• CHAPTER 5 – DIVINE POWER

Original source

Aquinas, Thomas (2016 [1920, 1265–1274]) *Summa Theologica*, First Part, Question 25, www.newadvent.org/summa/1025.htm.

Extracts are reprinted in the following anthologies:

Davies, Brian (ed.) (2000), 415–421; Eshleman, Andrew (ed.) (2008), 70–71; Meister, Chad (ed.) (2008), 119–122; Peterson, Michael et al. (eds) (2014 [1996]), 244–246.

Original source

Morris, Thomas V. (1991) *Our Idea of God* (Notre Dame, IN: University of Notre Dame Press), Chapter 4.

Reprinted in the following anthology:

Davies, Brian (ed.) (2000), 402–414.

• CHAPTER 6 – DIVINE WISDOM

Original source

Boethius (1957) *The Consolation of Philosophy*, ed. James T. Buchanan (New York, NY: Frederick Ungar).

Extracts are reprinted in the following anthologies:

Meister, Chad (ed.) (2008), 108–118; Peterson, Michael et al. (eds) (2014 [1996]), 256–258; Zagzebski, Linda and Miller, Timothy D. (eds) (2009), 246–250.

Original source

Aquinas, Thomas (2008) *Summa Theologica*, First Part, Question 14, www.newadvent.org/summa/1014.htm.

Extract reprinted in the following anthology:

Davies, Brian (ed.) (2000), 446–455.

• CHAPTER 7 – DIVINE ACTION

Original source

Hume, David (1748) *An Enquiry Concerning Human Understanding*, Section X; reprinted in L. A. Selby-Bigge (ed.) (1975) *Enquiries Concerning Human Understanding and Concerning the Principles of Morals* (Oxford: Clarendon Press).

Extracts are reprinted in the following anthologies:

Davies, Brian (ed.) (2000), 430–435; Hick, John (ed.) (1990), 107–120; Meister, Chad (ed.) (2008), 397–408; Klemke, E. D. (1992), 530–541; Peterson, Michael et al. (eds) (2014 [1996]), 465–471; Stump, Eleonore and Murray, Michael J. (eds) (1999), 320–330; Taliaferro, Charles and Griffiths, Paul J. (eds) (2003), 565–573; Zagzebski, Linda and Miller, Timothy D. (eds) (2009), 572–582.

• CHAPTER 9 – ARGUMENTS FOR THE EXISTENCE OF THE DIVINE: COSMOLOGICAL ARGUMENTS

Original source

Craig, William Lane (1991) 'The Existence of God and the Beginning of the Universe', *Truth: A Journal of Modern Thought* 3 (1991): 85–96. Available on Craig's website at: www.reasonablefaith.org/the-existence-of-god-and-the-beginning-of-the-universe.

Reprinted in the following anthology:

Peterson, Michael et al. (eds) (2014 [1996]), 161–169.

Original source

Aquinas, Thomas (2008 [1920, 1265–1274]) *The Summa Theologica of St Thomas Aquinas*, trans. Fathers of the English Dominican Province, www.newadvent.org/summa/ Part I, Question 2, Article 3.

Reprinted in the following anthologies:

Meister, Chad (ed.) (2008), 193–196; Zagzebski, Linda and Miller, Timothy D. (eds) (2009), 71–72; Hick, John (ed.) (1990), 37–42; Klemke, E. D. (ed.) (1992), 23–27; Eshleman, Andrew (ed.) (2008), 142–143.

Original source

Taylor, Richard (1991) 'A Cosmological Argument for God's Existence' in Richard Taylor *Metaphysics*, 4th edn (Englewood Cliffs, NJ: Prentice Hall), 100–107.

Reprinted in the following anthologies:

Klemke, E. D. (ed.) (1992), 240–248.

Original source

Mackie, J. L. (1982) *The Miracle of Theism: Arguments For and Against the Existence of God* (Oxford: Clarendon), Chapter 5.

Reprinted in the following anthologies:

Eshleman, Andrew (ed.) (2008), 102–106; Taliaferro, Charles and Griffiths, Paul J. (eds) (2003), 242–253; Peterson, Michael et al. (eds) (2014 [1996]), 170–176; Meister. Chad (ed.) (2008), 215–226; Davies, Brian (ed.) (2000), 213–229.

Original source

Edwards, Paul (1959) 'A Critique of The Cosmological Argument' in Hector Hawton (ed.) *The Rationalist Annual* (London: Pemberton Publishing Company), 63–77.

Reprinted in the following anthology:

Davies, Brian (ed.) (2000), 202–212.

• CHAPTER 10 – ARGUMENTS FOR THE EXISTENCE OF THE DIVINE: DESIGN ARGUMENTS

Original source

Paley, William (1802) *Natural Theology, or Evidences of the Existence and Attributes of the Deity Collected from the Appearance of Nature* (Philadelphia, PA: Printed for John Morgan, No. 51, South Second-Street by H. Maxwell, No. 25, North Second-Street).

Reprinted in the following anthologies:

Peterson, Michael et al. (eds) (2014 [1996]), 177–179; Meister, Chad (ed.) (2008), 251–255; Davies, Brian (ed.) (2000), 253–259; Eshleman, Andrew (ed.) (2008), 144–145; Zagzebski, Linda and Miller, Timothy D. (eds) (2009), 28–30.

Original source

Hume, David (1947 [1779]) *Dialogues Concerning Natural Religion*, ed. Norman Kemp Smith (Indianapolis, IN: Bobbs-Merrill).

Extracts are reprinted in the following anthologies:

Hick, John (ed.) (1990), 68–106; Klemke, E. D. (ed.) (1992), 90–112; Stump, Eleonore and Murray, Michael J. (eds) (1999), 94–99; Taliaferro, Charles and Griffiths, Paul J. (eds) (2003), 254–258; Eshleman, Andrew (ed.) (2008), 146–150; Meister, Chad (ed.) (2008), 279–287; Zagzebski, Linda and Miller, Timothy D. (eds) (2009), 31–38.

Original source

Swinburne, Richard (1968) 'The Argument from Design', *Philosophy* 43, 165: 199–212.

Reprinted in the following anthologies:

Stump, Eleonore and Murray, Michael J. (eds) (1999), 100–109.

Original source

Swinburne, Richard (1996) *Is There a God?* (New York, NY: Oxford University Press), 56–68.

Reprinted in the following anthology:

Eshleman, Andrew (ed.) (2008), 107–112.

• CHAPTER 11 – ARGUMENTS FOR THE EXISTENCE OF THE DIVINE: MORAL ARGUMENTS

Original source

Kant, Immanuel (1985 [1788]) *Critique of Practical Reason*, trans. Lewis White Beck (London and Basingstoke: Macmillan).

Extracts are reprinted in the following anthologies:

Hick, John (ed.) (1990), 140–148; Klemke, E. D. (ed.) (1992), 40–46.

• CHAPTER 12 – ARGUMENTS FOR THE EXISTENCE OF THE DIVINE: ARGUMENTS FROM RELIGIOUS EXPERIENCE

Original source

James, William (1923) *The Varieties of Religious Experience* (New York, NY: Longmans, Green and Co.).

Extracts are reprinted in the following anthologies:

Hick, John (ed.) (1990), 169–195; Klemke, E. D. (ed.) (1992), 47–69; Meister, Chad (ed) (2008), 476–484; Taliaferro, Charles and Griffiths, Paul J. (eds) (2003), 141–145.

Original source

Alston, William (1998) 'God and Religious Experience' in B. Davies (ed.) *Philosophy of Religion: A Guide to the Subject* (London: Cassell), 65–69.

Reprinted in the following anthology:

Davies, Brian (ed.) (2000), 382–386.

Original source

Alston, William P. (2004) 'Religious Experience Justifies Religious Belief' in Michael Peterson and Raymond J. Van Arragon (eds) *Contemporary Debates in Philosophy of Religion* (Malden, MA: Blackwell Publishers), 135–144.

Reprinted in the following anthology:

Eshleman, Andrew (ed.) (2008), 183–190.

• CHAPTER 13 – ARGUMENTS FOR THE EXISTENCE OF THE DIVINE: ONTOLOGICAL ARGUMENTS

Original source

Anselm (1962a) *Proslogium*, in *St Anselm: Basic Writings*, trans. S. N. Deane (La Salle, IL: Open Court Publishing Company), 47–80.

Extracts are reprinted in the following anthologies:

Davies, Brian (ed.) (2000), 311–312; Eshleman, Andrew (ed.) (2008), 141; Meister, Chad (ed.) (2008), 291–294; Hick, John (ed.) (1990), 28–36; Klemke, E. D. (1992), 20–22; Peterson, Michael et al. (eds) (2014 [1996]), 133–134; Stump, Eleonore and Murray, Michael J. (eds) (1999), 65–66; Zagzebski, Linda and Miller, Timothy D. (eds) (2009), 81–83.

Original source

Gaunilo (1962) *In Behalf of the Fool*, in *St Anselm: Basic Writings*, trans. S. N. Deane (La Salle, IL: Open Court Publishing Company), 303–311.

Extracts are reprinted in the following anthologies:

Davies, Brian (ed.) (2000), 313–317; Meister, Chad (ed.) (2008), 295–299; Klemke, E. D. (1992), 82–86; Peterson, Michael et al. (eds) (2014 [1996]), 135–137; Stump, Eleonore and Murray, Michael J. (eds) (1999), 66–69.

Original source

Descartes, René (1967 and 1968) 'Meditation V, Objections I, Reply to Objections I' in *The Philosophical Works of Descartes*, trans. Elizabeth S. Haldane and G. R. T. Ross, Vol. 1, 180–183 (Cambridge; CUP, 1968), Vol. 2, 6–8, 18–22 (Cambridge: CUP, 1967).

Extracts are reprinted in the following anthologies:

Davies, Brian (ed.) (2000), 327–329; Hick, John (ed.) (1990), 63–67; Klemke, E. D. (1992), 28–31; Zagzebski, Linda and Miller, Timothy D. (eds) (2009), 84–89.

Original source

Kant, Immanuel (1965 [1787/1781]) *Critique of Pure Reason*, trans. Norman Kemp Smith (New York, NY: St Martin's Press).

Extracts are reprinted in the following anthologies:

Davies, Brian (ed.) (2000), 337–341; Hick, John (ed.) (1990), 122–127; Klemke, E. D. (1992), 113–118; Zagzebski, Linda and Miller, Timothy D. (eds) (2009), 90–97.

Original source

Malcolm, Norman (1960) 'Anselm's Ontological Arguments', *The Philosophical Review* 69, 1: 41–62.

Extracts are reprinted in the following anthologies:

Hick, John (ed.) (1990), 350–366; Klemke, E. D. (1992), 276–289; Taliaferro, Charles and Griffiths, Paul J. (eds) (2003), 271–281.

Original source

Plantinga, Alvin (1977) *God, Freedom, and Evil* (Grand Rapids, MI: Wm. B. Eerdmans Publishing Co.).

Extracts are reprinted in the following anthologies:

Davies, Brian (ed.) (2000), 342–352; Peterson, Michael et al. (eds) (2014), 338–356 [1996]; Zagzebski, Linda and Miller, Timothy D. (eds) (2009), 98–111.

• CHAPTER 14 – ARGUMENTS AGAINST BELIEF IN THE DIVINE: THE PROBLEM OF EVIL

Original source

Mackie, J. L. (1955) 'Evil and Omnipotence', *Mind* 64: 200–212.

Reprinted in the following anthologies:

Mackie, J. L. 'Evil and Omnipotence' in the following: Adams, Marilyn McCord and Adams, Robert Merrihew (eds) 25–37; Kessler, Gary E. (ed.), 224–233; Eshleman, Andrew (ed.) (2008), 232–239; Peterson, Michael et al. (eds) (2014 [1996]), 329–337; Zagzebski, Linda and Miller, Timothy D. (eds), 342–349.
Mackie, J. L. 'Evil Shows That There is no God' in Davies, Brian (ed.) (2000), 581–591.

Original source

Alvin Plantinga (1974) *The Nature of Necessity* (Oxford: Clarendon Press), Chapter 9, 'God, Evil and the Metaphysics of Evil', 164–193.

Reprinted in the following anthology:

Adams, Marilyn McCord and Adams, Robert Merrihew (eds) (1988), 83–109.

Original source

Plantinga, Alvin (1977) *God, Freedom and Evil* (Grand Rapids, MI: Wm. B. Eerdmans Publishing Company), 12–49.

Reprinted in the following anthologies:

Meister, Chad (ed.) (2008), 550–563; Peterson, Michael et al. (eds) (2014 [1996]), 338–356; Zagzebski, Linda and Miller, Timothy D. (eds) (2009), 350–368.

Original source

Hick, John (2010 [1966]) *Evil and the God of Love* (Basingstoke: Palgrave Macmillan).

Reprinted in the following anthology:

Adams, Marilyn McCord and Adams, Robert Merrihew (eds) (1988), 168–188.

Original source

Hick, John (2001 [1981]) 'Soul-Making Theodicy' in Stephen T. Davis (ed.) *Encountering Evil: Live Options in Theodicy* (Atlanta, GA: Westminster, John Knox), 39–52.

Reprinted in the following anthologies:

Zagzebski, Linda and Miller, Timothy D. (eds) (2009), 369–379; Peterson, Michael et al. (eds) (2014 [1996]), 357–364; Eshleman, Andrew (ed.) (2008), 245–255; Hick, John (ed.) (1990), 391–405; Stump, Eleonore and Murray, Michael J. (eds) (1999), 222–227; Meister, Chad (ed.) (2007), 537–549.

Original source

Rowe, William (1979) 'The Problem of Evil and Some Varieties of Atheism', *American Philosophical Quarterly* 16, 4: 335–341.

Reprinted in the following anthologies:

Meister, Chad (ed.) (2008), 526–536; Adams, Marilyn McCord and Adams, Robert Merrihew (eds) (1988), 126–137; Stump, Eleonore and Murray,

Michael J. (eds) (1999), 157–164; Taliaferro, Charles and Griffiths, Paul J. (eds) (2003), 368–374.

Original source

Rowe, William (1988) 'Evil and Theodicy', *Philosophical Topics* 16, 2: 119–132.

Reprinted in the following anthology:

Peterson, Michael et al. (eds) (2014 [1996]), 365–373.

Original source

Rowe, William (2001) 'The Evidential Problem of Evil' in *Philosophy of Religion: An Introduction*, 3rd edn (Belmont, CA: Wadsworth), 98–110.

Reprinted in the following anthology:

Eshleman, Andrew (ed.) (2008), 256–264.

Original source

Rowe, William L. (2006) 'Friendly Atheism, Skeptical Theism, and the Problem of Evil', *International Journal for Philosophy of Religion* 59, 2: 79–92.

Reprinted in the following anthology:

Zagzebski, Linda and Miller, Timothy D. (eds) (2009), 380–388.

Original source

Adams, Marilyn McCord (1989) 'Horrendous Evils and the Goodness of God', *Proceedings of the Aristotelian Society*, supp. vol. 63: 297–310.

Reprinted in the following anthologies:

Peterson, Michael et al. (eds) (2014 [1996]), 374–382; Stump, Eleonore and Murray, Michael J. (eds) (1999), 250–257; Zagzebski, Linda and Miller, Timothy D. (eds) (2009), 389–397.

Original source

Adams, Marilyn McCord (1988) 'Horrendous Evils and the Goodness of God' in Marilyn McCord Adams and Robert Merrihew Adams (eds) (1988), 209–221.

Reprinted in the following anthologies:

Meister, Chad (ed.) (2008), 564–575; Taliaferro, Charles and Griffiths, Paul J. (eds) (2003), 407–414.

Original source

Jonas, Hans (1987) 'The Concept of God after Auschwitz: A Jewish Voice', *The Journal of Religion* 67, 1: 1–13.

Reprinted in the following anthology:

Eshleman, Andrew (ed.) (2008), 265–272.

• CHAPTER 16 – ARGUMENTS AGAINST BELIEF IN THE DIVINE: THE PROBLEM OF RELIGIOUS DIVERSITY

Original source

Hick, John (1985) *Problems of Religious Pluralism* (New York, NY: St Martin's Press, LLC).

Extracts from this and a range of alternative sources are reprinted in the following anthologies:

Eshleman, Andrew (ed.) (2008), 364–373; Meister, Chad (ed.) (2008), 9–25; Hick, John (ed.) (1990), 418–432; Peterson, Michael et al. (eds) (2014 [1996]), 614–622; Taliaferro, Charles and Griffiths, Paul J. (eds) (2003), 517–522.

• CHAPTER 17 – VOLUNTARIST THEORIES OF RELIGIOUS BELIEF

Original source

Pascal, Blaise (1966 [1669]) *Pensées*, trans. with an introduction by A. J. Krailsheimer (Harmondsworth: Penguin Books), 150–153.

Extracts reprinted in the following anthologies:

Helm, Paul (ed.) (1999), 182–185; Taliaferro, Charles and Griffiths, Paul J. (eds) (2003), 544–545; Stump, Eleonore and Murray, Michael J. (eds) (1999), 298–300; Meister, Chad (ed.) (2008), 389–393; Peterson, Michael et al. (2014 [1996]), 100–102.

Original source

James, William (1896) *The Will to Believe and Other Essays in Popular Philosophy* (New York, NY: Longmans, Green and Co.).

Extracts reprinted in the following anthologies:

Eshleman, Andrew (ed.) (2008), 162–171; Helm, Paul (ed.) (1999), 240–244; Klemke, E. D. (ed.) (1992), 501–514; Meister, Chad (ed.) (2008), 366–378; Peterson, Michael et al. (eds) (2014 [1996]), 109–115.

Original source

Clifford, William Kingdon (1901) *Lectures and Essays* (New York, NY: Macmillan), 163–176.

Reprinted in the following anthologies:

Helm, Paul (ed.) (1999) 238–240; Klemke, E. D. (ed.) (1992), 496–500; Meister, Chad (ed.) (2008), 359–365; Peterson, Michael et al. (2014 [1996]), 103–107; Stump, Eleonore and Murray, Michael J. (eds) (1999), 269–273; Taliaferro, Charles and Griffiths, Paul J. (eds) (2003), 196–199.

• CHAPTER 18 – REFORMED EPISTEMOLOGY

Sources include:

Plantinga, Alvin (1982) 'The Reformed Objection to Natural Theology', *Christian Scholar's Review* 11, 3: 187–198.

Extracts from a number of Plantinga's books and articles are reprinted in the following anthologies:

Davies, Brian (ed.) (2000), 42–94; Eshleman, Andrew (ed.) (2008), 172–178; Hick, John (ed.) (1990), 484–499; Klemke, E. D. (ed.) (1992), 414–431; Meister, Chad (ed.) (2008), 379–388; Stump, Eleonore and Murray, Michael J. (eds) (1999), 285–297; Taliaferro, Charles and Griffiths, Paul J. (eds) (2003), 200–225.

Original source

Hasker, William (1998) 'The Foundations of Theism: Scoring the Quinn-Plantinga Debate', *Faith and Philosophy* 15, 1: 60–67.

Extracts reprinted in the following anthology:

Peterson, Michael et al. (2014 [1996]), 223–227.

• CHAPTER 19 – LIFE, DEATH AND HOPE

Original source

Swinburne, Richard (1986) *The Evolution of the Soul* (Oxford: OUP).

Extracts reprinted in the following anthologies:

Peterson, Michael et al. (eds) (2014 [1996]), 497–505; Stump, Eleonore and Murray, Michael J. (eds) (1999), 367–375.

Original source

Price, H. H. (1953) 'Survival and the Idea of "Another World"', *Proceedings of the Society for Psychical Research* Vol. L, Part 182: 1–25.

Extracts reprinted in the following anthologies:

Hick, John (ed.) (1990), 280–301; Peterson, Michael et al. (eds) (2014 [1996]), 489–496.

Original source

Hick, John (1976) *Death and Eternal Life* (London: HarperCollins Publishers Inc).

Extracts reprinted in the following anthology:

Peterson, Michael et al. (eds) (2014 [1996]), 513–521.

appendix 4: glossary

Abduction: Inference to the best explanation.

Abrahamic religions/traditions: Religions which hold that the Hebrew patriarch Abraham was an important spiritual ancestor – i.e. Judaism, Christianity and Islam.

Actual infinite: A set of things the number of which cannot increase.

Agnostic: Someone who does not know – in this context, whether the Divine exists.

Altruism: Acting for the good of others without concern for oneself.

Analogical language: Language in which the words are literally true, but their sense is stretched.

Analytic philosophy: A philosophical style in which hypotheses are tested for deductive or inductive validity.

Analytic statement: A statement the truth of which can be determined by analysing the meanings of the words of which it is comprised.

Anti-realism: See 'non-realism', with which it is often used interchangeably.

Apophatic: Using negative terms to describe the Divine.

***A posteriori* argument:** An argument derived from (posterior to) experience.

***A priori* argument:** An argument based on analysis of a concept or concepts (that is, prior to experience).

Arhat: In Theravada Buddhism, a perfected person who has achieved liberation.

Atman: In Hinduism, the human Self or universal consciousness which is identical with *Brahman*.

Bhakti movement: In Hinduism, worship of the divine Person which began in the ninth century CE. Its main scripture is the *Bhagavad Gita* (date of composition uncertain, but thought be to be between 400 BCE and 200 CE). The theologian Ramanuja (c. 1017–c. 1137) has been particularly influential for the Bhakti movement.

Boddhisattva: In Mahayana Buddhism, an 'enlightenment being', a person who could achieve enlightenment but chooses to help other sentient, suffering beings achieve this.

Brahman: In Hinduism, the Absolute or Ultimate Reality which underlies everything. *Nirguna Brahman* is beyond our understanding and has no attributes, while *Saguna Brahman* does have attributes.

Coherence theory of truth: A statement is true if its components cohere with each other (internal coherence) and with other statements about the world (external coherence).

Compatibilism: The view that freedom and determinism are compatible.

Continental philosophy: A philosophical style which examines common ways of thinking to show how they lead to social and/or spiritual disadvantage and attempts to offer a new and liberating vision.

Contingent event: An event which depends on a cause external to itself and which therefore may or may not happen.

Counterfactual: An event which would happen if certain circumstances were to arise but in fact does not because those circumstances do not arise.

Correspondence theory of truth: The theory that statements are true if they correspond with (link up with) a mind-independent reality.

Creation *ex nihilo*: Creation out of nothing.

Critical realism: Our language refers to a mind-independent reality, but the way we perceive the world to some extent affects what we see.

Deductive reasoning: A form of argument from premises (statements) to a conclusion which is logically certain.

Defeater: Something which counts against an argument to such an extent that the argument is unsound.

Determinism: All events and human choices are ultimately caused by an external cause, perhaps the Divine.

Divine, the: The supreme being or value. This may be God or Allah, but the term is intended to be inclusive of traditions in which the ultimate being or value is something other than God.

Dukkha: In Buddhism, suffering. Caused by *samsara*, the cycle of birth, suffering and death and rebirth.

Efficient cause: From Aristotle (384–322 BCE), something which causes the existence of something, or a change to something – e.g. the potter who makes the pot.

Emanation: A theory of creation in which created things gradually spread out from and manifest their Divine originator.

Epistemology: The study of how and what we can know.

Epistemological non-realism: Truth consists in coherence with other true statements.

Epistemological realism: Truth consists in correspondence with a mind-independent reality.

Equilibrium, state of: A state in which the quantities which specify its properties – e.g. temperature – remain unchanged.

Equivocal language: Language which has different meanings in different contexts. For example, a screen is both something which enables us to see pictures and/or text and a means to prevent us from seeing something. If religious language is understood to be equivocal, it means something entirely different from its meaning in our human world when it is applied to the Divine.

Euthyphro dilemma: From Plato's dialogue *Euthyphro*, the question of whether the Divine must conform to what goodness requires, in which case there is a standard of goodness which exists independently of the Divine, or whether the good is what the Divine wills, and is therefore arbitrary.

Falsifiable: We can specify what would show a claim to be false. If there is no way in which a statement could be falsified, it is unlikely to be true in any meaningful sense.

Form of the Good: Originally from Plato, the property of goodness which is shared by all good things.

Formal cause: From Aristotle, the form or structure of a thing.

Global realism: Realism about every aspect of our world.

Immanence, doctrine of divine: The belief that the Divine is present everywhere and in everything.

Immutable: Unchangeable.

Inductive reasoning: A form of argument in which the premises support the conclusion but cannot show that the conclusion is true beyond doubt.

Inference: A conclusion arrived at by means of evidence and analysis.

Instantiated: If a concept is instantiated, it has an actual, real-world existence; it is not just a concept.

***Ishvara*:** Various meanings but, in the Upanishadic literature of Hinduism, the immanent aspect of God.

***Karma*:** In Hinduism and Buddhism, the sum of a person's actions.

Knowledge of approbation: Knowledge which causes the thing which it knows.

Liberty of indifference: Human actions are not determined in any sense and are therefore free choices in the broadest of senses.

Liberty of spontaneity: Human beings are free to act according to their natures, but their actions are determined by their upbringing, education, and so on.

Logic: The study of good and bad reasoning.

Mahayana Buddhism: '*Mayhayana*' is Sanskrit for 'Great Vehicle' and is the later of the two existing forms of Buddhism, dating, it is thought, from about the first century CE. It teaches the *Bodhisattva* Path, the main focus of which is to liberate all sentient beings from suffering.

Material cause: From Aristotle; the material of which something is made – e.g. the clay from which a pot is made.

Meliorism: The belief that the effort of humankind can make the world a better place.

Metaphorical language: Speaking about one thing as if it were something which is not literally the case, but with which it shares some attributes – e.g. 'God is my rock'.

Metaphysics: The study of abstract concepts such as the nature of being, or time.

Metaphysical non-realism: The claim that nothing exists independently of human minds, or that we cannot know whether anything exists independently of human minds.

Metaphysical realism: The claim that something exists independently of human minds.

Methodology: The study of the methods commonly used in philosophical inquiry.

***Moksha*:** In Hinduism, liberation from life in this world which is eventually achieved when the soul merges into *Brahman*.

Naïve realism: The view that there is a direct link between human language and that which it describes.

Naturalism: The belief that everything is the consequence of natural causes; there are no supernatural causes.

Necessary: Either the nature of our world is such that something must exist in it (metaphysical necessity), or the nature of the laws of logic entail that something must exist (logical necessity).

Necessary and sufficient conditions: A necessary condition is a set of circumstances which must exist for an event to occur; a sufficient condition is one which may enable an event to occur, although there may be other possible causes of the event.

Negative way: Speaking about the Divine by saying what it is not.

***Nirvana* (Sanskrit) or *nibbana* (Pali):** In Buddhism, the end of suffering with the extinction of the individual.

Non-realism: Human language cannot describe a mind-independent reality.

Ockham's Razor: A philosophical principle developed by William of Ockham (1285–1347) which requires that we do not multiply causes without necessity.

Omnipotent: All-powerful.

Omniscient: All-knowing.

Postulate: To put forward as a hypothesis for testing by means of argument.

Potential infinite: A set of things the number of which could increase to infinity.

Pragmatist theory of truth: The theory that a statement is true if it has beneficial practical consequences.

Premise or premiss: A statement which forms a step in an argument.

Principle of sufficient reason: Everything has a reason which is sufficient to explain its existence.

Realism: The claim that something exists independently of our perceptions of it.

Reductionism: In the case of religion, reducing religion to something which is no longer clearly religious.

Samsara: In Hinduism and Buddhism, the cycle of birth, death and rebirth which causes *dukkha*, suffering.

Satchitananda: In Hinduism, of *Brahman*, having the attributes of both consciousness and bliss.

Sceptical theism: The claim that, since human beings do not have the capacity to understand the Divine mind, there may be reasons why the world is arranged as it is (in particular, why there is suffering) which we cannot reasonably expect to be able to understand.

Sound: An argument is sound if it is valid and all its premises are true.

Sunyata: In Mahayana Buddhism, usually translated 'Emptiness'. An attempt to see the world as it is in itself, empty of the evaluations, comparisons and concerns of individuals.

Synthetic statement: An informative statement – that is, one which is not simply true by definition.

Theravada Buddhism: '*Theravada*' means 'the doctrine of the Elders' and is the oldest form of Buddhism. It teaches its followers how to achieve liberation from *samsara* and become an *Arhat* by means of meditation and following the way of life described in the Noble Eightfold Path.

Timelessness, divine: Time does not pass for God; God sees everything which, for us, is past, present or future in one simultaneous 'present'.

Torah: In Judaism, the divine law as revealed to Moses in the first five books of the Hebrew Bible (the Pentateuch).

Transcendent: Existing beyond or external to our human world.

Ultimism: From J. L. Schellenberg; the claim that there is some reality which may be called religious.

Univocal language: Language which means the same in two different contexts – e.g. when applied to something in our human world and when applied to the Divine.

Upanishads: Collection of texts written in India, probably between c800 BCE and 500 CE, containing some of the central teachings of Hinduism.

Valid: An argument is valid if its conclusion must follow from its premises. It may not be sound, however, if its premises are not true.

Vedas: Foundational scriptures of Hinduism dating from c. 1700 BCE to c. 500 CE and consisting of the Rig Veda, the Yajur Veda, the Sama Veda and the Atharva Veda. Each is divided into the Samhitas (mantras and benedictions), Brahmanas (concerned with rituals, ceremonies and sacrifices), the Aranyakas (commentaries on the Brahmanas) and the Upanishads (on meditation, philosophy and spiritual knowledge).

Verifiable: Is either true by definition or can be tested by means of experience.

Zen Buddhism: A combination of Indian Mahayana Buddhism and Taoism which focuses on the practice of meditation as a means to understand the meaning of life without reliance on written texts or logical thought.

index